DEMOCRACY UNDER SIEGE

Essays from the Trump Years
(2017–2024)

Curt Strickland

ISBN: 979-8-9920322-1-5

Published by Rogers Drive Publishing

First Edition

For Anne:
my heart, my love, my soulmate and muse.

Contents

Preface

In 2016, Donald Trump was elected President. I was shocked that a man of his character could win the presidency. His ascendancy revealed the dark underbelly of America, the racism and white supremacy which had laid dormant, festering below the surface. As a society, we labored under the delusion that we had stopped America's cancer of racism from growing any further. It was shrinking, even. After all, didn't we just elect a Black president? Yet, instead of the code words and dog whistles, the racism became overt, courtesy of Donald Trump's stamp of approval.

But it wasn't just Donald Trump. For a man like Donald Trump to exist, an army of enablers had to conspire to legitimize the hate, the racism, the white supremacy. I began to see friends in a different light as this bottled-up racism began to ooze out. I saw that American's racism ran deep; its foundations were structural, institutionalized. I realized our nation's divide was intentional, employing the same playbook that has worked for thousands of years: divide and conquer.

As each outrage became normalized, or sane-washed, I felt impelled to make sense of our democracy, our culture. The silver lining to Hillary losing the election was it drove home the truth that democracy is a living, breathing beast that has to be fought for daily, worked on daily, and created daily. We can lose it in a whisper. Americans were complacent. "Why vote? Our votes don't matter. Who cares who the President is? It doesn't affect me. Politicians are all corrupt."

It was with this backdrop that I wrote my first essay, and found I had struck a chord, both good and bad. I found that writing about America is vital, therapeutic, because it generates dialogue, which is the first step to our country healing.

We can't stay silent. Silence condones cruelty, violence. These essays are an attempt to begin the conversation.

Curt Strickland,
October, 2024

1

War Ends

November 1, 2017

What if all war ended November 13, 2017?

Our new emperor just brokered a 110-billion-dollar arms deal with Saudi Arabia.

There's no way this can end well. It's like dousing a fire with gasoline and turning it into a raging inferno.

Since our new emperor assumed office, the word "nuclear" has been bandied about way too frequently. During the Reagan years, the United States and Russia possessed enough nuclear weapons to destroy the world 67 times. It appears this administration would like to reenact the Cold War, maybe bump our nuclear arsenal to triple figures.

Destroy the world 67 times over? I'm thinking we should get this down to single digits.

If you destroy the world once, isn't another 66 times a bit redundant?

Here's the thing: I believe our new emperor is hell-bent on waging war. I believe that he thinks war can salvage his poll numbers, and perhaps jumpstart the middle-class economy. His childlike insecurity motivates him to act tough.

We don't have to accept this scenario. We can write our own script, be proactive. At the end of the day, we have more power than our leaders, more power than our new emperor. We just need to seize it.

So, in honor of my late father's birthday, I hereby declare that all war will end on November 13th, 2017. Any wars being waged that day will be declared a tie, with all soldiers free to return to their families.

Yes, November 13th, war will end.

We can decide this.

We can do this.

November 13th, war will end.

Ain't nothing more powerful than an idea. An idea can diffuse and dismantle force when it appeals to our humanity, our collective souls, and the innate goodness that resides in all of us. The Berlin Wall was dismantled not through force but through the idea of freedom. No shots were fired; people just exerted their power, insisting on freedom.

And ain't nothing more powerful than the idea of peace.

In 1960, President Eisenhower warned the nation about the proliferation of the military-industrial complex. His prophesy has borne fruit. This insatiable beast needs to be fed, and it can only be nourished by conflict, carnage, body counts, and huge purchase orders for instruments of death—purchase orders that generate millions of jobs, mountains of cash, and multigenerational fortunes. This structure is hot-wired to sabotage peace.

In his *Chance for Peace* speech, Eisenhower said, "Every gun that is made, every warship launched, every rocket signifies, in the final sense, a theft from those who are cold and are not clothed. This world in arms is not spending money alone. It is spending the sweat of its laborers, the genius of its scientists, the hopes of its children. This is not a way of life at all in any true sense. Under the cloud of threatening war, it is humanity hanging from a cross of iron."

So, the beast must be confronted because it serves to divide us and promotes the propaganda that we are not connected, that there is no commonality between our collective souls.

And we only have till November 13th.

As Eisenhower warned, our economic underpinnings became more and more dependent on the military-industrial complex, and this dependency has evolved into a full-borne addiction. Too many jobs, payrolls, and fortunes are dependent on this machine. But how does the world put down this golden goose? Look how hard it was to outlaw slavery. There was an economic addiction to slavery, which resisted it from being vanquished, and despite the passage of the Thirteenth Amendment, we are still infected by that virus: i.e., the prison-industrial complex, which has evolved because there is still money to be made through the incarceration of the powerless.

By ending all war on November 13th, we can begin to dismantle this demonic structure.

We can decide this.

We can do this.

November 13th, 2017, war ends.

Get the word out.

Now, don't think for a moment the military-industrial complex will quietly fold and go gently in the night. Payrolls, livelihoods, and economies are sustained by this structure. People don't voluntarily surrender their golden goose.

But we can do this because the idea of peace is more powerful than any force. History has taught us that lesson.

War ends November 13, 2017

Now, there are a few contingencies/housekeeping chores to be taken care of before we execute our mission.

1. If a nation's leaders insist on engaging in combat after November 13th, a fighting match would be staged between the two leaders of the warring

factions, a battle royale if you will, the winner of the fight claiming victory for their nation. Perhaps it could even be a cage-match. Think of the pay-per-view killing that could be made, the proceeds going to support the peace efforts. (This all may come down to a fight between our emperor and the emperor of North Korea. They both have small hands, so it should be a very even fight.)

2. After November 13th, the munitions industry will experience massive layoffs. We, as a nation, need to hire and train these laid-off workers. These are good, hardworking people, the soul of America. Like all parents, they labor to support their families and put food on the table. They will never allow their kids to go hungry and will work in a munitions factory if that's the only choice they have. We will need industrialists to step up and hire the people affected by the new peace economy. And why should they do this? It's the patriotic thing to do. We are Americans; we take care of our own. Even if you don't need them or can't afford them, be a job creator and find work for these laid-off workers—it will pay off in the end. We need to have a peacetime economy where the unemployment rate is 3%. We can do this. We have some of the most brilliant economic minds in the world. Surely, we can figure how to create a thriving, viable economy not based on carnage. And please, be more creative than constructing a casino. Do it as a favor to me.

3. We need to get the word out:

   A. Ads, both TV and radio, "War ends, November 13th."

   B. We need huge billboards all over the world declaring, "War ends, November 13th." Times Square should be blanketed by electronic billboards declaring, "War ends, November 13th." And we should have a countdown clock in Times Square so warring nations know how much longer the fighting will be permitted.

   C. We need a massive mailing campaign declaring, "War ends, November 13th."

D. We need extensive email blitzes, Facebook posts, monumental sharing, and Twitter feeds, all declaring, "War ends, November 13th."

E. We can start selling t-shirts professing, "War ends, November 13th," the proceeds going to programs that help train laid-off workers in new, employable skills. We must take care of these laid-off workers. New jobs are the key to this whole thing.

4. A lot of soldiers will be entering the peacetime economy. Business owners need to step up and hire these veterans. There's no better employee than a veteran. I know from experience.

5. We need gigantic dumpsters hauled out to battlefields where soldiers can deposit their weapons on November 13th. (This could create a whole new industry of weapons recycling.)

6. Teams of mediators need to leave immediately for areas of conflict with the express purpose of diffusing combatants, thereby achieving our November 13th deadline.

7. Athletes can refuse to play any games until all war has ended.

8. Get celebrities to spread the word, "War ends, November 13th, 2017." Have it be the talk of the town.

9. At Tupperware parties, people can say, "Did you hear? All war ends November 13th."

10. At weddings, funerals, and tailgate parties, the topic of conversation should be, "War ends, November 13th."

November 13th, 2017—it's gonna be great!

This is crazy, right?

Yup.

But, we can do this.

What if a new war was declared and nobody showed up to fight?

Yes!

Let's end this with a quote from Mister Rogers' Dartmouth commencement address in 2002. Yeah, the guy with the sweater.

> "Our world hangs like a magnificent jewel in the vastness of space. Every one of us is a facet of that jewel. And in the perspective of infinity, our differences are infinitesimal. We are all intimately related. May we never even pretend that we are not."

Trump Tweets This Morning

January 9, 2017

Our president-elect was tweeting this morning at 3:30 because Meryl Streep called him out for being a bully. Shouldn't our president-elect be concerned with more substantive issues, say, peace in the Middle East, America becoming an oligarchy, and helping heal the racial divide in our country? And if he is up at 3:30, shouldn't he be boning up on, say, foreign affairs, or perhaps his plan to replace Obamacare? Will he really take away healthcare from 20 million people who are very happy with their current health care?

These are the issues I want our president to be wrestling with at 3:30 in the morning, not commenting on an actress, a petty grievance, or a beauty pageant.

We will miss President Obama. He brought dignity and integrity to our highest office. He infused his tenure with honor, class, and deep courage. It takes tremendous courage—tremendous courage—to live a life of kindness, and empathy. He always had the American people in his heart and fought the forces that sought to divide us.

He believed in our shared humanity and believed that concept would ultimately prevail against our president-elect's message of hate, racial baiting, and scapegoating.

Our president-elect has never exhibited an ounce of kindness or empathy.

Bullies never do because they live in a hidden fear of others.

Let's Talk About Racism

August 3, 2018

It's uncomfortable, but necessary.

Our history is being whitewashed, and only through confronting the truth about our past, excavating America's original sins, can we achieve the high ideals as set forth in our Constitution. And given the fact that our president is a racist surrounded by white supremacists who foist a racist agenda of divisiveness and scapegoating upon us, while also condoning and enabling environmental disasters, and spearheading assaults on women's rights, LGBTQ+ rights, voting rights, and immigrant rights, I say, ain't no better time than the present.

Trump has emboldened carriers of this cancer, coaxing them out of the closet for a full-frontal attack on our Constitution, the press, marginalized groups, and the working poor.

But there's a silver lining. Before this, our nation labored under the delusion that the race issue had evaporated, no need to even bring it up for discussion. Didn't we just elect our first African-American president?

Trump got himself elected by appealing to the prejudices of this base, first by using the dog whistle of code phrases such as "law and order," and "our kind of people," and he then ratcheted up the rhetoric by labeling Hispanics as "rapists, drug dealers, and criminals," labeled Muslims as "terrorists," and African-Americans as people descended from "shitty" countries such as Haiti. Republican Senators and Representatives, instead of denouncing Trump for his blatant fearmongering and his moral depravity, doubled down on his hate, and railroaded legislation that deeply impacted people of color and the working poor.

And now we bear witness to Trump's racist agenda as it ramps up full throttle at the border with ICE separating kids from parents.

This sounds eerily familiar.

Imagine a child—a young girl—walking to the entrance gate of a plantation where people lived in bondage, under terror, waiting expectantly for her mother to return. She is too young to comprehend that her mother had been sold to another enslaver and would never see her again. And the child, who was too young to conceive such evil, continued to walk daily to the gate, expecting her mother to return, gazing hopefully beyond the horizon.

Or consider a child who would bear witness to his mother being sold on the auction block, and after the sale, his mother being carted away in chains. She watches as her child wails, calling out for his mommy who he would never see again.

And this horror was replicated all over the South as families were systematically and brutally split.

Imagine a Jewish child in Nazi Germany being told their mother was taking a shower and once showered, the mother would reunite with the child. What they didn't tell the child was that the shower rained poison gas, not water. But the child waited, patiently, wondering how long the shower might take.

Imagine a child, picked up by ICE, being told that her mother was taking a shower and would see the child later, but the shower ended up taking two months, sometimes more, and sometimes the shower never ended.

It breaks your heart. Or at least it should.

And the fact that ICE agents told the children lies about showers ... well ... let's not go there ....

When I was in high school in Maryland, there was an African American who was on the football and basketball teams. He was an okay football player and didn't play much on the basketball team. He was very personable, well-mannered, intelligent, well-liked, and probably came from a strong nuclear family.

In other words, he was just a regular guy who probably went on to lead a life of achievement and purpose. He had all the prerequisites that would predict success.

And then the incident.

One day at lunch, this handsome Black teenager was spotted walking around school grounds with a beautiful teenage blond, arms draped over each other, their new romance in full bloom. In an instant, he went from being one of the guys to a "fuckin' ni…r". And this hatred came from his teammates, his brothers in arms.

His partner wasn't spared either and was quickly labeled as a "goddamn whore" and "ni…r lover". The speed with which he went from being one of the guys to a social leper was shocking. A Black boy flouting a relationship with a white girl in suburban Maryland ignited a deep reservoir of hatred and vitriol. Minutes before, they were your typical suburban teenagers discussing sports, girls, and Friday night parties. The next moment they were consumed by this cauldron of hate, implanted by fathers—a family legacy passed on like a family heirloom. And it was only a couple of guys, the rest sat quiet, condoning the attack with their silence. As Dr. Martin Luther King Jr. said, "In the end, we will remember not the words of our enemies, but the silence of our friends."

These guys were a typical mix of suburban kids. Most were average students, some were above-average, and they went to church—or their parents demanded they attend—and they grew up to be citizens of their communities, their racism and hatred simmering just below the surface, ready to be mined by politicians who served up scapegoats, igniting their racism by floating the code words and phrases that excavated the bile.

But what is it about white guys and their insistence on this concept of white purity, their fragile psyches, their fragile character that shatters upon seeing an interracial couple?

Where does this fear come from? And why does it exist?

Our history is saturated with tales of African American men and boys being tortured, mutilated, and murdered for benign acts like looking at a white woman. Emmitt Till was tortured, his body mutilated, and buried in a lake for the crime of smiling at a white woman—and this was only in 1955, not the antebellum period. There was nothing that set off a white man more than just the hint of interracial interaction—didn't even have to be sex. It could be a wink or a smile, and a Black man would quickly have a noose around his neck.

Senator Calhoun, a Senator from South Carolina in the 1850s said,

> "Interfering northern whites would demand for ex-slaves 'the right of voting and holding office,' resulting in 'the prostration of the white race'—political servility and forced interracial marriage—'a degradation greater than has ever yet fallen to the lot of a free and enlightened people.'"

> ~ Edward E Baptist
> *The Half Has Never Been Told*

And he said this out loud.

In a conversation with then-staffer Bill Moyers, President Lyndon B. Johnson had this to say,

> "If you can convince the lowest white man he's better than the best colored man, he won't notice you're picking his pockets. Hell, give him somebody to look down on, and he'll empty his pockets for you."

That, my friends, is the Southern strategy exhumed by Richard Nixon, polished off by George Bush (remember the Willie Horton campaign ads?), piloted by Sarah Palin, and executed by Donald Trump. In the antebellum South, as long as a white man could put their foot on a Black man's neck, they felt whole. Then and now, they didn't know who their suppressor was. Then, as now, their suppressors had brainwashed the white folk into thinking that people of color were keeping them down, stealing their jobs, and taking their women.

A white man's last visage of manhood, their last shred of honor, centered around their control of women, coupled with their implanted patriarchal view of the world. It was their last cord of dignity and they readily resorted to violence in order to preserve that identity. Back in the day, even white people were illiterate. Enslavers, who controlled the landscape, fought against public education, sensing it was a vehicle for change and revolution. Jobless, because all of the menial jobs were held by slave labor, their last straw of dignity rested on the fact that they could control their women, and exact violence upon them as an outlet for their suppressed existence. It was their last shred of control and if a Black man even hinted at a relationship with their women, it would ignite a cauldron of rage and violence, and oftentimes murder.

In America, these festering, racist volcanoes have never been extinguished, much less confronted. The Civil Rights movement achieved political rights, but it never penetrated the suppressed, manipulated souls of a wide swath of whites, their hatred nourished by their family's legacy.

So, this unexamined heirloom has been allowed to smolder to the present day. A *Washington Post* reporter recently interviewed a Trump supporter who continues to be all in on the President, despite her being a devout Christian, and turning a blind eye to her President's moral degradation.

The article had this to say, "The evidence was all the black people protesting about the police, and all the talk about the legacy of slavery," which Sheila never believed slavery was as bad as people said it was. "Slaves were valued," she said. "They got housing. They got fed. They got medical care."

In other words, being a slave was the equivalent of a leisurely stay at Trump Towers. It was practically a Brady Bunch existence, coupled with the free food and lodging and primo healthcare … well, there might have been a few hiccups like torture, hangings, lashings, rape, murder, malnutrition, multination families torn apart in an attempt to erase a collective race and culture, and that doesn't even mention the fact that many were forced to pick cotton in 100-degree heat for 14 straight hours at a time and if they didn't achieve their quota they were then whipped however many pounds their bags were short. In other words, if their quota was 100 lbs., and they picked 90 lbs., they were whipped 10 times. (Enslavers didn't use motivational speeches to get more production, they had the whip.) And I don't think their take-home pay was all that great.

So, except for these few minor indiscretions, plantation life was pretty much a Club Med experience, a front-runner for the "Best Places to Work" award, circa 1850.

But these implanted ideas have been passed on from generation to generation, as evidenced by Sheila and the Maryland boys. These are the people who delivered Trump to the Oval Office. He knew precisely what to say to ignite their cord of hatred and racism.

But we are all culpable.

Hate and racism not only damage the victim, it recoils on the soul of the perpetrator, and because people are basically good, hate undermines our basic nature. We are our brother's keeper, however, this stain on America's soul persists. It took a long time and a lot of horrid behavior by some and silence by many to construct this foundation.

In 1845, former governor James Henry Hammond of South Carolina insisted that slavery should be the cornerstone of all relations, and that class subordination was just as natural. Jefferson's "all men are created equal" was, Hammond insisted without shame,

> "... A ridiculously absurd concept. Now a circle of influential southern intellectuals was openly insisting that freedom was best achieved when people remained within their proper station."

> ~ Nancy Isenberg, *White Trash*

And earlier than that, slavery was the driving force behind an economy that enriched not only enslavers but northern investors, British industrialists, and French investors. Buttressing and justifying this terror, this juggernaut, this money-making industrial complex, were sermons from the pulpit that condoned the enslavement of fellow humans—apparently, being a slave was god's will, part of his divine plan. And then there were Supreme Court decisions that affirmed African Americans as property, not humans, which gave enslavers carte blanche to exploit a whole race of people.

But perhaps the original sin occurred when the Constitution was ratified, and enslaved peoples were deemed to be three-fifths of a person, the Southern enslavers winning out, the Northern delegates caving in for the purpose of preserving the union.

Even earlier, someone had the idea that slavery was ordained from the heavens. And once it got entwined with commerce, with money, it became harder and harder for America to extract itself from its addiction. We see this today with guns, as America can't pull itself away from this addiction, despite the slaughter of kids at Sandy Hook, despite the body counts across America, because payrolls are dependent upon these instruments of death. As long as the sale of AK-47s fills the coffers of corporations, AK-47s will sprinkle America's landscape. Cash trumps morality every time.

Many of us saw how hard the cigarette industry fought regulation and transparency despite manufacturing a product that kills. Too much money on the table. Slavery was allowed to flourish because it fueled the economy and the people all over the world who were making money off the sweat of slaves buried their moral scruples with their monthly dividend checks.

Lincoln wrote that we need to have empathy for the 'slaveholder.' Today, we need to have empathy for those mired in the vice grip of hate and racism. (And not from a patronizing viewpoint.) We are all complicit in allowing racism to fester. We either took the blood money or stood silent. Germans stood silent during Hitler's rise to power. He also had a problem with the press, until he did away with them. (I seem to recall another world leader having issues with the press) The fact that people like Shelia view slavery as benign is a scathing indictment of our educational system and our nation's leadership. In Germany, they continue to breed Nazi apologists. Shouldn't we be better than that?

Perhaps we can follow South Africa's lead and conduct Truth and Reconciliation hearings where citizens were able to confess their sins which in turn began the healing process.

So yes, let's talk about race.

We, as a country, have a lot to discuss.

Racism: Is It Still with Us Today?

February 2, 2018

Here's the thing: I'm a white guy. I hang around with white guys. Most of my friends are white guys. So, I hear things, and because I'm a member of this tribe, I listen in on unfiltered communications, unfiltered conversations.

And because my pigment offers me this intimate access, it is with great sadness that I report—racism is alive and well in America.

I bring this to the table because of postings I read excoriating President Obama for poking this bear, for having the gall to speak on the subject of race. According to these social media postings, the subject of race should be locked in the closet, its cancer ignored, so it doesn't disturb our busy lives.

Well, that's one way to go.

But if you have a cancer, ignoring it lets it spread. It's a malignancy that needs to be confronted, otherwise it will kill the body, much like racism will kill the American dream. Electing an African American President didn't vanquish racism in our country; it only served to stoke what had been left dormant.

Racism manifests itself in many forms, many colors and shades. From the extreme of using the "N word" to the subtler renderings like rants about welfare queens, free cell phones, rap, and speeches about white tax dollars supporting "these people" who don't want to work, racism is pervasive. And then there's the insulting jokes about Ebonics—really? All of these attributes could easily be applied to white people I have known.

I have been sent emails where President Obama has been dressed as a monkey, promoting some economic worldview, citing the travails of the top one-percenters. And then there are the more insidious, invisible structural forms: The Voter Suppression Laws, for example, which simply replaced the popular Poll Tax prevalent in the South after reconstruction. Now we have gerrymandering being exhumed by the Republican hierarchy. The intent of these actions is the same: prevent people of color from voting, from participating in our democracy. In 2013, a guy told me that in his Long Island township, they block any African American from moving into their white enclaves. They do this by keeping secret which homes are on the market. And if an African American somehow managed to put an offer on a house, it suddenly became unavailable.

And this was 2013, on Long Island, not 1952, in Mississippi.

But here's the rub, a lot of these racist rants emanate from some of the finest people I have known, who wouldn't hesitate a second to race into a burning building to save your kids, no matter what color they were. Nevertheless, they have been infected with this racist virus, both subtle and overt. They have been sold a bill of goods on the concept of scarcity, that if another culture or race rises, their position, their livelihood, and their neighborhood, will be compromised, threatened, and maybe wiped away. They have been fed the concept of a dangerous environment, that their anxiety and fear is not of their own doing or responsibility, but stems from some other nefarious group or race. They are a sponge for scapegoats, their prejudices having been implanted, nourished, and sitting dormant until a politician harvests and exploits their resentment into office, which is precisely what our new emperor did to win the election.

People are basically good; they are not basically racist. Racism is a learned behavior. But the teachers of hate no longer wear white hoods; they wear Brooks Brothers suits and have slick websites that name names: Muslims, Afro-Americans, Mexicans, and Jews.

Right now there is a battle for the hearts and minds of Americans. Right now, there is a concerted campaign to separate us, label fellow Americans as boogie men, much like McCarthyism did in the 1950s and Hitler did in the 1930s.

Our new emperor's most trusted advisor is a white supremacist. Think about that for a second. We already see his handiwork in the Trump Administration's relentless drumbeat of what a dangerous environment we live in, that only *they* can save us from the barbarians. On the White House website, they publish crimes committed by Muslims. They don't publish crimes committed by white people ... oh wait, maybe white people don't commit crimes. When Hitler was taking power, he published crimes committed by Jews.

These powerful forces are seeking to divide us by appealing to our baser instincts, and their intent is to disarm our compassion, our humanity, and our empathy.

The traits that make us human.

There is so much that connects us, so much that binds us. And it is these connections that will make us whole, make us great. My wife has infinite love for our children, just as a Syrian mother has infinite love for her children. Mexican parents desire the same thing for their children as my white friends want for their children—a better life than they had, a life filled with purpose and passion.

This is the hard part: there is money to be made by dividing us, money to be made through the creation of conflict. Munitions industries would evaporate, along with the enormous profits, if conflict was removed from the world. They would have a very difficult time making payroll.

Unfortunately, there are dollars to be reaped through bloodshed.

So how do you respond to this hate, the exploitation, and the witch hunts?

In a sermon delivered at a church in 1957, Martin Luther King Jr. said we should love our enemy even when they throw hot coffee in our faces or firebomb the buses we are riding in. Gandhi responded to force and hatred with nonviolence, and by so doing, he brought the mightiest nation on the planet to its knees. Abraham Lincoln said we should have deep empathy for slave owners. Love should be our weapon to combat the hatred and racism spewing from this administration.

We must resist the scapegoats offered up by the new emperor, and we must resist the propaganda that seeks to divide us.

Right now, this administration is coming for Muslims. They have already come for the Mexicans. The African American community has a staggering incarceration rate. Don't think for a moment that they won't come for you.

For John Lewis, Freedom Wasn't a Future Goal; It Was an Immediate Moral Imperative

February 6, 2018

John Lewis, one of our most courageous citizens and civil rights icon, found himself the target of a Twitter rant from our new emperor. He labeled Lewis, "All talk, talk, talk—no results ..."

Lewis, all talk??? If ever there was a man of action, it was Lewis. He rode the buses during the Freedom Rides, not backing down after firebombs, violence, and angry mobs descended on the buses. During the Freedom Marches, Lewis always planted himself in the front row, including Selma, knowing full well he was an easy target for a lunatic with a gun. When the NAACP lawyers counseled civil rights soldiers that they were moving too fast, that achieving freedom requires time, diplomacy, and patience, Lewis simply said, "I'm marching in the morning and you can join me or not." He marched.

For Lewis, freedom wasn't a future goal; it was an immediate, moral imperative.

Lewis was a man of action, not talk. Our country owes him a huge debt for confronting our American Taliban, the KKK, and for being on the front lines in the fight against America's cancer, racism.

Our new emperor should not be denigrating this man, but instead should be petitioning Congress to have a statue erected in his honor. Maybe the emperor's charity could fund it? I mean, why not? It previously funded a 6-foot-tall portrait of our emperor to the tune of $20,000.

You can't make this shit up.

Our new emperor further stated that Lewis's district was "crime-infested and falling apart." Not quite the truth. Well, let's call it like it actually is, a lie. Most of Lewis's district is doing very well. A small section is still disabled by institutional racism, a structure fueled and nourished by our new emperor, perpetuated by gerrymandering, new voter suppression laws, the Citizen United Supreme Court decision, lobbyists, and men such as the Koch brothers whose wealth is sustained by these insidious structures.

America's greatness will fully blossom when we remove the shackles from all Americans, when the power of the underserved, the disenfranchised, are unleashed.

Dismantling the structures which suppress large sections of our society will usher in a Renaissance for America, an unprecedented explosion of innovation, prosperity, and growth.

But I digress. This is about John Lewis. We all know what he did during the Civil Rights era, but how about our new emperor, where did he apply his vision and energy during this pivotal time in our nation's history?

Allow me to refresh your memory. During that time, he was convicted of systematically and intentionally denying African Americans the right to live in his housing projects. If you were a person of color and wanted to live in a Trump structure, well, suddenly the apartment was no longer available. In other words, our new emperor was one of the architects of institutional racism, an institution that Lewis continues to fight.

So, a tale of two cities, or men, and how they spent their time during the Civil Rights Movement.

I guess you could say our emperor was a man of action—he worked very hard to keep people of color out of his buildings.

More and More People Died of Gun Violence and They Did Nothing

February 6, 2018

After the Las Vegas massacre that left 59 people dead, the Republican Representatives and Senators offered up their thoughts and prayers for the victims.

And they did nothing.

After the Orlando nightclub massacre, 49 dead, the Republican Representatives and Senators offered up their thoughts and prayers for the victims.

And they did nothing.

After the San Bernardino massacre, 14 dead, the Republican Representatives and Senators offered up their thoughts and prayers for the victims.

And they did nothing.

After the Charleston church massacre, 9 dead, the Republican Representatives and Senators offered up their thoughts and prayers for the victims.

And they did nothing.

After the Sandy Hook massacre, 27 dead, the Republican Representatives and Senators offered up their thoughts and prayers for the victims.

And they did nothing.

There are hundreds more lives lost, but you get the point.

Lots of thoughts and prayers.

Every week, weapons pour into our inner cities through gun show loop-holes, resulting in staggering body counts.

And for the inner city blood baths, the Republican Representatives and Senators can't even take the time to offer up their thoughts and prayers, because the victims of this carnage are the disenfranchised, the working poor, and people of color. And their political power has been gerryman-dered out of existence.

Who are these spineless people who condone these American massacres? Have they no conscience, no compassion, no soul?

Is there nobody in the Republican Party strong enough to stand up to our merchants of fear and violence? American carnage is happening before their very eyes and all they will do is offer up their thoughts and prayers. And nothing else.

We will get no leadership on this issue from our new emperor. During the campaign, he suggested that perhaps there was a 2nd amendment solution to Hillary. In other words, he floated the idea that someone should assas-sinate Hillary.

Where was the outrage?

These Americans of the Republican Party will do nothing because they have sold their souls to the NRA. If they were not moved by the crimes at Sandy Hook elementary school, nothing can move them.

These were 5- and 6-year-olds, for God's sake.

But there's also this concept in the United States—the bigger the gun, the bigger the man, symbolized by our emperor who lives in a hidden fear of others. It takes tremendous courage to be non-violent, as evidenced by the lives of many people who were agents of real change and a positive force for this country I call home.

We need America to confront the NRA. They are bullies who willingly sacrifice 5-year-olds for profit.

Our Democracy and the Press: Two Quotes, Two Visions

February 6, 2018

Today we have a quiz.

Below are two quotations, one by President Trump and the other by his predecessor President Obama. A prize will be awarded to the person who correctly identifies the author of each.

Here's the first quotation:

"America needs you and our democracy needs you.

"We need you to establish a baseline of facts and evidence that we can use as a starting point for the kind of reasoned and informed debates that ultimately lead to progress. And so, my hope is that you will continue with the same tenacity that you showed us, to do the hard work of getting to the bottom of stories and getting them right and to push those of us in power to be the best version of ourselves and to push this country to be the best version of itself.

"You're not supposed to be sycophants, you're supposed to be skeptics, you're supposed to ask me tough questions. You're not supposed to be complimentary, but you're supposed to cast a critical eye on folks who hold enormous power and make sure that we are accountable to the people who sent us here, and you have done that.

"And you have done it for the most part in ways that I could appreciate for fairness, even if I didn't always agree with your conclusions. And having you in this building has made this place work better. It keeps us honest, it makes us work harder.

You have made us think about how we are doing what we do and whether or not we're able to deliver on what's been requested by our constituents.

"That is part of how this place, this country, this grand experiment in self-government has to work. It doesn't work if we don't have a well-informed citizenry. And you are the conduit through which they receive the information about what's taking place in the halls of power. So, America needs you and our democracy needs you."

And the 2nd set of quotations:

"The FAKE NEWS media (failing @nytimes, @CNN, @NBCNews and many more) is not my enemy, it is the enemy of the American people, 'SICK'.

"With all of the Fake News coming out of NBC and the Networks, at what point is it appropriate to challenge their License? Bad for country!

"Why isn't the Senate Intel Committee looking into the Fake News Networks in OUR country to see why so much of our news is just made up—FAKE!"

OK, there you have it, two visions as to the role of the 4th estate. Because there is such a subtle difference to the quotes, I feel compelled to offer a couple of hints:

1. The 1st quotation was from a man who deeply studied our Constitution and our Bill of Rights, and from that scholarship, he came to embrace the fundamentals upon which our democracy is based, including the vital role of the press in preserving and nourishing our democracy.

2. The 2nd quotation was said by a guy who failed 3rd grade civics, but whose father, upon seeing the report card, stormed into the

school and threatened to shut down the entire school unless his high IQ son received a grade more commensurate to his class and IQ—the threat was further punctuated with threatened multi-million dollar lawsuits against both the school district and the perpetuator of the outrage, 70-year-old teacher Mrs. Dowling who had recently been widowed. (So as not to be accused of being the purveyor of fake news: full disclosure, I have not received confirmation that this little incident occurred in 3rd grade. It may have been 4th grade.)

Okay, fellow friends, cast your votes.

The winner will receive a DVD of the first five seasons of *Keeping Up with the Kardashians*. I wonder how Kim K. did in civics?

I am going to end this with another quotation from Nina Khrushcheva, Nikita's granddaughter. (A quick primer, Nikita Khrushchev ruled Russia through terror, murder, spying, and squashing any semblance of a free press.)

"Here, President Trump defined 'fake news' the way Joseph Stalin defined 'enemies of the people': if they offer a slightest objection to his rule, they must be wrong. And they must be silenced.

"Somewhere on the way to his real estate/reality TV career he forgot his lessons in civics and American democracy from high school. Or maybe he always had an 'F' in those subjects; being rich, he didn't and still doesn't think they apply to him. For that we are all paying dearly.

"And the longer he stays in, offering more and more somewhat Stalinesque amendments to American democracy, the more autocratic erosion to this once wonderful system we will experience."

OK, when the granddaughter of a maniacal Cold War dictator starts lecturing us about our democracy, well, you might say, "something's rotten in the state of Denmark."

P.S. I would be remiss if I didn't address this week's hot topic—the Harvey Weinstein cesspool.

I believe that because of the women coming forward, there is now a website where men can go and unburden themselves and confess their sins of acts of domestic abuse and sexual harassment of women. When I heard about the site, the first person I thought of was our emperor. Finally, a safe place Don T. can go to. A sanctuary where he can unburden himself of his sins against women. Once he confesses his transgressions, he can then begin the process of making amends with the ultimate goal of rejoining the human race.

I think it will be a long, painful process for him as the number of women claiming to be harassed and abused by him are starting to rival the numbers posted by Harvey Weinstein.

Here's are the questions: Who can we send, who will he listen to? Who is the one person who can convince him to avail himself of this bridge to redemption?

Steve Bannon perhaps? Well, maybe not. He appears to have some similar issues of his own.

His buddy Bill O'Reily? Well, maybe not … some issues there, too.

Roger Aires? Oh, forgot. Diseased, and he posted some Weinsteinesque numbers.

Are there no old white guys we can send? This is a mission of redemption for our president. I think he would totally do this—the timing couldn't be better.

OK, I will reach out to him and cold call the White House—I probably should delete some of my previous Facebook posts, but I'm sure he'll take my call.

If he doesn't, well, I often call him emperor but I may have to switch to Predator in Chief.

Our President Is a Racist

February 6, 2018

Evil is hard to confront.

The signs were all there:

1. The demonization of Muslims

2. The denigration of Mexicans

3. The embracing of voter suppression laws specifically aimed at African Americans

4. The scapegoating of immigrants, similar to Hitler's blueprint in the 1920s

And he would throw us curveballs, about wanting to unite the country, about how he is the most least racist person anybody could know.

But the signs kept coming.

He became the first president to decline an invitation to speak at the NAACP convention. He surrounded himself with white supremacists like Steve Bannon and Stephen Miller, massaging his ego while validating his white privilege worldview. The total absence of any people of color in his administration spoke volumes about his agenda. And he carried forward a history of discrimination: in the 1960s and 70s he was convicted of systematically denying people of color residency in his housing developments. The appointment of Jeff Sessions as the Attorney General, that good old boy who was denied a judgeship because of his history of racism, whose first big Civil Rights initiative was to crack down on reversed discrimination, that beleaguered victim, your average white guy.

Really?

And it was all revealed after the Charlottesville tragedy when he just couldn't bring himself to denounce the KKK, the neo-Nazis, and the white supremacists. All he had to do was to follow the script, and he would be free to continue his assault on the working poor, the disabled, women, people of color, the LGBTQ+ community, education, the EPA, etc., etc. And most importantly, he could continue his assault on his imagined enemies.

But he just couldn't bring himself to denounce the neo-Nazis or the KKK, and in so doing fully revealed both his character and his agenda.

Our president is a racist. And it saddens me to say those words.

We couldn't bring ourselves to see it because we want/we assume our president to be the most ethical, humble, intelligent, compassionate, courageous person in the room. Instead, we are infected with a man-child who is immoral, a sexual pervert (remember the "Grab 'em by the pussy" tape), paranoid, vengeful, a bully, and a coward. When you strip off the guise, a bully is revealed to be a coward, living in a hidden fear of others.

During the campaign, we ignored his message of hate and divisiveness and relished the theatre. But he was very overt in declaring what he would do, and we ignored it, much like the German people ignored Hitler's demonization and scapegoating of the Jews during his ascent to power. Hitler fed the German people a scapegoat, and they devoured the meat because it absolved them of any responsibility for their condition, of having lost the war and trying to survive in a broken economy. And Trump executed the same playbook, offering up to his base the meat of Muslims and Mexicans.

We ignored the signs. We ignored his sordid past (6 bankruptcies to go along with over 4,000 legal cases. Who does that—4,000 and counting ????) The demonization of Hillary kept the press chasing after red herrings instead of doing their job and investigating the truth, the truth behind his straw house.

His method of conflict resolution is to file a suit, and this is the guy we gave the nuclear codes to.

We patted ourselves on the back after we elected the first African American President. Racism was dead—look who we just elected. It turned out that Obama's election only served as a Band-Aid to the festering cancer called racism. Trump ripped off the Band-Aid, allowing the cancer to erupt, nourishing the disease by empowering groups such as the KKK, neo-Nazis, and white supremacists.

He still can't bring himself to denounce David Duke.

The issue of race continues to haunt our country. Until we confront this cancer, we will never be whole.

Here's the problem: playing the race card can get you elected. In the past, code words were the vehicle. Nixon used the phrase "Law and Order." Reagan used the Willie Horton ads, Sarah Palin talked about "our kind of people." Trump threw away the code words and brought racism out of the closet. He legitimized it. He started naming new groups to target: Muslims and Mexicans. He told his base the reason they are miserable, unemployed, sick, and patronized was because of people of color. Because of the others.

He served up the "who" for their discontent, and disillusionment, much like McCarthy did in the 1950s.

We are still unwilling to confront this disease because we are unwilling to confront our sins, and our lack of responsibility. In South Africa, after apartheid was dismantled, they convened "Truth and Reconciliation Hearings." These were public hearings which gave its citizens a haven to confess their sins, to take responsibility, allowing the country to begin the healing process.

Maybe it's time for the United States to hold its own Truth and Reconciliation Hearings.

Here's the thing: the children being brought up in KKK and neo-Nazi groups are being manipulated and brainwashed. Hate is taught. Nobody is born a racist; it is a learned behavior. The KKK and the neo-Nazis have historically fought against people of color in the same socio-economic class. Ironically, they should be a band of brothers because the forces that keep them poor, uneducated, and suppressed are the same. It is not people of a different pigmentation.

They have the wrong who, but the infighting guarantees the working poor will remain cemented in their class for generations to come. By fighting each other, they fail to see the puppeteer who is pulling their strings; they fail to see the force that exploits them, uses them, and flushes them out when they are no longer useful to the puppeteer. The reason they are poor and vulnerable and expendable is not the person across from them; it is the economic structure whose underpinnings are dependent on the poor fighting each other.

And we now have a president who sanctifies this economic engine of hate and divisiveness, pitting the working poor against each other, fighting for the leftover crumbs as our president fights for tax breaks for the rich.

He has legitimized the American Taliban, also known as the KKK!

Don't get me wrong; I'm a business owner, I believe in capitalism.

Capitalism works best when the playing field is level, when fairness reigns. And even high-powered businesses have to pay taxes.

Pitting races and the powerless against each other has a long track record. It had a free rein during Reconstruction and during Boston's busing crisis, young Black and white kids being pitted against each other by community leaders and politicians. You got elected in South Boston and Charlestown by fanning the flames of racism. White kids were told to boycott school by politicians such as Louise Day Hicks, resulting in a generation of unemployable dropouts who were often addicted to drugs.

And these were shitty, neglected schools. Instead of addressing why the schools were shitty, poor whites and poor Blacks took the bait and engaged in internecine warfare.

And so, our current president continues to fan the flames of race, hatred, and divisiveness. By embracing this hate and scapegoating, it only serves to erode our humanity: our inherent connection with each other.

We are all connected. When we deny these connections, we become less human, less empathetic, and our humanity is compromised.

One of the saddest things about all of this is Trump can't see that America's glory, strength, and soul spring forth from its diversity. We are the greatest country on Earth and will be even greater once the shackles of hate have been unlocked and the full power of our diversity manifests itself.

I'll end by quoting myself—is that arrogant or what?

Well, I do have the mic.

"We must resist the scapegoats offered up by the new emperor, and we must resist the propaganda that seeks to divide us.

"Right now, this administration is coming for Muslims. They have already come for the Mexicans. The African American community has a staggering incarceration rate. Don't think for a moment that they won't come for you."

P.S. How's that wall coming? Did the Mexicans ever pony up that cash?

What Makes America Great?
Our Diversity

February 6, 2018

When Trump made racist remarks about Hispanics, the Republicans were silent.

When Trump made racist remarks about Muslims, the Republicans were silent.

When Trump denigrated our Veterans, the Republicans were silent.

When Trump made antisemitic comments, the Republicans were silent.

When Trump made racist remarks about African Americans, the Republicans were silent.

But when Trump made disparaging remarks about white women, they couldn't get off the bandwagon fast enough. This country has a sullied history in preserving the sanctity of white women—lynching in the Deep South was often the vehicle for preserving this concept.

You see, Trump miscalculated. He figured that by appealing to our baser instincts he would get elected. He didn't realize that America is already great and what makes us great is our diversity. But what makes us even greater is our SHARED HUMANITY.

This is why America is the greatest country in the world.

Trump provided us with a great public service by shining the light on AMERICA'S GREATNESS.

Thank you, Donald!

The Bullying and Racism Where I Grew Up in Maryland

February 13, 2018

When I was about 14, my team had just played a basketball game and I referred to a player on the other team as that "Black guy." The two teammates I was riding with turned to me and said: "he's not a Black guy, he's a ni...r." And they insisted I say the word, out loud, as some kind of loyalty test, much like a fraternity pledge ritual.

Well, I didn't say the word, but I remember feeling shaken and bullied.

I grew up in Maryland, right outside of D.C. and I would often go back and ask about my high school classmates. A surprising number of them became police officers in Prince George's County, a county north of D.C., well populated by working-class and middle-class African Americans. And the ones who became cops were often the ones marginalized in high school: not quite good enough to play varsity sports, not quite smart enough or rich enough to go to college, and not quite accomplished enough to attract girls.

But they were well qualified to become cops in Prince George's County, including my two teammates who administered my loyalty test.

As the years passed, I read newspaper accounts of strife and racial tension between the citizens of Prince George's County and the police— reports about brutality, violent confrontations, and 'driving while Black.'

Not really a spoiler alert, as I grew up with these guys and I knew that putting on that uniform had not purged them of their racial animus. I also knew that putting on the uniform empowered them, validated their racial indoctrination, and their racial implants, and perhaps provided them, for the first time in their life, a winning identity.

I also remember those guys as kids. They were kind, loyal, funny, full of heart, and devoid of prejudice. By the time they were 14, those qualities seemed to have vanished, or were crushed, infected with hateful racial propaganda, the DNA that was passed down to Maryland boys back in the day. Remember, George Wallace ("segregation today ... segregation tomorrow ... segregation forever") received close to 200,000 votes in his Presidential bid in Maryland back in 1968.

One of the joys in life is realizing connections, and recognizing the commonality between yourself and the citizens of the world. It makes your life richer and deeper, your soul nourished by the rainbow, the richness of other cultures. There is so much that connects us. But back in my high school years, Maryland boys were force-fed racial stereotypes, scapegoats for all that ailed them. And the ones who became cops, their behavior programmed by their childhood indoctrination, came to view people of color as objects, and when you objectify someone, it becomes easy to exact cruelty upon them.

Now I have great respect for cops. They are similar to other professions—some good, some bad, but mostly good. Today, because of all the budget cuts to social services, we have dumped the tasks of social worker, counselor, and mental health worker, onto the police. All of that in addition to their primary job of keeping the peace. And, like teachers, they are grossly underpaid.

In the 1930s, when the Nazi SS rolled into Polish towns with orders to exterminate Jews, they lacked the personnel to execute their mission. To make up for their personnel deficiencies, they recruited townspeople to participate in their local holocaust. So, your local baker, mail carrier, civil servant, and carpenter spent the day executing Jewish men, women and children (yes, children) and afterward enjoyed a nice family dinner at night. They were willing executioners, having been infected by a steady diet of propaganda, including decades-long rants from pulpits about how Jews were animals, less than human, and were the principal reason for Germany's defeat in World War I. (The source for this data is: *Hitler's Willing Executioners* by Daniel Goldhagen.) The pump had been primed.

Hitler didn't create antisemitism; he exploited the cancer that had been planted and after laying fallow for decades.

We have a great capacity for evil when our soul is infected by the cancer of propaganda, infected with the disease of scapegoating. When this disease courses through our veins, shaping our behavior, and burying our inherent goodness, we become capable of astounding acts of cruelty.

During the 1900s, in many southern towns, the hanging of an African American in the town square served as a social event for the community, much like a spring dance, or when the circus came to town. Actually, it was more of a social event for the white community, with kids frolicking in the town square while a human being swung from a tree. The town's leaders, often the leading elders of the church, spearheaded this entertainment ritual. And like the citizens in those Polish towns, they viewed their victims as objects, not quite human, soulless, a threat to the social order, fortified by their interpretation of scripture. They felt they were doing God's work, much like the German citizens who would attend church the following day after engaging in genocide, comforted by their certainty they were executing God's will by executing their fellow humans.

And these acts of violence were condoned, and granted absolution by the silence of both German citizens and the white citizens in those Southern towns.

Back to my Maryland story and the Prince George's police force.

There are two tragedies in play here: a community laid siege with physical violence, intimidation, and suppression perpetuated against people of color by the police. But there is another victim: people like my buddies who were force-fed, indoctrinated with hateful racial stereotypes and scapegoats during their formative years. And the degree to which the teachings stuck was the degree to which their humanity became contaminated, compromised, and decayed, allowing them to remove themselves from the community of man and woman with all its inherent riches.

The perpetuators of violence don't walk away free and clear, for each act of cruelty performed recoils against their soul. There is a price to be paid because it is a crime against one's innate goodness.

Here we are 30 years later, and candidate Trump is running for president. Instead of appealing to the inherent goodness of our citizens, instead of appealing to the high ideals as set forth in our Bill of Rights and Constitution, instead of appealing to America's strength as embodied by its diversity, instead of appealing to the glory of the American dream and all it represents, he appealed to America's vast reservoir of prejudice, hate, and intolerance. He chose to take the cowardly path by pandering to America's deepest fears and prejudices. And like Hitler, and like the Southern Christian elders, he offered up a scapegoat. He pummeled the American people with the concept that we live in a dangerous environment, and that the fear and terror that blankets the land has one source—Muslims. Muslims are serving the same purpose that Jews served for Hitler, that African Americans served for the Southern Christian elders.

Trump recently called the press the enemy of the people. I wonder what politician coined that term … Oh yeah, it was Joseph Stalin. You know, the guy responsible for the deaths of 20 million Russians. (Some historians have pushed the figure to 80 million.)

Our president doesn't quote Thomas Jefferson, Alexander Hamilton, John Quincy Adams, Martin Luther King Jr., or Abraham Lincoln. No, his go-to guy is Joseph Stalin, the man responsible for The Great Purge.

Trump is systematically infecting America with his white supremacy agenda, the Republican Representatives and Senators are complicit in their silence. What was said behind closed doors is now becoming public policy throughout the land. White supremacists now run our country and they have an agenda, and people of color are in their scopes.

Trump is a bully.

American can no longer afford to be silent. This insecure bully has the nuclear codes.

From here forward, nobody should ever say the words, "I didn't vote; they are all bad."

Well, they're not. And our silence, our apathy, has elected a guy who thinks a maniacal dictator had the right idea about the press.

And for my basketball buddies and the rest of Trump's base, we must work to restore their innate humanity, their innate goodness. They fell for the wrong boogie man. We must work to combat intolerance because it sabotages the promise of America.

This is a real test for our democracy and our institutions. The administration's white supremacy agenda is no longer hidden. They hold power, and secret code words to communicate their message of intolerance are no longer required. Their racism is overt; they feel empowered, which in turn empowers the white supremacists, neo-Nazis, and other hate groups.

This race thing has a chokehold on America. We either confront it or the virus injected by our president will become the law of the land.

Our Democracy Is Under Siege, Not by a Foreign Power, but by Our Own Greed

July 1, 2018

I love basketball.

Not only do I believe that basketball demands more skill than other sports, but I consider it the most aesthetically pleasing—players improvising artistic riffs reminiscent of Baryshnikov, Michael Jackson, or the Alvin Ailey dancers. At its best, it's a choreographed ballet, a transcendent dance interspersed with improvisational solos, almost spiritual, and oftentimes inspirational.

And this year's NCAA tournament symbolized this transcendence, saturated with inspirational stories, David repeatedly slaying Goliath. We witnessed a sport in all of its splendor, and were reminded as to why we watch.

Above all else, Americans have an innate sense of justice and fairness. It's part of our DNA, our soul. We recoil, we protest, and we fight when confronted by injustices, inequities, unequal playing fields or unequal opportunities, circumstances that simply don't pass the smell test. Our DNA demands fairness. It's what built this country and is what makes our country great.

Greed has infected college basketball. It has been festering for decades, its pestilence rotting the core of amateur sports. Greed has spurred coaches, school presidents, and athletic directors to circumvent and break rules, lie, and cover up, all in an effort to un-level the playing field, to stack the deck. There is money to be extracted from teenagers, and as a consequence, collegiate athletic coaches and administrators have flushed away their integrity in a sordid attempt to preserve their jobs while cashing in on the tainted money, the golden goose of free labor—collegiate athletes who produce the product but who earn nothing from their labors. Greed has fostered cheating creating a system in which 18-year-old kids are exploited and preyed upon by sophisticated predators seeking their pound of flesh.

So, it was interesting in this year's March Madness to see that the schools racked by scandal, schools visited by the windbreakers, were eliminated by lower-seeded schools, often with 2% of the recruiting budget of the blue bloods.

David continually slayed Goliath in this year's March Madness, and it was glorious.

When I was young, my buddies and I formed a basketball team. We would go to a local playground to compete. Our team would get to the court early in order to secure a game. It was single elimination; if your team lost, you would have to wait 3 hours to get another game. And since we didn't want to wait 3 hours, our will to win was off the charts. But it was a level playing field and no one wanted to wait for another spot to open up. Game point was a virtual bloodbath, but it was an honest competition. We always shook hands after the game, and respect was earned.

The deck was not stacked.

But there was another issue at play during these games—race. Since the court was right on the border between D.C. and Maryland, there would often be games between Black and white teams, the race issue hovering overhead like a cloud. But it never got racial because the playing field was level. What mattered was your game and how hard you competed in order to avoid the three-hour wait. Honest competition dissolved any potential racial animus, because honest competition fosters respect, the kryptonite of racism.

But every once in a while, a guy showed up after having recruited a team of All-City players, All-Stars, even college players—in other words, a dream team, a stacked deck. I could tell he was afraid to compete, using his recruits to camouflage his fear. And I would say to myself, "I don't care who's on your team, even if you have pros, I'm still gonna beat your motherf...... ass."

It would make my blood boil. I always considered it cowardly, like breaking an unspoken covenant. But I welcomed the challenge, which unearthed even deeper reservoirs of will I didn't know I had.

And sometimes we beat the dream team, and it was glorious.

But I always wondered about these guys who felt the need to stack their decks. What were they afraid of? What was it about their character, their deep insecurities, that they were unwilling to put in the work to compete. They were cheaters, but more importantly, they cheated themselves out of the character growth that results from honest competition, and honest striving for one's goals. Instead, they choose the path of least residence and dishonesty, which probably became their default operating system in navigating their life.

At its core, these guys had a hidden fear of others, a disability that unconsciously demanded they compulsively stack the deck. They obsessively suppress others because if the people around them flourished, they might be found out.

And I began to wonder if these people had any influence on the world today. Had they somehow ascended to positions of power?

And then I realized who our president was. That people with a hidden fear of others, people who squash anyone around them who they fear will become more powerful, and who surround themselves with sycophants whose sole redeeming quality is loyalty to a bully, can often rise to positions of power. And they are put there by the political apathy of our citizens.

You can almost view America's history as a battle between those who cowardly stack the deck and those who fight for a level playing field. Or more simply, those who believe in America's basic principle—"We hold these truths to be self-evident, that all men are created equal, that they are endowed by their Creator with certain unalienable Rights, that among these are Life, Liberty and the pursuit of Happiness,"—and those who don't. (I am aware that this basic principle ignores women and others, but that's an essay for another day.)

This battle has raged since our country's inception, the dream team architects ratcheting up their agenda over the past 30 years.

> "In the United States, for example, 'trickle down' economic policies that support tax cuts for the rich with the aim of boosting economic growth and jobs have led to a $2 trillion annual redistribution of wealth from the bottom 99 percent of earners to the top 1 percent over the last 30 years,' said Nick Hanauer, a former venture capitalist and now head of Civic Ventures."
>
> ~ Laurie Goering, Reuters, *Growing wealth inequality 'dangerous' threat to democracy: experts*, April 15, 2016

The consequence of this exploding wealth gap poses the gravest threat to our country's founding principles.

> "We can either have democracy in this country or we can have great wealth concentrated in the hands of a few, but we can't have both."
>
> ~ Louis Brandeis,
> U.S. Supreme Court Justice (1856–1941)

> "An imbalance between rich and poor is the oldest and most fatal ailment of all republics."
>
> ~ Plutarch,
> ancient Greek biographer (C. 46–120 CE)

"There's no more central theme in the Bible than the immorality of inequality. Jesus speaks more about the gap between rich and poor than he does about heaven and hell."

~ Franklin D. Roosevelt,
United States President (1882–1945)
Second Inaugural Address, 1937

The fact of the matter is this: we are our brother's keeper.

Ain't no getting around that.

The ever-widening wealth gap wrecks the idea of our shared humanity, and sabotages the idea that we are our brother's keeper. Our innate humanity and goodness can only blossom when we take responsibility for our fellow humans. Living in a gated community does not immunize us from our responsibility to the citizens of the world. America's salvation, our greatness, is linked to how we treat and serve all of our citizens, especially the ones less fortunate, the ones trying to find their way with the cards stacked against them.

Before we go any further, I need to comment on this concept of wealth redistribution and its reporting.

Now if you listen to Fox News, the propaganda wing of the White House, you hear this drumbeat, one of FOX's big lies, pounded down Americans' throats: President Obama was a socialist, intent on redistributing the wealth, which served to distract the American public with what was really happening in regard to wealth distribution.

And make no mistake about it—the American public was pummeled by this 'fake news'.

Pummeled.

Here is what Joseph Goebbels said about the concept of telling big lies:

"If you tell a lie big enough and keep repeating it, people will eventually come to believe it. The lie can be maintained only for such time as the State can shield the people from the political, economic and/or military consequences of the lie. It thus becomes vitally important for the State to use all of its powers to repress dissent, for the truth is the mortal enemy of the lie, and thus by extension, the truth is the greatest enemy of the State."

Can't help but think that our emperor was an avid student of Goebbels. But here is what was really happening with wealth distribution:

"If the trend continues, by 2030, the top 1 percent of Americans will earn 37 to 40 percent of the country's income, with the bottom 50 percent getting just 6 percent. Globally, half of the world's wealth is now held by just 1 percent of the world's population, according to a 2015 report by Credit Suisse, a financial services company."

~ Laurie Goering, Reuters, *Growing wealth inequality 'dangerous' threat to democracy: experts*, April 15, 2016

We are spiraling toward an economy that is reminiscent of the antebellum South, embodied by enslavers, exploiting a stacked deck through the torture and enslavement of African Americans, backed by the financial investments of the North and Europe. This was perhaps the ultimate stacked deck, the exploitation of slave labor in order to expand and grow an industry.

And like the enslavers, who justified the torture, the terror, the subjecting of an entire race to bondage—condoned from Catholic, Baptist and Episcopalian pulpits—today, these justifications for crimes against humanity emanate from the pulpit of Ayn Rand, the Republicans' wet dream. (By the way, it's ironic how the religious right continues to support our new emperor and the depravity of his character: the constant lying, the sexual assault boastings, the bullying, and the racism. They continue to line up behind him in lockstep because their selective reading of scripture validates a patriarchal worldview, ethics, and compassion be damned. Their admiration of a man who degrades women and people of color eclipses Bible scriptures about morals and empathy.)

"The disposition to admire, and almost to worship, the rich and the powerful, and to despise, or, at least, to neglect persons of poor and mean condition is the great and most universal cause of the corruption of our moral sentiments."

~ Adam Smith,
Scottish Political Economist (1723–1790)

Repudiation of responsibility for one's fellow humans requires a philosophic rationale and Ayn Rand delivers the goods.

A philosophical system that sees workers' rights as a barrier to business, that ignores macroeconomic reality, that always blames the poor for being poor, and that elevates the rich to the status of economic saviors, that is the new reality for America's conservatives. It is slowly but consistently seeping into the mainstream conservative outlook on this side of the Atlantic. Any political party that promotes tax cuts for the rich while simultaneously cutting protections for workers and the poor is on the outer edge of the Ayn Rand economic death spiral.

"Today, Rand's policies are embodied by US politicians like Rand Paul (yes, he was named for her) and Ted Cruz, both potential Republican presidential candidates. Cruz wants to abolish the IRS and the minimum wage, Paul wants to get rid of laws that stop businesses from committing racial discrimination. The message is simple: 'let the rich do whatever they want, and everyone will benefit.'"

~ Darragh Roche

Back in the antebellum South, preachers served the role of Ayn Rand, proclaiming that slavery was part of God's will, his divine plan.

Today we have our modern-day Goebbels in the form of Sarah Saunders who justifies the trauma being enacted upon the children of immigrants by suggesting the Bible offers reasonable explanations for this outrage.

And reminiscent of slave markets, we are now separating kids from parents—courtesy of our new immigration initiative, similar to what happened on the slave blocks where families were splintered, crying children removed from the clutches of their parents.

Trump's immigration policy has set in motion a replay of our original sin—the splintering of families as parents were separated from children, a drama we saw play out by the Nazi's during the Holocaust.

Our democracy is under siege, not by a foreign power but by our own greed. The widening wealth gap is undermining the very foundations of our democratic institutions. At some point, these chickens will come home to roost. And for people of color living in this country, the trends are looking truly alarming.

> The Institute for Policy Studies's recent report: *The Road to Zero Wealth: How the Racial Divide is Hollowing Out the American's Middle Class* showed that between 1983 and 2013, the wealth of the median Black household declined 75 percent (from $6800 to $1700) and the medium Latino household declined 50 percent (from $4,000 to $2,000). At the same time, wealth for the median white household increased 14 percent (from $102,000 to $116,800).

Our president has emboldened white supremacists to rise up from the swamp (maybe that is what he meant by his campaign pledge of draining the swamp), fueling and giving validation to their racism, and hatred, affirming their scapegoats.

But their true objective is to fuel a pestilence that has been eroding our democracy since its inception: the widening wealth gap which has accelerated over the last 30 years.

Today, there is a systematic agenda to revert the United States back to the dynamics of the antebellum South. Same playbook, different players but the intent is the same—rule by an oligarchy. Here are the basics of the playbook:

1. Make sure education isn't funded. Before the Civil War, there was no public education in the South. They systematically kept both poor whites and slaves illiterate. It was calculated as a vehicle of control and suppression. People were hanged from trees if they were caught in possession of abolition literature.

Today, we have education budgets and teacher's salaries continually slashed by legislatures. More money is being funneled into our prison industrial complex, a living breathing monster that needs to be fed and have its beds filled, often by a disproportional amount of people with higher levels of melanin. Empty beds don't generate dividends for investors. And suppressing education makes sense to feed the prison system: the less educated our citizens are, the more likely they will be to resort to crime, so I guess we need to get those beds ready for their incarceration. We can invest in education, or we can invest in prison beds. Trump and the Republicans have put their money into prison beds. To my Florida friends, your governor is a big supporter of prison beds, and the prison industrial complex—lots of campaign contributions from that industry go into the Governor's coffers.

2. Work to separate the races. Prior to the Civil War, there was a growing awareness by Southern whites that they were screwed because they were competing against slave labor. Slave owners toiled to keep poor whites and slaves separated, lest they figure out who their enemy was. Ultimately, slave owners were able to brainwash poor whites into believing that Black people were their enemies, not their allies. And through this brainwashing, the KKK evolved. Poor whites were kept ignorant, destitute, and oblivious as to whom their suppressor was. They were kept oppressed by the instruments of control: law enforcement and the courts, which could sentence a white man to slavery for transgressions such as loitering, unpaid debts, etc. (Can't help but think of Ferguson.)

Today, our administration has saturated the airwaves with the concept that America is a dangerous environment, offering up Muslims, Mexicans, and African Americans as the dangers. The less educated a person is, the more likely they will be to embrace scapegoats, no matter who the scapegoat is. At the end of the day, Trump's administration has served to separate Americans, with hate crimes being up 67% since he took office.

3. Control the voting booths. During the antebellum South, voting was a sham. You had to own property in order to vote and your vote was public. If one voted against the slaveowner's candidate, he could lose his job, maybe his life. (Yes, you also had to be male.)

Today we have the proliferation of the voter suppression laws, spearheaded by the Republicans and condoned by our emperor, all calculated to deny people of color and the working poor the right to vote. We also have obscene gerrymandering, calculated to ensure Republican dominance in the House and Senate, again blessed by the current administration. Their goal is a stacked deck. Republicans have publicly stated that the fewer the voters, the more successful they will be.

4. Use the law to incarcerate anyone who might challenge the power structure. Poor whites were continually incarcerated for trumped-up violations such as loitering, debt, distributing handbills talking about workers' rights, etc. Some whites were even hanged for these misdemeanors, as were abolitionists, or anyone who promoted the idea of freedom for all races.

So, here's my point. (I know you're saying to yourself, "It's about god-damn time.") Sports reveal character. People who have played golf with Trump say he cheats. You have to be pretty degraded to cheat at golf. And it's doubly degrading if you are the president and you find the need to cheat. And it wasn't just a few people.

I've written many things about our president, but you really need to know only one thing: he cheats at golf.

14 Early Signs of Fascism

November 11, 2018

There is a plaque at the Holocaust Museum that lists the early signs of fascism. Got me thinking: I wonder how this current administration measures up to the warnings.

1. Powerful and continuing nationalism. Well, he did run on the mantra of *Make America Great Again*. That phrase sounds familiar ... oh yeah, Hitler promised to *Make Germany Great Again*. Was Trump's phrase just a coincidence? Trump's nationalistic message also came armed with scapegoats: Muslims, Hispanics, and African Americans. Hitler used Jews and communists.

2. Disdain for human rights. We need to look no further than the assault on children and immigrants at the border. Their rights are trampled as families are systematically separated, children are herded into cages, and people are sometimes forced to take psychotropic medications. I seem to recall another movement that separated families. I think they were Jewish families ... cages ... ovens ...

3. Identification of enemies' scapegoats as a unifying cause. Well, that's an easy one: it ain't a good time to be a Muslim, African American, or Hispanic in the United States. According to our emperor, they are all terrorists, drug dealers, criminals, rapists, or come from shitty countries like Haiti. He fed this red meat to his followers, much like Hitler fed Jews to the Germans.

4. Obsession with national security. Well, it's more of an obsession with loyalty, or shall we say, a selective obsession with national security. He did prop open the door to Russia, enabling them to compromise one of our most sacred democratic institutions—the right to vote. And he has closed the door to asylum seekers, people seeking sanctuary from fascist regimes, forgetting the fact that America is the world's haven for people fleeing fascism, forgetting the fact that the soul of America is composed of immigrants. It's what made us great. And there is that wall he can't seem to stop talking about. Yes, quite the obsession.

5. Supremacy of the military. Our defense budget has exploded, fueled by the gutting of social programs, including education. And let's not forget the military parade our new emperor wants to orchestrate, eerily similar in scope to the Third Reich's goose-stepping militaristic displays, or his buddy Putin's weapons arsenal parade. And let's not forget his bro, Kim Jong Un, and his nuclear dick wave. So ironic given the fact that our president was a draft dodger.

6. Rampant sexism. Well, kind of an easy one. One word, Stormy. And don't forget about the Access Hollywood tape. And I lost track on how many sexual harassment suits he has been (and is) involved in. And not to mention his verbal assault on the LGBTQ+ community, as well as anyone with—what he considers—a disability.

7. Controlled mass media. Trump continually labels the media as the "Enemy of the People." Stalin originally coined that phrase and again I have to ask the question, is this a coincidence? From Day 1 of his administration, he has sought to intimidate the media, blocking access to the mainstream media and only granting access to the White House's propaganda arm, Fox News, while labeling them purveyors of fake news which only served as a smoke screen for his assault on the American Constitution.

8. Religion and government are intertwined. The religious right has easy access to the White House and is now preaching its right-wing agenda from pulpits across the country. Our Founding Father's concept of separation of church and state is under siege.

9. Corporate power is protected. The current administration unleashed a campaign to roll back regulations that were enacted to protect American consumers. Corporations can now operate with impunity.

They can now pollute the environment with impunity. Trump bestowed upon corporations the largest tax break of this century, fueled by the middle class and working class, and despite what he says, he made out really well personally with the tax breaks.

10. Labor power is suppressed. Well, we can start with Trump's hotel employees whose efforts to organize were met with extreme countermeasures. And then there's the fact that all of Trump's products are manufactured overseas, with slave wages, child labor, toxic work environments, and in countries where the concept of unionizing is suppressed.

11. Disdain for intellectuals and the arts. Trump's administration is saturated with sycophants, good old boys, and major campaign donors—no mention of intellectuals. In order to pay for the escalating war machine, the arts budget has been gutted.

12. Obsession with crime and punishment. He wants to execute drug dealers but gives a pass to the drug companies who have saturated our nation with their deadly poisons. He has labeled immigrants as criminals, rapists, and drug dealers and continually broadcasts that message with the implication that only he can save America from the dark hoards.

13. Rampant cronyism and corruption. The list of associates under indictment is staggering. His collusion with Russia to steal the election is unprecedented. His use of Trump properties to bilk the government is beyond arrogant. His appointing friends, major donors, and family members to positions of power despite their being totally unqualified is a slap in the face of the American people—Betsy DeVos being the prime example. His financial crimes are slowly oozing out from the infection; the revelations in his tax returns will provide the final roadmap to his sordid crimes and misdemeanors.

14. Fraudulent elections. Kind of an easy one. He invited Russia into our house. He even fired the guy whose job it was to investigate the collusion, James Comey.

There you have it.

The question now becomes will we respond like Neville Chamberlain did with a policy of appeasement, or will we respond as Churchill did with a forceful, patriotic assault?

Do we really need any more evidence?

Trump and Responsibility

October 30, 2018

Remember when Trump suggested to his base that there might be a Second Amendment solution to Hillary?

Remember that?

And the not-so-veiled threats to reporters for being 'enemies of the people'?

Remember that?

And his suggestions to police that it was okay to break the law when arresting a suspect?

Remember that?

And telling his base that he would pay any legal fees incurred if one of his base roughed up a protester?

Remember that?

And how about decades ago, when five African American teenagers were accused of raping a white woman in Central Park, Trump responded by taking a full-page ad in four daily newspapers calling for a return of the death penalty, fanning racial tensions in the city.

When the five teenagers were acquitted decades later, Trump offered no apologies.

Remember that?

And he wants to take no responsibility for inciting violence, no responsibility for planting seeds of violence.

Actually, I have never heard him utter the words, "I'm responsible." That concept is not in his vocabulary. I've heard him say numerous times, "I'm not responsible."

Then last week he finally confessed to being a nationalist. When asked if he was a *white* nationalist, he feigned ignorance, saying he didn't know what that was. He responded in the same tone and manner as when asked if he would denounce David Duke and he responded that he didn't know who David Duke was.

Really? I thought he was such a smart guy??? You really don't know who the former head of the KKK is, the American Taliban???

Really? Since taking office, it has been documented that he has lied 5001 times and counting.

5001. It's not fake news because it is all on video. Anyone can check it.

5001 times. And we as a nation condone this.

For the president's edification, here is the definition of a white nationalist. According to Merriam-Webster dictionary, a white nationalist is "one of a group of militant whites who espouse white supremacy and advocate enforced racial segregation."

But even if you are just a nationalist, it does have sinister connotations, including links to the Third Reich where it was used as a weapon in their antisemitic playbook.

> "The book argues that growing extremism in nationalist attitudes afforded a suitable ideological and social background for anti-Semitic activity, as manifested by calls for discriminatory legislation against Jews, the pogroms of Eastern Europe and, ultimately, the Nazi Holocaust."
>
> ~ Shmuel Almog & Lyael Maman, *Nationalism and Antisemitism in Modern Europe, 1815–1945*

Part and parcel of nationalism is the manufactured hatred, demonization, and scapegoating of immigrants for all that might ail a nation. Trump has been tapping out this drumbeat since the moment he announced his candidacy.

Speaking of immigrants, I stand in awe of the people who walk, sometimes thousands of miles, often with their children, fueled solely on faith and hope, striving against impossible odds to reach the promised land, a country by its creed that embraces the immigrant: "Give me your tired, your poor, your huddled masses yearning to breathe free, The wretched refuse of your teeming shore."

The fortitude and the resiliency of those people is based solely on the faith that by reaching the US, a better life is possible for their children. The courage, the love, the sheer willpower that must reside in the souls of these immigrants is truly an inspiration.

I am humbled by their courage. These are the people I would want in my country, in my town, on my street, in my company. These are the people who make a country great. It takes unbelievable courage and stamina to travel thousands of miles toting your kids, fueled by the vision as set forth by our Founding Fathers—FREEDOM. And they keep walking, despite the resistance, despite the odds and uncertainty, despite Trump sending 5,000 troops to the border, armed to the gills, ready to do battle against a mother holding a one-year-old child.

Will we once again separate children from parents?

As a nation, can we just stop doing that?

Please!

Trump has labeled these freedom seekers as criminals and drug dealers. Really? Hate to break it to you, but drug dealers and criminals don't walk a thousand miles for anything. In case you haven't heard, criminals and drug dealers are lazy cowards. They always take the easy route, and the easy route is never a thousand-mile odyssey with 5,000 hostile troops waiting at the finish line.

The greatness of America was forged through the souls of our immigrants, (including the immigrants who didn't enter through Ellis Island). Alexander Hamilton, a homeless immigrant from the Caribbean, was one of the first who had a profound impact on our nation. Immigrants built this nation, built this economy, found cures, invented technological breakthroughs, fought in our wars to preserve our freedom, built the roads, designed our cities, designed and built our skyscrapers, enhanced our culture, and built enduring monuments to capitalism. Our greatness has always manifested itself through the hearts and souls of our immigrants.

It would be shortsighted of us to deny a whole generation of people who would embody the ideals of America as set forth in our Constitution, whose children might find a cure for cancer, or world peace, or compose a symphony that could stir the souls of our citizens. America is a nation of immigrants. They built this country into the most admired experiment in democracy in the world. Denying our soul, our history, our ancestry, dilutes our strength as a nation, and poisons our humanity.

Until about a week ago, this caravan was labeled immigrants. They are now being labeled 'invaders' by Fox News, a label now parroted by our president. The more you can dehumanize and demonize the freedom seekers, the easier it will be to enact violence and suppression toward them, including the infants.

Dare I mention Pittsburgh? Dare I mention the pipe bomber?

One might ask, "Well, what are you going to do with all these immigrants?"

Well, you just figure it out. It ain't rocket science. It reminds me of the story when our Dust Bowl refugees descended on labor camps on the west coast, emaciated and starving, and the question was asked, "How are we gonna feed them?"

Someone answered back and said, "You just feed them."

And they did.

There is tremendous power in us when we embrace humanity.

Same thing with the caravan refugees, fleeing suppression and starvation. We embrace them. Help them. For they are the future citizens of this great nation, infusing our culture with their souls as they work to create a better life for their children, and in so doing strengthen the fabric of America.

The Sad Relationship Between Misogyny and Violence

August 26, 2019

In continuing our lively discussion on gun control, one element we have not discussed is misogyny.

From *The Handmaid's Tale*:

> "Someone once said men are afraid that women will laugh at them. Women are afraid that men will kill them."

Julie Bosman, Kate Taylor, and Tim Arango, Aug. 10, 2019, *N.Y. Times*:

- "The man who shot nine people to death last weekend in Dayton, Ohio, seethed at female classmates and threatened them with violence."

- "The man who massacred 49 people in an Orlando nightclub in 2016 beat his wife while she was pregnant, she told authorities."

- "The man who killed 26 people in a church in Sutherland Springs, Tex., in 2017 had been convicted of domestic violence. His ex-wife said he once told her that he could bury her body where no one would ever find it."

"The motivations of men who commit mass shootings are often muddled, complex, or unknown. But one common thread that connects many of them—other than access to powerful firearms—is a history of hating women, assaulting wives, girlfriends and female family members, or sharing misogynistic views online, researchers say."

"Most mass shootings are rooted in domestic violence," Ms. Watts said.

"Most mass shooters have a history of domestic or family violence in their background. It's an important red flag," said Shannon Watts, founder of Moms Demand Action for Gun Sense in America.

We know that most killers are male … and white. In a previous installment, we talked about the emasculation of American males, and how that factor plays a key role in the escalation of violence. But perhaps underpinning this condition is a deep layer of misogyny, deeper than the manufactured racist hatred fueled by white supremacist websites and manifestos that percolate in the minds of these killers, lying dormant until ignited by demagogues.

But let's dig deeper. Between 1882 and 1968, 3446 African Americans were hanged, often for the crime of looking at a white woman, smiling at a white woman, being friendly to a white woman, looking cross-eyed at a white woman, helping a white woman—you get the picture. The murder of Emmitt Till symbolized this horrific, vigilante justice. The perpetuators of this violence were often poor, illiterate, force-fed a legacy of racist ideology, convinced that their fragile manhood and self-esteem rested upon the subjugation and murder of people of color, as well as the suppression of women, similar to our mass shooters: both embraced a false ideology whose purpose was to preserve white privilege, white supremacy, and a white patriarchal social order. There was no greater sin than interracial marriage. As part of that culture, women were cast as 2nd class citizens, victims of terror and violence by their emasculated men and husbands. As with the mass shooters, both were ignited and manipulated by demagogues, puppet masters who sought to keep their hands clean while placing the gun or noose into the hands of the manipulated executioners—the puppet masters being the plantation owners, NRA executives, and elected officials who sought to preserve their money train even at the expense of the vulnerable.

Mass shootings are our modern-day hangings, and both were fueled by manufactured hate. Until we disable the disinformation infrastructure that infects our citizens, why can't we remove military assault weapons, high-capacity magazines, or gun stocks from the American arsenal? (I believe the Ohio shooter killed 9 people in 30 seconds.) Why are we putting our police forces at such a competitive disadvantage by sanctioning military-type weapons? How many dead kids/citizens will it take for Republican representatives to finally say no more? Or more importantly, when will Republican representatives stand up and stop repressing half of the population of this country through religious misogyny?

Misogyny is needs to be rooted out. As a country, we can remove this cancer. But it takes all of us.

Slowing Down to See the Beauty Around Us

December 17, 2019

I have Interstitial Pulmonary Fibrosis (IPF). What that means is my lungs are compromised, the air passages become more and more constricted, making it harder and harder to breathe. The medical community hasn't discovered a cause or a cure. I recently received stem cell therapy, and it has given me a new life. (If you are interested yourself, or for your loved ones, please contact me, and I can put you in touch with the medical group that performed my procedure.)

I was diagnosed with the disease in 2014, and as a consequence, I began to view time differently: it was no longer infinite, but a precious commodity. Coupled with that sobering realization, my disease granted me a precious gift: it taught me to slow down and look, and by looking, I discovered there is a heaven, here on earth, full of grace, surrounded by beauty, love, and wonder.

I discovered that God's gifts, his bounties, are hiding in plain sight; we just need to look, to exalt in the love and grace we are all surrounded by.

Slowing down releases you to revel in the festival of grace that envelops us all. The beauty and love surrounding us, screams at us to embrace, to savor its sustenance: a child's smile, a belly laugh from a friend, a gesture of kindness, the breathless beauty of a flower, a random act of kindness, a knowing smile from a stranger, community, a child's first step, a child's first word, a song so good you listen to it on repeat, an intimate conversation with a friend, a sunset, a sunrise, a good book, making love, connecting with the soul of another human, your team winning after being down 20 points, an opportunity to help—perhaps the most precious gift—kindness, beauty, and love.

By slowing down you begin to see the inherent goodness of people, you begin to see their soul, which always responds to kindness, love, and truth.

The beauty that surrounds us is hiding in plain sight.

The love that surrounds us is hiding in plain sight.

And sometimes it takes forgiveness to unlock this treasure trove of grace.

Forgiveness and responsibility remove the blinders that shroud God's handiwork.

Open your heart to the glory and wonder around you. We live in a heaven, surrounded by beauty, love, and grace. We only need to look, and accept the riches that are on display, sent there to nourish our souls.

I Believe …

February 5, 2019

I believe that any occupation, vocation, or passion should be done with the viewpoint of changing the world.

I believe in the power of art to heal, inspire, provoke, challenge, offer hope and, most of all, to connect—to remind us of our common humanity.

I believe that grandkids were put on earth to rekindle the souls of grandparents.

I believe in the power of a smile, its ability to melt barriers; its ability to disarm hate.

I believe that in any endeavor, we should all strive for greatness.

I believe that non-violence is the most militant, revolutionary, and effective weapon to be used against merchants of violence and hate.

I believe Bill Russell is the world's greatest athlete—23-0 in elimination games, 11 championships, Olympic gold medal and two NCAA championships. Lebron and Michael aren't even in the conversation.

I believe that racism is a cancer that has infected America from its inception, and that America will never be made whole until we confront its history, its structure, its perpetuation, and its manipulation by politicians who seek to divide us. This includes the way we manipulated and murdered the people who were here before us and how we still treat them today.

I believe advocates of the Second Amendment care more about their guns than about the lives of children. I wish they showed the same passion for the Thirteenth, Fourteenth, and Fifteenth Amendments. Our democracy would be the better for it.

I believe hate is artificial and manufactured and that love is natural and instinctual in our souls.

I believe peace can be achieved only by confronting industries of death: the gun industry, drug companies, munitions industry, the military-industrial complex, and the prison industrial complex. This will be extremely challenging given the fact that a lot of jobs are created by these industries, not to mention the fortunes generated for owners and executives. (You can't tell someone not to provide for their family.) It will have to be done on a gradient scale, but it can be done. We put people on the moon, didn't we?

I believe having kids is a soul-enriching gift that enhances ones' humanity.

I believe being married to the same woman for 39 years is an answered prayer, that 39 years makes a love richer, deeper, stronger, nourished by a shared history of struggles and triumphs. It also helps to marry the right person.

I believe in the music of John Coltrane, and its ability to inspire and to heal.

I believe we are surrounded by little slices of heaven, we just have to look.

I believe in the integrity of Robert Mueller.

I believe that tearing down Fenway Park would be the equivalent of destroying the Vatican or dismantling the Wailing Wall in Jerusalem. Many a prayer has been whispered on that sacred baseball ground, many a tear has been shed, and many a soul has sung in ecstasy.

I believe that once Republicans stop their campaign of sabotaging citizen's right to vote, it will usher in a new era of democracy that will truly transform our country.

I believe in our democracy, a beacon that is the envy of the world, whose foundation is only as strong as our citizen's participation.

Honoring Victims of Gun Violence

July 15, 2019

Well, another day, another shooting, and another recitation of 'thoughts and prayers' by our Republican Congress members and Representatives.

Our administration's chief of staff, Mick Mulvaney, said now is not the time to discuss gun violence.

Didn't he say that after the previous shooting?

I guess if the mass shootings continue, there will never be time for meaningful dialogue on this issue. Right now, Senator McConnell is sitting on 100 bills that he refuses to bring up for a vote in the Senate, including gun control legislation.

At what point can McConnell be charged with manslaughter? I think it's a fair question. He knows the carnage will continue and he chooses to do nothing.

Twenty years since Columbine, America averages one mass shooting a day when defining mass shooting as any incident that kills or wounds four or more people.

Each!

Day!

Since Sandy Hook, we have allowed 2043 mass shootings to occur.

What is the body count of American lives that it will take for Republican lawmakers to stand up to the NRA and pass gun control legislation?

Just give me a number so we can alert the children that we choose the NRA and gun manufacturer's profits over their lives. Gun control laws work. There's no debate on that fact any longer. Now people will say that the Second Amendment is being trampled upon, that the taking away of guns is the first step to tyranny. I could have more respect for these gun advocates if they didn't cherry-pick the Amendments. For example, where is the outrage from these people for the sabotaging of the Thirteenth, Fourteenth, and Fifteenth Amendments? Citizens from all over the country are being denied their right to vote, which is the bedrock of our democracy.

Where is the outrage?

This latest shooter had a silencer. Second Amendment advocates wail about gun control and not being able to hunt—nobody wants to take your rifle away. But when someone goes deer hunting, do they really need a silencer? Aren't they already at a competitive advantage? I mean, they have a gun and the deer doesn't. Really, how much more do hunters need to tip the scales? (It's like Kevin Durant joining the Warriors. Couldn't help myself: I always root for the underdogs—deer, the Toronto Raptors, defenseless kids.)

AFTER SANDY HOOK, WE SAID NEVER AGAIN. AND THEN WE LET 2043 MASS SHOOTINGS HAPPEN. (Gunpolicy.org United Nations Development Programme.)

"One of those killed at Borderline—his name was Telemachus Orfanos—also had been in Las Vegas when a gunman there went on a rampage last year. That this young man survived the worst mass shooting in recent U.S. history, only to die in another slaughter, speaks volumes about gun violence in the United States and the unspeakable failure of national lawmakers to do anything."

His mother: "My son was in Las Vegas with a lot of his friends, and he came home. He didn't come home last night, and I don't want prayers. I don't want thoughts. I want gun control, and I hope to God nobody sends me any more prayers. I want gun control. No more guns."

Below is a partial list of Americans that have been executed since Columbine. This list only runs through 2018. The 2019 tally is at a staggering level already.

Perhaps we need a wall, similar to the Vietnam Wall, to honor these victims.

April 20, 1999, at Columbine High School in Littleton, Colo.: Cassie Bernall, 17; Steven Curnow, 14; Corey DePooter, 17; Kelly Fleming, 16; Matthew Kechter, 16; Daniel Mauser, 15; Daniel Rohrbough, 15; William "Dave" Sanders, 47; Rachel Scott, 17; Isaiah Shoels, 18; John Tomlin, 16; Lauren Townsend, 18; Kyle Velasquez, 16.

Dec. 26, 2000, at Edgewater Technology in Wakefield, Mass.: Jennifer Bragg Capobianco, 29; Janice Hagerty, 46; Louis "Sandy" Javelle, 58; Rose Manfredi, 48; Paul Marceau, 36; Cheryl Troy, 50; Craig Wood, 29.

March 21, 2005, at Red Lake High School on the Red Lake Indian Reservation in Red Lake, Minn.: Derrick Brun, 28; Dewayne Lewis, 15; Chase Lussier, 15; Daryl Lussier, 58; Neva Rogers, 62; Chanelle Rosebear, 15; Michelle Sigana, 32; Thurlene Stillday, 15; Alicia White, 15.

Oct. 2, 2006, at an Amish schoolhouse in Lancaster County, Pa.: Naomi Ebersol, 7; Marian Stoltzfus Fisher, 13; Lena Zook Miller, 7; Mary Liz Miller, 8; Anna Mae Stoltzfus, 12.

April 16, 2007, at Virginia Tech in Blacksburg, Va.: Ross Abdallah Alameddine, 20; Christopher James "Jamie" Bishop, 35; Brian Bluhm, 25; Ryan Clark, 22; Austin Cloyd, 18; Jocelyne Couture-Nowak, 49; Daniel Perez Cueva, 21; Kevin Granata, 46; Matthew G. Gwaltney, 24; Caitlin Hammaren, 19; Jeremy Herbstritt, 27; Rachael Elizabeth Hill, 18; Emily Hilscher, 19; Jarrett Lane, 22; Matthew J. La Porte, 20; Henry Lee, 20; Liviu Librescu, 76; G.V. Loganathan, 51; Partahi Lumbantoruan, 34; Lauren McCain, 20; Daniel O'Neil, 22; Juan Ramon Ortiz,

26; Minal Panchal, 26; Erin Peterson, 18; Michael Pohle, 23; Julia Pryde, 23; Mary Read, 19; Reema Samaha, 18; Waleed Shaalan, 32; Leslie Sherman, 20; Maxine Turner, 22; Nicole R. White, 20.

Dec. 5, 2007, at the Westroads Mall in Omaha, Ne.: Beverly Flynn, 47; Janet Jorgensen, 66; Gary Joy, 56; John McDonald, 65; Gary Scharf, 48; Angie Schuster, 36; Dianne Trent, 53; Maggie Webb, 24.

April 3, 2009, at the American Civic Association immigration services center in Binghamton, N.Y.: Parveen Nln Ali, 26; Almir O. Alves, 43; Marc Henry Bernard, 44; Maria Sonia Bernard, 46; Hai Hong Zhong, 54; Hong Xiu Mao, 35; Jiang Ling, 22; Layla Khalil, 57; Roberta King, 72; Lan Ho, 39; Li Guo, 47; Dolores Yigal, 53; Maria Zobniw, 60.

Nov. 5, 2009, at Fort Hood, near Killeen, Tex.: Michael Grant Cahill, 62; Libardo Eduardo Caraveo, 52; Justin Michael DeCrow, 32; John P. Gaffaney, 56; Frederick Greene, 29; Jason Dean Hunt, 22; Amy S. Krueger, 29; Aaron Thomas Nemelka, 19; Michael S. Pearson, 22; Russell Seager, 51; Francheska Velez, 21; Juanita L. Warman, 55; Kham See Xiong, 23.

Jan. 8, 2011, in the parking lot of a grocery store near Tucson, Az.: Christina Taylor Green, 9; Dorothy Morris, 76; John M. Roll, 63; Phyllis Schneck, 79; Dorwan Stoddard, 76; Gabriel Zimmerman, 30.

Feb. 27, 2012, at Chardon High School in Chardon, Ohio: Demetrius Hewlin, 16; Russell King, Jr., 17; Daniel Parmertor, 16.

April 2, 2012, at Oikos University in Oakland, Cal.: Tshering Rinzing Bhutia, 38; Doris Chibuko, 40; Sonam Choedon, 33; Grace Eunhea Kim, 23; Katleen Ping, 24; Judith O. Seymour, 53; Lydia Sim, 21.

July 20, 2012, at the Century Aurora 16 movie complex in Aurora, Colo.: Jonathan Blunk, 26: A.J. Boik, 18; Jesse Childress, 29; Gordon W. Cowden, 51; Jessica Ghawi, 24; John Thomas Larimer, 27; Matthew McQuinn, 27; Micayla Medek, 23; Veronica Moser-Sullivan, 6; Alex Matthew Sullivan, 27; Alexander Teves, 24; Rebecca Ann Wingo, 32.

Aug. 5, 2012, at the Sikh Temple of Wisconsin in Oak Creek, Wis.: Satwant Singh Kaleka, 65; Suveg Singh Khattra, 84; Paramjit Kaur, 41; Prakash Singh, 39; Ranjit Singh, 49; Sita Singh, 41.

Dec. 14, 2012, at Sandy Hook Elementary School in Newtown, Conn.: Charlotte Bacon, 6; Daniel Barden, 7; Rachel D'Avino, 29; Olivia Engel, 6; Josephine Gay, 7; Dylan Hockley, 6; Dawn Hocksprung, 47; Madeleine F. Hsu, 6; Catherine V. Hubbard, 6; Chase Kowalski, 7; Jesse Lewis, 6; Ana M. Marquez-Greene, 6; James Mattioli, 6; Grace McDonnell, 7; Anne Marie Murphy, 52; Emilie Parker, 6; Jack Pinto, 6; Noah Pozner, 6; Caroline Previdi, 6; Jessica Rekos, 6; Avielle Richman, 6; Lauren Russeau, 30; Mary Sherlach, 56; Victoria Soto, 27; Benjamin Wheeler, 6; Allison N. Wyatt, 6.

Sept. 16, 2013, at the Washington Navy Yard in Washington, D.C.: Michael Arnold, 59; Martin Bodrog, 54; Arthur Daniels, 51; Sylvia Frasier, 53; Kathy Gaarde, 62; John Roger Johnson, 73; Mary Frances DeLorenzo Knight, 51; Frank Kohler, 51; Vishnu Bhalchandra Pandit, 61; Kenneth Bernard Proctor, 46; Gerald Read, 58; Richard Michael Ridgell, 52.

April 2, 2014, at Fort Hood near Killeen, Tex.: Daniel M. Ferguson, 39; Carlos A. Lazaney-Rodriguez, 38; Timothy Wayne Owens, 37.

April 13, 2014, at the Jewish Community Center of Greater Kansas City and the Village Shalom Retirement Center, both in Overland Park, Kan.: William Lewis Corporon, 69; Terri LaManno, 53; Reat Griffin Underwood, 14.

June 17, 2015, at Emanuel African Methodist Episcopal Church in Charleston, S.C.: Sharonda Coleman-Singleton, 45; DePayne V. Middleton Doctor, 49; Cynthia Graham Hurd, 54; Susie Jackson, 87; Ethel Lee Lance, 70; Clementa C. Pinckney, 41; Tywanza Sanders, 26; Daniel Simmons, 74; Myra Thompson, 59.

July 16, 2015, at an armed services recruiting center and a Navy reserve center in Chattanooga, Tenn.: Carson A. Holmquist, 25; Randall Smith, 26; Thomas J. Sullivan, 40; Squire K. "Skip" Wells, 21; David A. Wyatt, 35.

Oct. 1, 2015, at a community college in Roseburg, Ore.: Lucero Alcaraz, 19; Treven Taylor Anspach, 20; Rebecka Ann Carnes, 18; Quinn Glen Cooper, 18; Kim Saltmarsh Dietz, 59; Lucas Eibel, 18; Jason Dale Johnson, 33; Lawrence Levine, 67; Sarena Dawn Moore, 44.

Nov. 27, 2015, at a Planned Parenthood clinic in Colorado Springs, Co.: Jennifer Markovsky, 36; Ke'Arre M. Stewart, 29; Garrett Swasey, 44.

Dec. 2, 2015, at an office park in San Bernardino, Cal.: Robert Adams, 40; Isaac Amanios, 60; Bennetta Betbadal, 46; Harry Bowman, 46; Sierra Clayborn, 27; Juan Espinoza, 50; Aurora Godoy, 26; Shannon Johnson, 45; Larry Daniel Kaufman, 42; Damian Meins, 58; Tin Nguyen, 31; Nicholas Thalasinos, 52; Yvette Velasco, 27; Michael Raymond Wetzel, 37.

June 12, 2016, at Pulse nightclub in Orlando, Fl.: Stanley Almodovar III, 23; Amanda L. Alvear, 25; Oscar A. Aracena Montero, 26; Rodolfo Ayala Ayala, 33; Antonio Davon Brown, 29; Darryl Roman Burt II, 29; Angel Candelario-Padro, 28; Juan Chavez Martinez, 25; Luis Daniel Conde, 39; Cory James Connell, 21; Tevin Eugene Crosby, 25; Deonka Deidra Drayton, 32; Simón Adrian Carrillo Fernández, 31; Leroy Valentin Fernandez, 25; Mercedez Marisol Flores, 26; Peter Ommy Gonzalez Cruz, 22; Juan Ramon Guerrero, 22; Paul Terrell Henry, 41; Frank Hernandez, 27; Miguel Angel Honorato, 30; Javier Jorge Reyes,

40; Jason Benjamin Josaphat, 19; Eddie Jamoldroy Justice, 30; Anthony Luis Laureano Disla, 25; Christopher Andrew Leinonen, 32; Alejandro Barrios Martinez, 21; Brenda Marquez McCool, 49; Gilberto R. Silva Menendez, 25; Kimberly Jean Morris, 37; Akyra Monet Murray, 18; Luis Omar Ocasio Capo, 20; Geraldo A. Ortiz Jimenez, 25; Eric Ivan Ortiz-Rivera, 36; Joel Rayon Paniagua, 32; Jean Carlos Mendez Perez, 35; Enrique L. Rios Jr., 25; Jean Carlos Nieves Rodríguez, 27; Xavier Emmanuel Serrano-Rosado, 35; Christopher Joseph Sanfeliz, 24; Yilmary Rodríguez Solivan, 24; Edward Sotomayor Jr., 34; Shane Evan Tomlinson, 33; Martin Benitez Torres, 33; Jonathan A. Camuy Vega, 24; Juan Pablo Rivera Velázquez, 37; Luis Sergio Vielma, 22; Franky Jimmy DeJesus Velázquez, 50; Luis Daniel Wilson-Leon, 37; Jerald Arthur Wright, 31.

Jan. 6, 2017, at the baggage claim of Fort Lauderdale-Hollywood International Airport in Florida: Mary Louise Amzibel, 69; Terry Andres, 62; Michael Oehme, 57; Shirley Timmons, 70; Olga Woltering, 84.

June 5, 2017, at an awning company near Orlando, Fl.: Kevin Clark, 53; Kevin Lawson, 46; Brenda Montanez-Crespo, 44; Jeffrey Roberts, 57; Robert Snyder, 69.

Oct. 1, 2017, on the Las Vegas Strip in Nevada: Hannah Ahlers, 34; Heather Alvarado, 35; Dorene Anderson, 49; Carrie Barnette, 34; Jack Beaton, 54; Stephen Berger, 44; Candice Bowers, 40; Denise Burditus, 50; Sandy Casey, 35; Andrea Castilla, 28; Denise Cohen, 58; Austin Davis, 29; Thomas Day Jr., 54; Christiana Duarte, 22; Stacee Rodrigues Etcheber, 50; Brian Fraser, 39; Keri Galvan, 31; Dana Gardner, 52; Angela Gomez, 20; Charleston Hartfield, 34; Christopher Hazencomb, 44; Jennifer Topaz Irvine, 42; Teresa Nicol Kimura, 38; Jessica Klymchuk, 34; Carly Kreibaum, 33; Rhonda LeRocque, 42; Victor Link, 55; Jordan McIldoon, 23; Kelsey Breanne Meadows, 28; Calla-Marie Medig, 28; Sonny Melton, 29; Patricia Mestas, 67; Austin Meyer, 24; Adrian Murfitt, 35; Rachael Parker, 33; Jennifer Parks, 36; Carolyn Parsons,

31; Lisa Patterson, 46; John Phippen, 56; Melissa Ramirez, 26; Jordyn Rivera, 21; Quinton Robbins, 20; Cameron Robinson, 28; Rocio Guillen Rocha, 40; Tara Roe, 34; Lisa Romero-Muniz, 48; Christopher Roybal, 28; Brett Schwanbeck, 61; Bailey Schweitzer, 20; Laura Shipp, 50; Erick Silva, 21; Susan Smith, 53; Brennan Stewart, 30; Derrick Taylor, 56; Neysa Tonks, 46; Michelle Vo, 32; Kurt Von Tillow, 55; Bill Wolfe Jr., 42.

Nov. 5, 2017, at the First Baptist Church in Sutherland Springs, Tex.: Keith Allen Braden, 62; Robert Michael Corrigan, 51; Shani Louise Corrigan, 51; Emily Garcia, 7; Emily Rose Hill, 11; Gregory Lynn Hill, 13; Megan Gail Hill, 9; Crystal Marie Holcombe, 36; John Bryan Holcombe, 60; Karla Plain Holcombe, 58; Marc Daniel Holcombe, 36; Noah Holcombe, 1; Dennis Neil Johnson, 77; Sara Johns Johnson, 68; Haley Krueger, 16; Robert Scott Marshall, 56; Karen Sue Marshall, 56; Tara E. McNulty, 33; Annabelle Renae Pomeroy, 14; Ricardo Cardona Rodriguez, 64; Therese Sagan Rodriguez, 66; Brooke Bryanne Ward, 5; Joann Lookingbill Ward, 30; Peggy Lynn Warden, 56; Lula Woicinski White, 71.

Feb. 14, 2018, at Marjory Stoneman Douglas High School in Parkland, Fla.: Alyssa Alhadeff, 14; Scott Beigel, 35; Martin Duque, 14; Nicholas Dworet, 17; Aaron Feis, 37; Jaime Guttenberg, 14; Chris Hixon, 49; Luke Hoyer, 15; Cara Loughran, 14; Gina Montalto, 14; Joaquin Oliver, 17; Alaina Petty, 14; Meadow Pollack, 18; Helena Ramsay, 17; Alex Schachter, 14; Carmen Schentrup, 16; Peter Wang, 15.

May 18, 2018, at Santa Fe High School in Santa Fe, Tex.: Jared Black, 17; Shana Fisher, 16; Christian Riley Garcia, 15; Aaron Kyle McLeod, 15; Glenda Ann Perkins, 64; Angelique Ramirez, 15; Sabika Sheikh, 17; Christopher Stone, 17; Cynthia Tisdale, 63; Kimberly Vaughan, 14.

June 28, 2018, at the Capital Gazette newsroom in Annapolis, Md.: Gerald Fischman, 61; Rob Hiaasen, 59; John McNamara, 56; Rebecca Smith, 34; Wendi Winters, 65.

Oct. 27, 2018, at Tree of Life Synagogue in Pittsburgh, Pa.: Joyce Fienberg, 75; Richard Gottfried, 65; Rose Mallinger, 97; Jerry Rabinowitz, 66; Cecil Rosenthal, 59; David Rosenthal, 54; Bernice Simon, 84; Sylvan Simon, 86; Daniel Stein, 71; Melvin Wax, 87; Irving Younger, 69.

This is a man-made slaughter.

We need a wall to honor these innocent victims.

The Death of Mr. Oruma and the Cruelty of the Trump White House

July 15, 2019

A taxi driver named Luckinson Oruma, age 60, was shot dead in Boston last month, leaving 5 kids, all of whom he had put through college at UMASS Boston. He comes from Nigeria, one of those countries our president has labeled "shitty." His son Jeffrey said:

> "He always told me to work hard for the things you want and be kind to people."

Mr. Oruma is the type of person our president fights to deny access to the American dream. What he doesn't understand is that Mr. Oruma is the type of citizen who built and defended our country, he is of the stock that nourished and strengthened our democracy, the type of character that has and will continue to make America great.

> "He always told me to work hard for the things you want and be kind to people."

Our president is a white supremacist, and ungirding this philosophy is a belief in the psycho-science of eugenics, the belief in the superiority of the white race. The melding of eugenics and xenophobia has a long sordid history in this country, an amalgam which has proved potent in exporting fear while appealing to our baser instincts. A 1906 *Washington Post editorial* claimed: "They were coming to America to cut throats, throw dynamite, and conduct labor riots and assassination." The author of this piece was referring to Italians, but it reminds me of Trump's present-day demonization of Muslims and Hispanics.

> "He always told me to work hard for the things you want and be kind to people."

This racism even filtered up to the highest office in the land: Theodore Roosevelt said, "Someday we will realize that the prime duty, the inescapable duty of the good citizen of the right type is to leave his or her blood behind him in the world, and that we have no business to permit the perpetuation of citizens of the wrong type." The Guarded Gate by Daniel Okrent. Reminds me of Hitler, who drank deeply from the unholy cup of eugenics and xenophobia.

"He always told me to work hard for the things you want and be kind to people."

This weekend Trump has vowed to conduct raids in sanctuary cities, unleashing a reign of terror in those communities—can't help but be reminded of the Nazi raids of the Jewish ghettos back in the 1940s. I am already reminded of the Nazi camps when I see children separated from their parents and housed in cages. (By the way, certain American companies are making a killing in the warehousing of kids, a new cottage industry for the prison industrial complex.)

"He always told me to work hard for the things you want and be kind to people."

Eugenics seeks to measure everything physical: brain size, skin color, literacy, face structure, etc., but what they can't measure is a person's soul, their courage, their integrity. And these immeasurable qualities are the weapons that built and expanded this great country, that defeated the British despite impossible odds, that overcame wars, pestilence, riots, and attacks. It is the souls of such people that made America the most admired and powerful country in the world. Alexander Hamilton, one of the most impactful figures in American history, singlehandedly wrote the blueprint for our government and our financial system. If Hamilton tried to immigrate today, the door would be locked, having immigrated from a 'shitty country.'

"He always told me to work hard for the things you want and be kind to people."

There is a cruelty to this administration. It is led by a bully and it seeks to squash, to terrorize the most vulnerable, the powerless, people of color.

We're better than this.

> "He always told me to work hard for the things you want and be kind to people."

I've driven a cab and have taken countless taxi rides. Ain't nobody getting rich in this industry. It is a remarkable achievement for a taxi driver to put 5 kids through college. I stand in awe! I suspect there were many double shifts, extreme sacrifices, and a lot of praying, fueled by a passion for his kids to have a better life than himself, a passion for his kids to have a shot at the American dream.

Our country is richer from the immigration of Mr. Oruma. He has endowed our community with 5 kids, imbued with the teachings of their father:

> "He always told us to work hard for the things you want and be kind to people."

Our president pushes fear, paints the world as a dangerous environment, seeks to separate us, and seeks to squash the truth of our common humanity. We need to counterattack the fear with kindness and embrace Mr. Oruma's plea to "be kind to people."

Last week one of Trump's peeps, Jeffrey Epstein, was arrested for running an underage sex ring. In the past, Trump has referred to him as a 'terrific guy.' I don't know about that, but for my money, Mr. Oruma is actually a terrific guy.

> "He always told me to work hard for the things you want and be kind to people."

A Quest for Common Ground Against Disinformation

July 15, 2019

"Our ability to reach unity in diversity will be the beauty and the test of our civilization."

~ Mahatma Gandhi

A friend of mine recently posted a meme on Facebook that was racist. Its message was a denunciation of "parasites" (people living off the dole) and next to the broadside was a picture of an odd looking African American who seemed to be promoting a lifestyle of milking the government rather than earning a paycheck. The inference was clear.

Another friend and I called him out on it and he removed the post. He had received the post from another friend and he felt he was doing the community a service by forwarding the post. I think he is apolitical, and was just forwarding something a friend had sent. I suspect he doesn't study the issues and he lives in a community of Trump loyalists. The ironic thing is that he has spent the last few decades working to enhance the educational and moral levels of developing countries throughout the world—mostly countries with people of color.

After he posted the meme, a friend of his started a political debate with me: myself denouncing Trump, his character, and his policies. Her main argument for Trump was the economy, which appears to be the main virtue espoused by people when defending our current president. Now I feel Obama teed it up for Trump, economy-wise, which Trump has never acknowledged, and the rate of economic growth has actually slowed when compared to Obama's final year in office. And I won't even mention the 2 trillion added to our national debt since Trump took office. That will come home to roost at some point for our nation.

But that's not the point of this posting, whether I'm right about Trump or not.

Back to the friend. We went back and forth for a couple of days, neither achieving traction with each other. At the end, she said that neither of us would change, and there was no sense in carrying on the debate. In other words, we should both retreat to our bunkers and call it a day.

But I disagree.

I refused to think there was no common ground. Two rational people should be able to have a political debate in this country without each one retreating to their respective bunker. I refused to accept that change can't be affected through honest debate. And then I started to think about the meme my friend posted, and it dawned on me that its source was Russia. It was just too weird, starting with the odd looking African American and the almost illiterate and divisive copy.

And then I realized that there were hundreds of millions of these divisive memes choking our social media and airways. The stated purpose of the Russian hackers was to divide us and render America less powerful by injecting false data and disinformation. Russia even created a Black Lives Matter website with the purpose to create racial disharmony. And quarterbacking this campaign of divisiveness was our president, who fuels the flames of discord almost daily with his tweets and his policy initiatives. According to the FBI, hate crimes increased by 17% during Trump's first year in office.

By the way, the idea of compromising our elections was born out of a meeting between Hillary Clinton and Putin when Hillary lambasted Putin for conducting sham elections. (He definitely has a problem with strong women but gets along very well with our current president.) After that meeting, Putin vowed revenge. Too bad we don't have a president who has the courage to confront Putin.

But here's my point. America has been contaminated by a 2-year disinformation campaign from the Russian troll factory. It has so poisoned our discourse that we no longer engage in political debate, an exercise that is the lifeblood of our democracy.

People are always telling me, "Make sure you don't talk politics." I refuse to accept that. I believe political discourse nourishes the soul of America. I refuse to believe common ground can't be found. I refuse to believe I don't have a lot in common with a contemporary who resides in Iowa. I refuse to believe that someone from South Carolina doesn't have the same hopes and dreams for their kids as I do. I refuse to believe that Americans don't believe in justice for all.

We need a cleansing, a purification of the false data and disinformation that has polluted our discourse. Russia sought to divide us, and the Trump campaign gave them the passcode. We need to purge our airways and our social media. Our democracy has been compromised, and the perpetrators need to answer for their sins.

The Russian Troll Factory

July 15, 2019

A friend of mine recently posted this quotation from Ryan Fournier and I thought it apt for our times:

> "Being taught to avoid talking about politics and religion has led to a lack of understanding of politics and religion. What we should have been taught was how to have a civil conversation about a difficult topic."

I had lunch with a different friend recently. It was pleasant, and at one point it morphed into a who-has-the-cutest-grandkids battle. Needless to say, I won that battle hands down … well, she might be saying the same thing but really, I won.

No contest.

But that's not the point of this essay. But I did win—wasn't even close.

Here's my point. My lunch friend is a staunch Trump supporter. And I would love to discuss politics with her, but I sense a reluctance on her part to engage in any political or religious discussion. It feels like she is a closeted Trump supporter, a phenomenon I've noticed a lot lately—his supporters don't want to defend his character, defend his record, but they do send me links, often originating from Russia: you know, the ones that depict Hillary as the devil or Obama as a monkey. And after they send the Obama monkey one, they insist they aren't racist.

But a link is not a conversation, it's a cowardly method to persuade. My friend and her friends support the man but seem to shy away from honest debate. I wondered about that. Is it something about this president that stifles political discussion? Is there some other hidden factor at play?

Democracy is not forwarded or strengthened by link battles. Dialogue and honest debate are hard, but so is democracy. It takes constant vigilance—a constant fight against apathy and division. Our democracy flourishes to the same degree that our citizens participate, debate, and vote. Dialogue and honest debate are what nourish our democracy; it's the nutrient that strengthens our Founding Father's scriptures.

So, what the hell is going on?

And then it dawned on me:

The Russian troll factory was designed to sabotage our democracy. Their intent was to divide us, to create racial disharmony, and to elect Donald Trump. They have infected our airwaves and this infestation disables honest dialogue because the conversations are saturated with false data. How can we agree on anything when the data we present is false? As a result, we have retreated to our bunkers, fearing each other, our courage to engage neutered. Links have replaced dialogue.

We surrendered to the Russian disinformation campaign and our democracy is teetering on life support because the air we are breathing is funneled from Russia, and it is rendering our airwaves toxic.

Our nation needs a cleansing, a purification of the Russian disinformation campaign, and until that happens, public discourse will be compromised, which in turn will compromise our democracy.

I recently went to this event regarding DACU. One of the panelists, who is in DACU, noted there was a lot of conflict and disharmony creeping onto the DACU website. There is no group that should be more united than DACU, but then I realized this has Russia's footprints all over it. It aligns with their stated purpose which was to create disharmony, to destabilize our country. It reminded me of the fact that the Russian troll factory had created a Black Lives Matter website, their sole purpose being to create disunity within the African American community, to create racial discord, and to discourage African Americans from voting.

Back to my friend: the link she sent me could be traced to Alex Jones. He's the guy who promotes the idea that Sandy Hook was all some government conspiracy. So, you consider the source. Here's the problem. Russia implanted millions upon millions of these memes into America's bloodstream with the stated intent to divide us.

And it's working.

Here's the other problem. According to numerous news sources, President Trump has publicly lied to the American people over 10,000 times since taking office. OVER 10,000 TIMES!

This is a fact, not fake news because our President said all these things out loud. Anyone can verify this total. I suggest starting with his tweets. In addition to the Russian memes that infected our democracy, we also need to cleanse the lies our President has disseminated to our citizens. It's a necessary step in restoring our democracy. For example, he keeps extolling the virtues of Alex Jones. Yes, the Alex Jones that promoted the idea that Sandy Hook was a hoax orchestrated by our government and that no kids were killed.

And this is a man our president praises. Can you imagine being a parent of an executed child and the President of the United States promotes a guy who proclaims the executions never happened?

It breaks my heart that we have a president who is a compulsive liar. I take comfort in the fact that my oldest grandchild isn't old enough to follow politics and my prayer is that the next president exhibits a moral and ethical example of the standard we expect from the highest office in the land.

Our president should not only be our political leader but our moral beacon, inspiring our country with their moral leadership.

So, we should put the links down and start communicating with each other, no matter how uncomfortable and difficult it may be. The future of our democracy depends on it.

Finally, I hope to sit down with my friend and have a political conversation ... right after she admits that I do have the cutest grandkids.

Really, it was no contest.

The Trump Divide

October 6, 2019

"Being taught to avoid talking about politics and religion has led to a lack of understanding of politics and religion. What we should have been taught was how to have a civil conversation about a difficult topic."

~ Ryan Fournier

I recently reconnected with an old colleague on Facebook. It was nice to connect, and we eventually hit upon the subject of politics. It turns out he's a huge Trump fan, and me … not so much.

But a curious ritual began to take shape. I would write that Trump was a white supremacist, or that Trump believes global warming is some kind of hoax, or that Trump had lied to the American people over 12,000 times, or that Trump had been convicted for discriminating against people of color who wanted to live in his housing developments, etc., etc. Instead of writing back and debating the points, he sent me links.

So, I wrote back and told him I wasn't interested in links, I was interested in his thoughts, and I would then bring up more points: the suppression of the Mueller Report, his six bankruptcies, Russians guaranteeing his loans with Deutsche Bank, etc., etc. Instead of writing back and debating the points, he sent me more links, implying I didn't have the guts to confront the truth. He likes to patronize me.

So, I wrote back and told him I wasn't interested in links, I was interested in his thoughts, and I would then bring up more points: the seven people from his inner circle serving jail time, the numerous people from his administration under indictment, emoluments, the separating of kids from their parents at the border, the multiple sexual harassment suits against him, etc., etc. Instead of writing back and debating the points, he sent me more links.

So, I wrote back forbidding him to send more links, telling him I wanted to hear his thoughts on these issues.

And he sent more links.

What is a poor boy to do?

I did get him to admit that he believes Trump has never lied ... ever. Well, that left me speechless for a couple of days. And my friend is an intelligent man. Now I did view a couple of his links. They were filled with conspiracy theories fueled by QAnon—he's a big fan—but when you drill deep into these websites, they are based on white supremacist theories, with a dash of 19th-century eugenics undergirding their flimsy scientific foundation. It all comes down to this idea of a master race. That is what they hang their hat on.

At the end of the day, they feel so insecure that they need to look down on people to boost their ego, prop up their insecurity and their fragile self-worth, all the while fully embracing the propaganda that they are part of some master race. Here's the kicker, any dissatisfaction, shortcomings, or failures they feel in their life is really not their fault, not their responsibility. Their failures are the fault of others, in other words, scapegoats. Trump has a treasure trove of them: Hispanics, Muslins, African Americans, Dreamers, Immigrants—people who help make this country great. But Trump is certainly not the first. Offering up scapegoats by playing the race card can get you elected. The Republicans know this as they have been executing the Southern Strategy since Richard Nixon.

Back to my buddy: I'll keep sending him my political thoughts, hoping that at some point we can engage in a civil discourse of ideas. But this is an interesting phenomenon, original thoughts are being phased out, replaced by links steeped in conspiracy theories meant to replace critical thinking and debate. The heartbeat, viability, and health of our democracy are predicated on citizens engaged in civil discourse. This radical experiment of "All men are created equal ..." can only work with the full participation of our citizenry, a principle that flies in the teeth of the Republican voter suppression initiative.

Republicans believe that fewer votes means they will do better at the polls. When our citizens succumb to apathy, that politics doesn't matter, that voting doesn't matter, propaganda fills the void, usually in the form of video links, appealing to our baser natures, (and) stirring up dormant prejudices.

So, my friend could be described as a card-carrying member of Trump's base. Trump once said, "I could stand in the middle of 5th Avenue and shoot somebody and I wouldn't lose voters." I used to take that as a joke, but it's no longer funny. I think that is the essence of what we are dealing with when it comes to the Trump base—blind faith. This faith will excuse the deepest depth of moral depravity as long as their personal needs are catered to, as long as their personal prejudices are validated. Dictators have historically exploited this phenomenon, offering up scapegoats while slowly erasing the power of the press to hold politicians accountable. Hitler was the poster child for that stratagem.

It's very hard to pierce the blind faith fortress of the Trump supporter, because their faith validates their worldview that they are not responsible for their plight, for their condition—someone else is to blame. It guarantees no introspection, it takes the lazy route of providing scapegoats for all that ails.

There is a silver lining to the Trump presidency: it made us realize that our democratic institutions are fragile, easily dismantled by demigods through the apathy of our citizens. The easy thing would be to retire to our bunkers, sending out propaganda link salvos, rather than engaging in political discourse. We can't stop trying to break through the blind faith of our political opponents—there is common ground if we put in the work to find it. Our country and our airways have been infected by millions of Russian memes and this cancer has metastasized, driving a wedge between us. Russia's stated purpose was to divide us, and they are executing that playbook to a T. Today someone sent me a picture of Hillary Clinton with the words "50 years of killing babies". Really??? Russian fingerprints were all over this meme.

We can't surrender to this artificial divide. We have to roll up our sleeves and go into the bunkers and engage in civil, political discourse. People are innately good, and our country's healing can begin when we tap into that goodness—all the while cleansing our airwaves of the Russian memes. By excavating the goodness in each of us, this nectar can fuel a political renaissance, ushering in a golden age of peace and prosperity, and the United States can once again be a beacon of democracy for the rest of the world to admire and emulate.

Really, Steven Miller?

September 4, 2019

This breaks my heart!

I am astounded by this level of cruelty, this lack of compassion, empathy. And I am ashamed this outrage is being executed on American shores. America should be a beacon of light, a sanctuary, not the heart of darkness, a reservoir of hate and depravity.

> "Severely ill immigrants, including children with cancer, cystic fibrosis, and other grave conditions, are facing deportation under a change in Trump administration policy."
>
> ~ Michael Levenson, *Boston Globe* Staff,
> August 26, 2019, 11:17 a.m.

The Trump administration has axed a program that allowed immigrants with serious health conditions—including children and people with disabilities—and their families to remain in the United States while receiving life-saving medical treatment.

The "medical deferred action" program was recently eliminated by the US Citizenship and Immigration Services without warning. Immigrants and visitors—and their families—are being notified by letter that they must leave the country within 33 days of receipt. For many immigrants, this means leaving critical medical care behind, which could prove to be a death sentence.

> "I feel like I'm signing my son's death warrant."
>
> ~ Michael Levenson, the *Boston Globe*

I never thought this administration could sink lower than the racism, the bullying, the embracing of white supremacy, the condoning of neo-Nazi violence, the Islamophobia, the demonization of Hispanics, the splitting apart of families at the border, the labeling of immigrants seeking the American Dream as criminals and drug dealers.

I thought we were at the bottom of the Trump Administration's cesspool.

I was wrong.

They are now targeting kids with cancer, and terminal illnesses, sabotaging their lifelines in some cruel revenge agenda. Who even conceives of such cruelty—I suspect it is Stephen Miller, Trump's immigration consigliere.

With all the pressing problems confronting America today—gun control, peace in the Middle East, the North Korea situation, trade wars, racial conflict, etc., etc.—and this Administration finds time to send out letters to parents of severely sick children, giving them 33 days to leave the country, or be arrested and deported, which, in essence, serves as a death warrant for their sick children.

This level of cruelty, bullying, antisemitic, anti-immigration rhetoric is a reminiscence of Germany during the 1930s as a demagogue rose to power, promising he would make Germany great again.

Help Is Part of Our Basic Nature

April 10, 2020

Americans love to help. There is some primordial urge deep in our soul that seeks an outlet for this altruistic imperative. We are at our best when we help, when we comfort the afflicted, the most vulnerable, to provide aid, hope, and comfort. It is therapeutic and restorative, and it helps to heal our souls.

We come alive when we help.

The soul, the goodness, and the courage of America manifest themselves during a crisis. I am reminded of police and firemen rushing into the World Trade Center on 9-11. I am reminded of communities coming together to help each other during natural disasters. I am reminded of the persistent acts of kindness and courage during the pandemic as citizens watch over neighbors, especially the elderly. I am reminded of people on the front lines who fight drug addiction and human trafficking. Those who fight to stop global warming. I stand in awe of the courage of medical personnel who show up for work every day fighting the coronavirus.

This is who we are.

Helping also evaporates any prejudices, arrogance, and egos, all the while restoring our basic natures, our humility, and most of all, our humanity. Helping connects us, reminding us of our shared humanity, connecting us in a profound way. Helping dismantles the artificial divides constructed with the mortar of fear. We realize that we are all in this together, and that our ultimate survival depends on eradicating the lies that fan the divide.

In contrast, the Trump administration has spent the last 3½ years seeking to divide us by force-feeding us artificial scapegoats, usually citizens of color: they have labeled Hispanic Americans as drug dealers and rapists, American Muslims terrorists, African Americans as coming from shitty countries, and Nazi white supremacists as good people. We are better than that. When a tragedy presents itself, our better nature is resurrected; we help, and in so doing, our prejudices melt away. Helping is pure; it has been cleansed of fear, hate, and prejudice.

It is inspiring today to follow the heroic stories of Americans sacrificing their lives with a selflessness and compassion for others during this pandemic, usually complete strangers of different races, religions, and ethnicities. It is ironic that a crisis excavates the best in us. After 9-11, that feeling of fellowship expired way too fast. Let's pray that the goodness unleashed in our present crisis will never fade, that it strengthens and grows, and that it can disable the hateful rhetoric that spews forth daily from the White House.

Let us embrace our basic natures, goodness, rekindled in this crisis, and use it as a weapon to permanently eradicate the industrial complex of hate.

Nazism and Fascism
Require Enablers to Succeed

August 12, 2020

My five-year-old granddaughter has two refrains, "Watch this Papi," and, "That's not fair."

Recently, a friend of mine told me a story about his great uncle, a soldier in Germany during World War II. After the war, his unit would go into German towns, gather the citizenry, and offer them a choice to either watch a movie about the horrors of the Holocaust and German crimes against humanity, or go into the concentration camps and experience the horror first-hand. Most chose the movie, but each one emerged from the theater wailing, the weight of their culpability, their acts of omission, their enabling silence, and their compromised conscience, all weighing down upon them.

It had dawned on them they were enablers. They realized the deadly consequences of their silence, which served to lubricate the wheels of mass executions.

> "When the number of people who were parties to the genocidal enterprise, who must have staffed these institutions and occupied these roles, is considered and when the still far larger number who worked in the larger system of domination—the enormous extent of which is only suggested by the 10,000 camps so far identified—is also taken into account the inescapable conclusion is that the number of Germans who contributed to and, more broadly, had knowledge of this regime's fundamental criminality was staggering ...."

> ~ Daniel Jonah Goldhagen,
> *Hitler's Willing Executioners*, Page 168

"We must always take sides. Neutrality helps the oppressor, never the victim. Silence encourages the tormentor, never the tormented."

~ Elie Wiesel

I recently had a discussion with a Trump supporter. My basic point was that character matters, a person's integrity matters, and morality matters, especially with our leaders. Immoral people make decisions based on their own vested interests, or based on money, or based on sex. I brought up Trump's six bankruptcies, his conviction for not leasing apartments to people of color, his twenty-four sexual assault lawsuits, the Hollywood Access tape, the shutting down of his charity by the Attorney General of New York, the warehousing of kids in concentration camps—just a few of his greatest hits. She wouldn't respond, wouldn't even argue that what I was bringing up was not true. Afterward I realized I was dealing with blind faith, a surrendering to a false prophet, whose message resonated in the buried recesses of hate and racism.

This was something new that I had seen gestating over the last few years. Before this, political discussions were possible, ideas and policies were debated, sometimes passionately, but that was okay. Positions were changed because reason permeated the discussions. Name-calling and character assassination weren't needed and we were better for it because our ideas were challenged and debated.

I am voting for Biden because I consider him to be a strong, decent, and kind man who will help heal our country by dismantling the artificial divides constructed by the dominant caste. Now, I could find many things wrong with Biden if I scrutinized his voting record or his policy recommendations. These issues can be debated and that's the key point—they can be debated.

An enabler doesn't debate. Blind faith forbids debate. Debate nourishes our democracy and strengthens it. Blind faith is a lubricant for fascism.

Right now, we have a president trying to sabotage our November election with empty accusations of voter fraud, (per the Heritage Foundation, not exactly a left-wing think tank, there were 37 instances of proven voter fraud over the last decade—37!) Doesn't the president have bigger issues, like the goddamn pandemic? Putting a totally unqualified person in charge of the Post Office in order to slow down and sabotage mail-in ballots (who happens to be a huge donor to the Trump campaign), sending unmarked Storm Troopers into Portland to arrest peaceful demonstrators, having an Attorney General who believes the president is above the law, firing a United States Attorney General who was knee-deep in investigating Trump's criminal enterprises, suppressing the Mueller report, putting roadblocks in communities of color that suppress their vote, and it goes on and on.

We are on the brink of fascism. The playbook for fascism has been launched: declare the press an enemy of the people, rig the elections, make the future dictator above the law, offer the public scapegoats for whatever ails the country, create a special police force of Storm Troopers.

All this wouldn't be possible without a merry band of enablers. The Holocaust wouldn't have been possible without the enablers. Hitler had the vision, but the enablers executed the program. Today, Trump's enablers have stood silent as disinformation and outright lies spew forth from this White House. They have stood silent as Trump cozied up to dictators like Putin, condoning Russia's sabotaging of our last election. (Russia has made it clear they will again seek to sabotage our November election, feeling Trump will be better for them than Biden.) They have stood silent when ICE separated kids from parents and warehoused them in concentration camps. They stood silent when he called NEO-NAZIs "very fine people." They stood silent when he denigrated the memories of John Lewis and John McCain.

But Trump doesn't happen without the enablers. The corrosion of the office of the Presidency doesn't happen without the silence of his minions.

The president, emboldened by the silence of his followers, has taken his bile to a whole new, lower ground. Trump said about Biden in his Cleveland speech, "He's following the radical-left agenda: take away your guns, destroy your Second Amendment, no religion, no anything, hurt the Bible, hurt God." Trump also said, "He's against God."

What the hell does "no anything" mean? What the hell does "He's against God" mean?

This was said about a man of deep faith. Biden has leaned on his religion in times of unspeakable tragedies.

But Trump's enablers remained silent, as well as the Congressmen and Senators who condone this assault on our democracy.

> "History will have to record that the greatest tragedy of this period of social transition was not the strident clamor of the bad people, but the appalling silence of the good people."
>
> ~ Martin Luther King Jr.

Enablers will inevitably have to answer for their silence. There were the Nuremberg trials, and in South Africa they conducted Truth and Reconciliation Hearings where citizens could publicly confess their sins, serving as a therapeutic salve for both the individual and the country, becoming a vehicle that helped heal the horror of apartheid. Given the racial unrest in this country, Truth and Reconciliation Hearings might just be the prescription needed.

Back to my granddaughter. The first principle of our democracy is fairness:

> "We hold these truths to be self-evident, that all men are created equal, that they are endowed by their Creator with certain unalienable Rights, that among these are Life, Liberty and the pursuit of Happiness."
>
> ~ *Declaration of Independence*

Trump and his minions never seem to ask what is fair, what isn't fair, and how can we correct it? How can we correct the inequities that are entrenched in our institutions? How can we make the American dream accessible to all citizens and fulfill the promise of our Founding Fathers?

A fascist would never ask those questions. The question they usually ask is, what's in it for me? Or, how does this consolidate my power?

At some point, the chickens will come home to roost, and Trump's enablers will have to answer to this nation and to their Supreme Being.

So, look out! In the not-so-distant future my granddaughter will be unleashed into the world, and like her mother, she will cry out, "HEY, THAT'S NOT FAIR!"

I'm Tired of Trump's Hitleresque Actions

December 15, 2020

I wish I didn't have to write these words, but the Trump Administration and their enablers compel me to speak out, and I will not remain silent.

As stated in previous posts, there is an unfortunate parallel between the Trump phenomenon and Hitler's blueprint. Just when I say to myself it's all a coincidence, that he doesn't mean what he says, or doesn't mean what he retweets, or that his motives are altruistic, then something like this happens ... Corey Lewandowski:

> "Hey, this is a message for the Alpha Freedom Friends. This is Corey Lewandowski. You know me as President Trump's 2016 campaign manager and his current 2020 senior adviser. Look, I want to say freedom only for the members of the government or only for the members of the party is no freedom at all. We need to end the China virus lockdown, and WORK SETS YOU FREE. Let's get everyone back to work, let's get our economy growing again, let's send Donald Trump and Mike Pence back to the White House for four more years."

That phrase hangs over the entrance of Auschwitz: WORK SETS YOU FREE. It leaves me speechless, although it all makes sense, including the earlier parallels.

Both sought isolation from other democratic nations.

Both canceled treaties and agreements that bound nations together.

Both respected fascist leaders.

Both attacked the free press, stating criticism of their regime was tantamount to treason.

Both forged alliances with dictatorships.

Both sought support from white nationalists while targeting minorities and engaging in religious and racial scapegoating.

Both encouraged police to assault peaceful demonstrators.

Both attacked labor unions, using their powers to enrich the rich.

Both postured as strong military men while building up arms.

Both purged individuals from the government who sought to expose their crimes.

And then there is Trump's statement about admiring Hitler because he was perceived as a strong leader and the report by his ex-wife, who said he kept a copy of Hitler's speeches next to his bed. As his term in office moved forward, Trump's dog whistles, embraced by white nationalist groups, and embraced by conspiracy groups such as QAnon, were all emboldened as his dog whistles morphed into full-throated messages. "Stand down; stand by."

Like I said before, it is hard to confront evil. And, this evil has been spewing its bile, its hate, and we have been telling ourselves that it is all just benign, nothing happening here, nothing to look at. Just ignore those parentless kids at the border, ignore the condoning of violence by white supremacists, ignore his ignoring of science for both global warming and the pandemic. He doesn't mean it. He will save us. That's what the German people said. Evil hides itself in plain sight. Trump has been emboldened by his power, as well as by the Attorney General, and validated by all the white supremacy groups. He no longer feels compelled to hide his evil. He is validated by his enablers and his hate is legitimized by his propaganda loudspeaker Fox News. I pray that by November 4th, I will no longer have to write these essays.

History of Voter Suppression

December 27, 2020

African Americans were transported to this country over 400 years ago, chained, whipped, and raped, treated as property. The ships that transported them were not part of the Royal Cruise Line, all-you-can-eat buffet tables were nowhere to be found. Instead, hundreds of humans were stacked below deck, shackled, squeezed next to each other or on top of each other to save space. Air holes were drilled in the ships so the enslaved people could breathe, but they were plugged when the weather got rough.

The passage lasted one to six months, depending on the weather. Those who were to be enslaved were systematically starved, and many died. The dead, including women and children, were thrown from the ship like rubbish.

African Americans began their American experience as enslaved people. The right to vote was a fantasy. When our Founding Fathers were crafting our Constitution, the issue of voting rights, state taxes, and representation in the House of Representatives was raised, and enslaved people were deemed to be three-fifths of a person, which I guess is a step up from being a slave, but not really. Actually, it was determined they weren't human, but property, and enslavers could count their 'property' as three-fifths of a person, thereby giving more governmental representation to the slave states. The more people you enslaved , the more political clout your state wielded.

> "The domination of the slaveholders in politics and journalism was so complete that the non-slaveholding interests had little voice."

> ~ Kari Merritt, *Masterless Men*, Page 37

But before African Americans could vote, they would first have to be classified as human, and declassified as property. No one had the guts to stand up to enslavers, in other words, the bullies. Enslavers at that time were raking in obscene amounts of profit, with free labor forging the foundation for their wealth. Poor whites, possessing more rights than those who were enslaved, prayed that the spoils and trickle-down of the enslaver's wealth would somehow descend on them. This false hope motivated them to embrace the supremacy of possessing white skin.

From *The Broken Heart of America*, by Walter Johnson:

> "And importantly, thus has it been possible to make poor and working-class white people believe that their interests lie in making common cause with their political leaders and economic betters. Common cause in whiteness: the idea that they might eventually share in the spoils, and the understanding that the discomforts and anxieties of their own precarious lives were due—are due to—those below them rather than those above them. As the historian Robin D.G. Kelley suggests, guns and tanks and tear gas are sufficient to control the black people (or, for that matter, the Indians and immigrants); white supremacy is necessary to control the white people."

We still see this phenomenon today, whites blaming the scapegoats President Trump points to, camouflaging his policy's intentions which are designed to strip his constituents of their safety nets, pollute their communities, strip away their healthcare—2.3 million citizens so far have lost coverage. As in the Reconstruction Era, the white supremacy trickle-down lure is the trigger for self-sabotage. People are actually voting for a man who has battled for four years to take away their lifelines, healthcare, and Social Security.

In 1860, the Civil War launched, a war many in the South insist was all about state's rights, not slavery, not the exploitation, the torture, and the dehumanizing of an entire race of people. Riding on the state's rights con, the South sought to bury their complicity in the South's reign of terror on people of color. And the North was complicit in this, having financed and profited from the immoral exploitation of enslaved, men, women, and children; all justified and motivated by selected readings of scripture. This is similar to today where the evangelicals use scripture to promote racism, Islamophobia, homophobia, in other words, white supremacy, a plague alive and well in America.

> "God had created some people unfit for freedom. Slavery was God's will. To worry about slavery was to doubt God. To oppose it was heresy."
>
> ~ Edward Batiste, *The Half Has Never Been Told: Slavery and the Making of American Capitalism*, Page 211

The Emancipation Proclamation did free enslaved people … on paper at least. Officially, African Americans were free, and in 1867 men of all races could vote, but once the Compromise of 1877 was enacted, removing Federal troops from the South, voter suppression of African Americans and people of color was uncorked. Former enslaved people could now vote if they paid a toll tax, or passed a literacy test, or survived a public hanging, or survived their home being firebombed. (By the way, enslavers blocked public education for not only African Americans, but for poor whites. They knew an educated citizenry was a lethal weapon against homegrown fascism.) Polling station doors were wide open throughout the South, at least in theory. On a theoretical level, African Americans were allowed to vote, but realistically, they could be killed if they made the attempt—all under the guise of maintaining and supporting the money-making power structure.

The Broken Heart of America, by Walter Johnson:

> "The master class had a long-established, effective, and well-planned system of social control. They kept the white poor uneducated and illiterate on purpose. Refusing to invest in a system of public education, slaveholders used public money to

fund law enforcement departments, creating an intricate and bureaucratic criminal justice system. This system allowed masters to incarcerate (at will) whites who failed to follow their social dictates."

That playbook's legacy seems eerily familiar, with reruns occurring in the town of Ferguson, Missouri, among other places.

After the Reconstruction era was launched in the South, the enslavers' zeitgeist saturated the South, the KKK emerging as the dominant instrument of control. As the number of hangings of African Americans exploded, the number of African American men who voted was reduced to subterranean levels. Hangings became a blood sport in some towns, sometimes attracting over 10,000 citizens, including women and children, who witnessed the brutal executions. Hangings, fueled by the power structure and executed by poor whites, drove home the message that African Americans weren't human, they were animals that needed to be suppressed and controlled, otherwise the beasts would end up raping the ultra-pure wives and girlfriends.

Can you imagine a white child witnessing such horror? The imprint that it makes? The legacy of hate and racism seared into that child's soul? A kid mired and inculcated in this hatred, soaked in the racist propaganda, doesn't shed this stain in a generation. It becomes deeply embedded into a family's DNA, passed on to their offspring, offspring that perhaps becomes police officers in later generations, unwashed of the poison. Electing Barak Obama didn't evaporate America's racial cancer. It just poked the bear, with Trump shattering the hatch of white supremacy, exposing the untreated boil.

Denied education, poor whites lapped up the racist propaganda force-fed by former enslavers, whose land was returned to them by the Missouri Compromise. They became soldiers for fascism and white supremacy. Poor whites had been stripped of everything else—jobs, education, political power—all that was left of their identity was whiteness.

Praying that wealth would trickle down to them, poor whites ignored the common humanity they shared with poor Blacks, instead embracing the divisive, poisonous bile spewed forth from former enslavers and the KKK. Poor whites were the targets of the elite's propaganda, who sought to separate whites and Blacks, knowing full well that their power could only be maintained if poor people continued to fight each other. And they were able to run this con by keeping poor white people illiterate, illiteracy being a sponge for disinformation and racist propaganda.

"No one is born hating another person because of the color of his skin, or his background, or his religion. People must learn to hate, and if they can learn to hate, they can be taught to love, for love comes more naturally to the human heart than its opposite."

~ Nelson Mandela

For African Americans, it was illegal for them to read, subject to execution if discovered. So, if an African American was able to gain an education surreptitiously, they could possibly pass the literacy test and cast a vote. But if they could pass the literacy test, that would reveal they had broken the law regarding African American's literacy, which in turn opened them up to being executed.

HELL OF A DILEMMA: DO I VOTE AND OR DO I GET HANGED IN THE CITY SQUARE?

"The master class had created a legal system that allowed them to imprison, brutalize, and murder anyone who challenged the slave-based hierarchy, ... rising levels of incarceration, the 'selling' of convicts and debtors, and the spectacle of public corporal punishment force poor white men to reflect upon the status of their rights as white citizens within the slaveholding South, and the results of the reflection did not bode well for the future."

~ Kari Merritt, *Masterless Men*, Page 248

We see here the origins of the prison industrial complex; in other words, how can we make money off incarceration—poverty parasites. Slavery was outlawed but replaced by sharecropping, by prison labor, which is simply slavery smothered in make-up. And remember, if convicted of a crime, that makes you ineligible to exercise your most fundamental right, the ability to vote.

Today, these machinations are labeled voter suppression. The South, during Reconstruction, elevated that concept to a whole new plateau. And today, we no longer hang African Americans who try to vote. What we do is more subtle, systematic, using the insidious gerrymandering, grandfather clauses, and voter I.D. laws designed to block African Americans from voting, or to nullify their vote. Today we don't have enslavers suppressing the vote, we have mostly puppet Republican Congressmen, the one percenters pulling their strings, tainted with the South's cancerous legacy of racism igniting the machinations of voter suppression. Just last week in Georgia, Republicans were trying to nullify the registration of 75,000 new voters.

This insidious voter suppression morphs into all kinds of deceitful structures. In the 2016 election, we had Russian operatives creating Black Lives Matter websites, telling African Americans not to vote, that their vote didn't count.

The strategic legacy of Reconstruction was to keep the Black and white working poor separated, at odds with each other by implanting disinformation, while the power structure burglarized the cupboards of the working class.

> "Southern captains of industry quickly learned from slaveholders how to pit poor white and black laborers against each other, and commonly used enslaved people as strikebreakers."
>
> ~ Kari Merritt, *Masterless Men*, Page 99

"And even though small land-holders were hardly seen as equals to the large slave owners, the Genoveses concluded that because they aspired to become plantation owners themselves, yeomen 'were led step by step into willing acceptance of a subordinate position in society.'"

~ Kari Merritt, *Masterless Men*, Page 139

Hangings continued into the 20th century. From 1882 to 1968, 3446 African Americans were hanged, a ritual that hardly promotes free and fair elections. Despite the terrorism, the horror perpetuated upon them, African Americans made very small, incremental inroads into the voting booths. And in the 1950s and 60s, civil rights workers descended on the South, courageously getting Black people to register, despite death threats and executions: i.e. Cheney, Goodman and Schwerner. Robert Moses was another who did courageous work in Mississippi, somehow managing to escape the hangmen's noose.

"As previously discussed, antebellum courts functioned on a fee system from a sheriff's fee for the actual arrest itself, to accrued daily jail fees, to the payment of the solicitor general, the courts depended on the accused for reimbursement of their own legal costs, criminal convictions, could vary widely, from 5 to 110 dollars to hundreds of dollars for more serious offenses."

~ Kari Merritt, *Masterless Men*, Page 235

THIS IS THE PRISON INDUSTRIAL COMPLEX IN ITS INFANCY.

Industrialists craved prison labor as it generated obscene profits, and it behooved them to keep the incarceration count high for a few reasons: it provided slave labor for their firms, it kept African Americans from organizing, and it stopped African Americans from voting. Voting was the kryptonite to their power, and they used whatever means necessary to squash the assertion of rights by African Americans, the right to vote being the most impactful.

> "As late as 1908, Georgia's African American prisoners out-numbered white convicts almost ten to one."
>
> ~ Kari Merritt, *Masterless Men*, Page 336

And there were many machinations used to keep the Black and white poor separated, one of which was the threat of a race war. Industrialists and former slaveholders enlisted poor, degraded whites into their holy war, but it was really a war for profit, collateral damage notwithstanding. If Blacks and whites were allowed to connect, which they secretly did, (enslaved people often stole food from their masters to give to starving and degraded whites), they would discover their common humanity. If that were to occur on a major level, the power of the exploitative land-owners would start to erode.

> "By the eve of war, affluent Southerners used an insidious form of racism to try to scare lower-class whites into supporting se-cession predicting that the poor would be slaughtered by the thousands in an inevitable race war following emancipation."
>
> ~ Kari Merritt, *Masterless Men*, Page 35

This blueprint is being replicated today with QAnon and the Proud Boys, both prophesying a race war. Here is what a Trump supporter in Pennsylvania had to say,

> "A race war is coming. It will be black against white, Hispanic against white, and we will fight it out in the streets."
>
> ~ Jennifer Silva, *We're Still Here:*
> *Pain and Politics in the Heart of America*

The residue of slavery festers in our culture, lobbying for race wars, and cementing the divide that benefits the few.

"By predicting that poor whites would be massacred by the 'black plague,' masters tried to scare white laborers into supporting the institution of slavery—regardless of what it did to their jobs or wages."

~ Kari Merritt, *Masterless Men*, Page 292

After the demonstrations and horror accompanying the Civil Rights movement, a bill was passed in Congress in 1965, the Voting Rights Act, guaranteeing the right to vote for all citizens.

Hallelujah!

But not so fast. The systemic racist structures that perpetuated African American disenfranchisement were declared unlawful, unconstitutional—in theory. The legacy of disenfranchisement continues to this day. They no longer hang potential voters, or administer literacy tests, or require poll taxes. These systemic structures, now outlawed, have been replaced by the new set of voter suppression structures in the form of gerrymandering, voter I.D. laws, shutting down polling stations, removing mailboxes and voting boxes in certain communities.

After all of these decades of voter suppression directed toward people of color, Republicans twist the knife one more turn: Trump filed over sixty lawsuits after the 2020 Presidential Election seeking to nullify the ballots of primarily African American communities: Milwaukee, Philadelphia, Atlanta, Detroit.

WHEN WILL THIS STOP?

If you believe in democracy, this has to stop. If you don't believe in democracy, well, I get it. Just be honest about it and let your communist flag fly. Since the days of slavery, many leaders in this country haven't really believed in, or endorsed democracy. They have never embraced the maxim of "All men are created equal ..." (Which, again, is missing the female half of the population of our country.)

"It is their hope, and intention, under the guise of vagrant laws, etc. to restore all of slavery but its name. ... To deal with this lack of infrastructure, the old master class returned to convict leasing."

~ Kari Merritt, *Masterless Men*, Page 335

One big lie promulgated by Republicans is that Democrats embrace communism, which makes them unpatriotic, guilty of treason. It's the exact opposite: Democrats fight to install democracy, Republicans fight to suppress it, and there is no better evidence than their voter suppression campaign. Open and free elections are the oxygen, the fiber of American democracy. Without it, we're just another developing nation, ruled by the arbitrary whims of a dictator.

Forces today continue to drive a wedge between Black and white, its ringleader our current president. The subsequent chaos that ensues from disinformation guarantees the entrenchment of the current power structure, which is insidious, powerful, and will fight tooth and nail to maintain their privilege, their station, and their cash. It is a juggernaut whose power rests on exploitation and division.

"Historically, people in power have counted on hostility and division within the working class, particularly between African Americans and northeastern ethnic whites or southern white populists, to reduce the possibility of a strong united working class."

~ Jennifer Silva, *We're Still Here:*
Pain and Politics in the Heart of America

"... by encouraging the enemy of the poor, laboring white man against the black, the slaveholder 'succeeds in making the said white man almost as much a slave as the black slave himself.'"

~ Kari Merritt, *Masterless Men*, quoting Frederick Douglas

We need to stop falling for the con of scarcity, the trickle-down con. The greatness of our country rests on the foundation of inclusion and diversity; it rests on recognizing our common humanity, that our strength as a country rests on inclusiveness, not divisiveness. Leveling the playing field does not make us weaker; it makes us stronger as it invites the talents of all people to participate in this grand experiment called DEMOCRACY.

Our glory, our power, is neutered when we fall for the con that our scapegoats, our enemies, are people who don't look like us. Right now, poor whites and poor Blacks are fighting each other, believing desperately each is the source of their discontent, their poverty. The Trump administration has flamed, manipulated, and exploited, this artificial chasm since day one of its reign.

America's culture, its greatness, flourished from the infusion and richness of other cultures. We can't shut off that wellspring; it is our lifeline, lifeblood, the mana for our glory.

> "Forced migration to the frontiers of slavery took children from parents who named them and taught them to talk, brothers from sisters who carried them as babies, wives from husbands who had whispered to them in the night, men from friends who had taken whippings rather than betray them. Survival by means of joint effort would require strong bonds, and all existing strong bonds had been broken."

> ~ Edward Batiste, *The Half Has Never Been Told: Slavery and the Making of American Capitalism*, Page 148

According to Thomas Jefferson:

> "... separation from loved ones mattered little to African Americans."

> ~ Edward Batiste, *The Half Has Never Been Told: Slavery and the Making of American Capitalism*, Page 192

Yes, he said that.

There is a story, repeated thousands and thousands of times back in antebellum times, of a child who used to walk to the gates of the plantation every morning expecting to see her mother walking down the path, returning home to embrace her child. But the mother never came, having been sold off by her enslaver for profit. Imagine the hole in a five-year-old's heart, as she stands by the gate, patiently waiting for her mother to appear ... and she never does.

And two hundred years later, we have kids in cages at the border, staring through wire, yearning for their parents to return. Imagine the hole in these kids' hearts.

Has America not evolved since the antebellum days? Have kindness and empathy evaporated or been extinguished in our nation? Are we no better than enslavers from the antebellum period? Why does this level of cruelty persist in America?

This residue of enslavers' mindsets continues to stain our republic. America has yet to shed this legacy of hateful, suppressive, disinformation. As a result, African Americans are executed during traffic stops and we have administration officials who think putting kids in cages is a good idea. The fact that we have separated over a thousand kids from their parents poisons our nation to its core.

We are still fighting the Civil War, not with weapons, but with ideas. Too many Americans don't believe in democracy and don't believe that all people are created equal.

Until we shed this enslaver legacy, our greatness will forever be compromised as this cancer sabotages our strength, our greatness, and our Constitution.

My eyes have seen the glory of America every day, its promise: the glory of connection, the glory of shared humanity, and the glory of the American Dream!

The Industrial Drug Complex

January 23, 2020

Some time ago I ran into a former classmate, someone I hadn't seen for almost 20 years. After exchanging pleasantries, he told me, unsolicited, that he had smoked marijuana every day for the past 25 years. He communicated this particular statistic with pride, a sterling accomplishment, as if he had discovered a cure for cancer, or had won the Superbowl.

He was presently the manager of a 7-Eleven convenience store.

It broke my heart.

A young man, 19 years old, was recently interviewed on the radio. He was on his way to a medical marijuana shop to pick up his pot medication. He said that he had been experiencing anxiety and a doctor had written him a prescription for pot. He said he was too anxious to work.

Anxiety? If you step out your front door you are confronted with anxiety. It's part of the human condition. The tragedy here is that this man will be forever unemployable, made permanently disabled by his medical marijuana prescription. If you were a business owner, would you hire this guy?

This wasted potential broke my heart.

My old classmate was a guy who I remembered as being smart, ambitious, dynamic, possessed of an intelligence capable of accomplishing great things, but here he was planted at his apex, managing a 7-Eleven, and damn proud of it.

He had never married, had probably never experienced a deep, passionate relationship, or a deep intimacy with another person, had probably never sought a job that was fulfilling, or challenging, that was impactful on society—I doubt he even considered it. Because of his pot smoking, he shielded himself from the rich kaleidoscope of life, denying himself the experience of any raw, deep emotions such as heartbreak, or love. Because of his pot smoking, he would never give himself the opportunity to experience deep, ineffable joy, or passion that comes from active engagement in life. Pot afforded him a safe harbor, a lowered bar, denying him a life full of purpose, passion, and achievement. He was devoid of goals or plans for the future.

His journey was a twenty-five-year atrophy from people, family, goals, intimacy, and challenge—elements that forge character and growth, the good stuff. He just wanted to get high. He probably ceased asking himself the big questions long ago: who am I? What is my purpose? My destiny? These questions were all shrouded under the haze of pot smoke.

He was apolitical and considered all politicians corrupt. So why bother to vote, or to participate in this grand experiment of democracy?

Now, someone might say, well, your friend isn't hurting anyone, and he generates a paycheck, and pays his taxes.

That's true, but my point is this: why settle? Why not pursue greatness? It is the most fun. We as a society condoned mediocrity, a lowering of the bar, fueled by the industrial drug complex. Because it is legal, we let the pot, vaping, and pharmaceutical industries set the bar as to our aspirations and dreams. We offer no resistance and blindly ingest the propaganda that getting high and pursuing materialism is cool, and will produce fulfillment. And what's even more egregious, these attitudes trickle down to our children, which in turn puts their lives of meaning and purpose in final jeopardy.

This really is about our children, the people most vulnerable, most susceptible to the insidious sales pitch of the industrial drug complex. (For example, kids in foster care are on 27% more medications than other kids their age. Because they have no advocate, no rights, they are easily exploited, given their cash cow status. Would the pharmaceutical industry take advantage of a defenseless class solely for profit—you bet your ass they would.)

We do a disservice to our children if we allow their aspirations to settle to the ceiling of a 7-Eleven store manager. There is a battle for the hearts and minds of our children, and it is an information battlefield. Both the scientific community and the pot industry agree that marijuana inhibits the growth of the brain for those who are under 25 years of age. Making pot illegal is not a solution, so the burden falls onto parents, grandparents, and friends to reboot the inherent dreams and aspirations of our future generations. Given the challenges our society is tasked with, future generations need to be present, dedicated, and clear-eyed in order to confront society's enormous challenges: global warming, racial divide, gun control, the wealth gap, the military industrial complex, drug abuse, women's rights, etc., etc. We must appeal to, exhort, and insist on the development of character—character so fortified that it refuses to succumb to the sales pitch of lessened awareness and titillation.

Now I recognize that a lot of citizens could probably manage a 7-Eleven while smoking pot every night. I guess you could say they have every right to do that.

But why settle? Is this the level of aspiration we want for our kids? We need to restore and protect our children's ability to dream, to hope, to aspire to the impossible. Our future democracy's infrastructure is dependent on this preservation. We must do this before the industrial drug complex locks their vice grip around the souls of our children.

A person is alive to the degree they are saturated with hopes and dreams. Pot sabotages one's hopes and dreams. It subverts one's innate courage. We have an obligation to unleash onto the world a generation of dreamers, imbued with the idea that the impossible is possible, that being the manager of a 7-Eleven just won't cut it.

Let us unleash a generation of dreamers. There is no telling what impact that may have on the world.

The Storm Troopers of Portland

July 26, 2020

I recently sent out a clarion call regarding the Trump/Nazi synergism. Well, suffice to say, not everyone agreed with me as evidenced by their creative use of four-letter words directed at my character.

Ouch!

But here's the thing, we had a secret band of Storm Troopers unleashed in this country, employing tactics eerily similar to Hitler's personal security force, the SA. This is evidenced by the swat teams Trump has assembled in Portland where peaceful demonstrators are being tear-gassed and whisked away in unmarked cars by unmarked, masked agents. In other words, the Storm Trooper Playbook has been resurrected and is experiencing a rebirth on the streets in Portland.

Let me repeat, American, yes, American peaceful protesters are being rounded up in unmarked cars, by police (?) showing no identification, no charges, and threatened with assault weapons.

This is happening in the United States of America, right now, not in some fascist country. IN AMERICA!

"Donald Trump said reading *Mein Kampf* in college had a profound effect on him, and he has tremendous respect for Adolf Hitler as a leader."

~ David Emery, April 2019

"Last April, perhaps in a surge of Czech nationalism, Ivana Trump told her lawyer Michael Kennedy that from time to time her husband reads a book of Hitler's collected speeches, My New Order, which he keeps in a cabinet by his bed ... Hitler's speeches, from his earliest days up through the Phony War of 1939, reveal his extraordinary ability as a master propagandist."

~ Marie Brenner

All of this urban drama brings me to the 'maskless' protesters during the COVID-19 lockdown: remember those people who were protesting the right NOT to wear masks, you know, fighting to maintain the right to spread a deadly virus to friends, family, co-workers, and children? Remember those patriotic warriors, how passionately they were marching to preserve the right to inflate a burgeoning pandemic. Well, since they are such First Amendment freedom fighters, I would expect them to be on the first bus to Portland to help combat the reenactment of a SS Nazi purge on U. S. citizens. Surely, this would take precedence over preserving the right to spread a deadly virus. They're patriots, right?

You know it's funny, maybe not "ha-ha" funny, but I don't recall the maskless freedom fighters marching for civil rights, or human rights, laying down their lives to stop child trafficking, marching to preserve voting rights for all citizens. But hey, who am I to judge? I guess what is important is the fact they marched. Perhaps in the future, they could rally around a cause that promotes real freedom, rather than pushing an agenda that ends with Americans in body bags.

By the way, Trump has plans to inject these USA Storm Troopers into other major cities, Chicago being the next target.

Our democracy is under siege right now. It will take severe commitment, vigilance, and courage to squash the juggernaut of American-born MAGA fascism.

This leads me to another subject: patriarchal culture, a subset of fascism, which evangelicals have spread through our country. I always wondered why evangelicals embraced a man who had at least two-dozen sexual assault allegations against him. Don't you draw the line after one, two at the most? Doesn't that give you pause before you rally behind a candidate, especially if you are a man of God? What would Jesus say? What would Jesus do? How does this square with Jesus' teaching of kindness, compassion, and empathy? As recently as the 1980s, when Bill Clinton was in office, character mattered. Ralph Reed, religious right leader said, "We care about the conduct of our leaders, and we will not rest until we have leaders of good moral character."

Well, that took a sudden turn!

But this evangelical hypocrisy built its roots much earlier. Jerry Falwell, a close friend of the current president, was a segregationist and staunch believer in a patriarchal society, which very much aligns with our president's worldview.

> "A child of the South, Falwell was a segregationist. Rather than fearing that American racism would discredit the country globally, Falwell insisted that civil rights agitation was inspired by communist sympathizers ... Falwell helped lead local efforts to resist school integration, even when that meant defying the Eisenhower administration, both national parties, and Lynchburg's own business leaders."
>
> ~ Kristen Kobes Du Mez, *Jesus and John Wayne: How White Evangelicals Corrupted a Faith and Fractured a Nation*

> "This is our President's religious mentor, well-schooled in the patriarchal interpretation of scriptures. Across two millennia of Christian history—and within the history of evangelicalism itself—there is ample precedent for sexism, racism, xenophobia, violence, and imperial designs."
>
> ~ Kristen Kobes Du Mez, *Jesus and John Wayne*, Page 44

Buttressing this patriarchal vision were evangelical women. Marabel Morgan from her best-selling book, *The Total Woman*, writes, "The biblical remedy for marital conflict was the submission of wives to husbands. It was God's plan for women to be under a husband's rule."

And then there was the popular evangelical, Jack Hayes, who wrote in 1972:

> "... he commanded women to 'be in complete and total submission to their husbands and to male leadership.' Whereas boys must be trained to be leaders, girls should be trained to submit."

> ~ Kristen Kobes Du Mez, *Jesus and John Wayne*, Page 53

> "And another of Jerry Falwell's, our President's spiritual mentor, greatest hits: Falwell sparked controversy by characterizing AIDS as 'the wrath of God upon homosexuals' and recommending that those with AIDS be quarantined. He also forged connections with South Africa's apartheid regime."

> ~ Kristen Kobes Du Mez, *Jesus and John Wayne*, Page 135

According to my reading of the Bible, we are all God's children. There is no hierarchy.

Evangelicals, historically, seemed to be terrified of the LGBTQ+ community. They will do anything to suppress them, deny them rights, and discriminate against them. They don't feel they are human and view them as an abomination. Now this is funny, well, not "ha-ha" funny, but funny nevertheless:

> "In 2014, the Billy Graham Evangelistic Association's *Decision* magazine featured Putin on its cover, and Franklin Graham praised the Russian president for standing up to the 'gay and lesbian agenda.'"

> ~ Kristen Kobes Du Mez, *Jesus and John Wayne*, Page 302

Like I said, we are all God's children. Atheists are more a product of the Big Bang, I think. But why are evangelicals so threatened by gays, so threatened that they forge awkward alliances with fascists like Putin? They admire how Putin stands up to the LGBTQ+ community: he either kills them or lets them rot in prison. (Word of warning to gays: be careful about stepping into an evangelical church—no telling if some gung-ho parishioner, Putin-lover, decides to implement the Putin program on his own. God knows the NRA will ensure these guys are well stocked in AK-47s.)

But here's another thought, pastors being around gays may remind the pastor that he is gay, and he can't have that. There were a lot of pastor scandals in the 1980s and 1990s, especially the gay ones. I got two words for you: Ted Taggart.

Over the past decade, evangelical groups have funneled more than $50 million into right-wing European organizations.

Back to the Putin gay agenda: is that really a program a religious institution should want to emulate—the murder and imprisoning of a select group of citizens? Does Billy Graham wanna take another look at that? Now I know why Trump has a man-love for Putin—he likes his religiously sanctioned anti-gay platform (developed by Billy Graham himself).

As the Russian official, Ramzan Kadyrov stated, "… there are no homosexuals in this country."

The evangelicals pray for the same outcome in America.

Yes, We Have Institutional Racism, but This Feels Different

June 14, 2020

This feels different.

In the past, strides have been made by various Civil Rights initiatives, protests, sit-ins, marches, legislation, etc., etc., but at the end of the day, the demand for change encountered invisible brick walls: institutional racism. For example, Civil Rights legislation was passed in 1965, including voting rights, but when people in the South went to vote, they encountered a host of obstructions, including poll taxes, literacy tests, and terroristic threats from the local American Taliban KKK operatives. Despite it being the law of the land, the right to vote was sabotaged.

Today, we have all kinds of voter suppression machinations, including insidious gerrymandering, voting locations closed in inner cities, and the discriminatory Voter ID badge policies. Progress was made, but it was only symbolic, marginal, and superficial. As time passed, the mechanisms and institutions of racism retrenched, constructing even higher structures meant to preserve the golden goose.

But this feels different.

What all these progressive initiatives did was chip away at the epidermis of institutional racism. We celebrated the journey of Martin Luther King Jr. and his non-violent messages, his galvanizing speeches, and marches to integrate, but all of the milestones that were achieved were cosmetic. After being terrorized, Black people could now eat bad-tasting food at a Woolworth lunch counter, a bit of a hollow victory. They never did address the structures that manufactured the racism.

Dr. King only became truly dangerous when he started to speak about worldwide institutional structures designed to protect the entrenched power, when he talked about empowering the working poor, when he talked about world hunger and its causes, and when he shed light on the mechanisms of suppression.

Two months later he was assassinated.

But this feels different.

In 2017, people of color represented just 28% of the population but 56% of prisoners. This isn't the result of some rogue sheriff deciding to get tough on crime. This is institutional and structured. The common denominator to all these structures is money. These institutions generate money, and lots of it, while ignoring the human cost. The working poor, the underclass, are far too often victims of this greed.

But this feels different.

Today, schools are just as segregated as they were in 1965, despite the groundbreaking legislation meant to integrate schools. In Boston, politicians pitted poor whites against poor Blacks, flaming an artificial divide. Roxbury and South Boston both had shitty, underfunded schools. Instead of joining forces and becoming allies in advocating for superior educational institutions, they turned on each other, blaming the other for their suppressed conditions, egged on by hidden forces.

Today, educational structures of segregation remain firm, impervious to any laws on the books. By keeping races segregated, students are denied the opportunity to find common ground, denied the opportunity to discover their shared humanity, denied the opportunity to savor another culture, denied the opportunity to be inspired by another culture, and fed disinformation that their poor station in life is a result of that person across the aisle, that person on the other side of the tracks, who happens to reside in the same economic straitjacket as themselves. They don't look above them for the genesis of their suppression or the institutions that surround them; they look across the aisle or down. The structural engineers of these institutions of racism fabricate intricate mazes, obscuring the puppet masters that orchestrate and flame the artificial divide among different races and nationalities.

But this feels different.

Despite the sensibility of keeping AK-47s out of the hands of mentally ill people, or teenagers, or criminals, the pure reasonableness of common-sense gun laws; despite all of this, we continue to turn our backs on our children. After every mass shooting, we are offered thoughts and prayers but nothing is done to protect our children. Gun laws save lives. This isn't about some gun shop owner trying to make a few bucks. This is institutional and structured. The NRA has constructed an impregnable fortress to preserve their ATM with its unlimited cash withdrawals, condoned by their enablers in Congress, who readily take the NRA campaign contributions. Right now, the NRA is an impregnable racist structure, saturating our inner cities with weapons.

But this feels different.

Our industries of death—the tobacco industry, the pharmaceutical industry, the military industrial complex, and the drug industry—are enabled by the bankers who launder their cash, reminiscent of Northern bankers who invested and financed slavery in the 1800s. These are all structural, and the collateral damage is ignored. Our silence emboldens these institutions, letting them know we will willingly turn our heads when their collateral damage surfaces. We remain safe in our cocoon of irresponsibility, as did the good German people who remained silent as Hitler constructed Germany's concentration camps, ashes blowing in the wind as the ovens baked Jews. Silence is one of the most powerful enablers of evil.

But this feels different.

There is a common humanity among all of the people of this planet: we believe in family, we desire for our kids to have a better life than us, we love to help, we need community, and seek gainful employment that speaks to our passion. And we all have that crazy uncle that we tell our kids to avoid—but he's family, which forgives most sins, and we love him just the same.

But this feels different.

I say this because this is the first time in our history that white people are acknowledging our complicity in creating these institutions of structural racism. This is the first time in our history we are recognizing that our humanity, our personal integrity, our salvation, can never be fully realized if our fellow citizens aren't free, are denied opportunity, are denied equal access, are denied decent education, are denied health care, all because of the color of their skin or their socio-economic status. This is the first time in our history that we have recognized that many of our institutions are racist and that we have a responsibility to disable the pernicious effects of these structures.

This is why America is the greatest country in the world: we are the first country to figure out that our suppression is not coming from 'others.' Our suppression is not coming from people in our same socio-economic status. Our survival is inexorably linked to the survival of our fellow man. We can never be free if our fellow citizens remain in bondage. We have finally figured out that our enemy is not each other, and that there is a common humanity that binds us. No other country has figured this out yet; we are the first.

In the past, movements would achieve some measure of change, and studies would be commissioned, which served to placate the people, but after the dust settled, the institutions of oppression were left fully intact, racist institutional fortresses that fostered and generated inequities, wars, and hunger. It takes more than courageous civil rights protesters to dismantle and disable these structures. It takes a concerted effort by all races and religions to dismantle racist structures. For the first time, white Americans are willing to listen, to offer the keys, the combinations to the locks of these racist institutions. For the first time, all colors of Americans are realizing they need each other both for their own salvation, but for the nation as a whole.

This is definitely different.

One final note:

IF YOU DON'T VOTE, THERE AIN'T NO HOPE!

Hate Speech Is Disinformation

May 4, 2020

Allow me to start this by quoting Joseph Caputo, the recently appointed Department of Health and Human Services spokesperson.

March 8: "Coronavirus is the Democrats' new Russia, their new Ukraine. And nobody will believe them except their zombies. But know this: The Dems' strategy to defeat @realDonaldTrump requires 100s of thousands of American deaths. Will one of their nutjobs make it happen, a la Hodgkinson?"

March 11: "There must be a national pandemic tragedy for the Democrats to win. They're counting on it."

March 14: "100s of thousands must die and the US economy must collapse for the Democrat 2020 victory strategy to succeed. They're getting so excited for the carnage. Sick people."

March 14, doubling down: "This Democrat strategy, echoed by their conjugal media, will fail. Hoping your country fails and hundreds of thousands die so you can gain power is a sick and twisted strategy. American will punish them."

March 15: "Are you kidding? Soro's political agenda REQUIRES a pandemic."

March 16: "In response to the Stock Market losing all its gains since Trump took office, 'The Democrat celebration of the death and destruction will be held soon.'"

March 17: "The Chinese Communist Party has always been adept at lying to cover their murders. What's remarkable here is the US Democrats and their conjugal media repeating CCP propaganda because they hate

Trump more than they love America. The Wuhan virus has exposed them."

March 17, Caputo tweets a conspiracy that implies economist David Rothschild is a member of the European Rothschild family calling him, "...an inbred elitist sphincter whose family craves control. That's one reason why he constantly lies about President Trump." Rothschild told CNN he is not related to the banking family, which is frequently the target of antisemitic conspiracies. (Andrew Kaczynski, Nathan McDermott and Em Steck: CNN)

March 18: "Nobody should let Democrats and their conjugal media popularize Chinese Communist Party talking points. Democrats + Media=CCP."

March 22: "Power. It's the Democrats' oxygen and they'll destroy Americans for it."

March 22: "I'm serious. The Dem strategy for 2020 victory requires that @realDonaldTrump fail in his fight against the Chinese virus. Failure is measured in deaths and economic collapse. The only questions to ask a Dem are how many Americans must die, how many families must be destroyed?"

March 22, (he can't help himself): "They are literally cheering on the deaths of Americans and the destruction of our economy. They would rather see people die than see Trump successfully navigate this disaster."

March 23: "The Democrats have one motivation for holding Americans hostage in a global crisis: HATE." (Methinks, he protests too much.)

March 31: "The Left hate normal Americans and they want us dead and replaced. Act as if they mean it because they do."

Two weeks later he became HHS spokesman.

These are posts Mr. Caputo unleashed over a recent three-week span, and that is not all he spewed, just a sampling. But you gotta wonder what he's saying behind closed doors.

I'm a Democrat, and I don't remember praying for a mass graves in order for Democrats to win in November. And I don't remember any of my Democratic friends voicing a desire for national carnage as a strategy to get their candidates elected. And to be fair, if the shoe was reversed, none of my Republican friends would pray for body bags as a campaign blueprint. I know this because I know their heart; I know their goodness. Although we disagree politically, their overall humanity is what shines through.

So why are we so divided? On a fundamental level, we agree on basic truths: family, fairness, and justice. We all desire for our children to have a better life than we had. We connect on a human level.

So why are we so divided? We are all assaulted daily with a cesspool of disinformation, and, depending on the recipient, some of it will stick. We ingest this bile without examining the source or the motivation behind the message. Disinformation and hate propaganda have been with us forever. Now it is more sophisticated, laser-focused, based on mathematical algorithms designed to ignite maximum efficiency. It targets, manipulates, and ignites dormant prejudices. In the past, we would drop propaganda leaflets from planes over North Vietnam during the Vietnam War. Today we use the internet, but it has always been a battle for the hearts and minds, not much different than it is today.

Today, there is a meme going around that portrays Bill Gates, George Soros, and Dr. Fauci as part of an evil conspiracy poised to take over the world through mind control and various other nefarious mechanisms, tinged with the usual antisemitism. This is the Gates Foundation Mission statement:

> "THE PATH OUT OF POVERTY BEGINS WHEN THE NEXT GENERATION CAN ACCESS QUALITY HEALTHCARE AND A GREAT EDUCATION."

In developing countries, we focus on improving people's health and well-being, helping individuals lift themselves out of hunger and extreme poverty. In the United States, we seek to ensure that all people—especially those with the fewest resources—can access the opportunities they need to succeed in school and life.

It's hard to argue with that mission. And it's not just PR, the Gates Foundation has a proven track record of results. Compare the Gates Foundation results to the Donald Trump Foundation results. And George Soros is a man who has dedicated his life to helping refugees, the forgotten, the disenfranchised. And Dr. Fauci, he had the gall to introduce science to the administration's response to the pandemic.

Disinformation divides us, it serves up scapegoats for whatever ails us. Scapegoats act as smokescreens to prevent us from seeing the real source of our anxiety, our poverty, and our disenfranchisement.

Disinformation tells us that we are not responsible for our condition, perhaps the vilest consequence of the propaganda.

> "And importantly, thus it has been possible to make poor and working-class white people believe that their interests lie in making common cause with their political leaders and economic betters. Common cause in whiteness: the idea that they might eventually share in the spoils, and the understanding that the discomforts and anxieties of their own precarious lives were due to—are due to—those below them rather than those above them."
>
> ~ Walter Johnson, *The Broken Heart of America*, Page 7

Perhaps this pandemic can serve as a reboot for our culture, the first step in restoring grace. Kindness is the superpower that can do this.

Let's be kind to one another.

Racism and Racehorse Theory, Where Is Your Line in the Sand?

October 13, 2020

To all of my Trump friends and enablers, where is your line in the sand?

After my last post, calling out the president for his endorsement of white supremacy, my Trump friends doubled down on his increasingly blatant racism. Their main counterargument was basically, "Biden's a racist."

Really, and that's your argument?

But I have to ask again: what is your line in the sand? If he murdered someone on 5th Avenue, would he still have your support?

Where's the line?

This is the same guy who called neo-Nazis "very fine people."

Where is your line in the sand?

As Peter Seager once sang, "Which side are you on boys? Which side are you on?"

If you are a white supremacist, or endorsed white supremacy, just say it. It's okay. Be honest; you'll feel better. Don't let your argument be that Biden's a racist. Fly your colors and show the courage of your convictions. Martin Luther King Jr. once said that the most pernicious, hateful racism he ever encountered was in the North. It was insidious, hidden, but violent. In the South there was a certain honesty about their racism; it was blatant; you knew where you stood: challenge, protest, or question the institutional racism and they would hang you. Date a white girl and they would hang you.

But you knew where you stood.

As Trump's layers of racism have been stripped over the past four years, what has emerged is the foundation upon which his racism arises.

He believes he has superior genes, and springs from superior stock. He believes in the racehorse theory. Seema Mehta from the *LA Times* reported:

> "President Trump has alarmed Jewish leaders and others with remarks that appeared to endorse 'racehorse theory'—the idea that selective breeding can improve a country's performance, which American eugenicists and German Nazis used in the last century to buttress their goals of racial purity.
>
> "'You have good genes, you know that, right?' Trump told a mostly white crowd of supporters in Bemidji, Minn., on Sept. 18. 'You have good genes. A lot of it is about the genes, isn't it? Don't you believe? The racehorse theory. You think we're so different? You have good genes in Minnesota.'
>
> "This is at the heart of Nazi ideology ... This has brought so much tragedy and destruction to the Jewish people and to others. It's actually hard to believe in 2020 we have to revisit these very dangerous theories."

Trump touts his genes, his breeding, and per the first debate, how smart he is. Well, he inherited $34 million from his father and parleyed that into six bankruptcies.

How smart is that?

He doesn't believe in science, and per his pandemic performance, he thinks global warming is a hoax.

How smart is that?

But his whole persona is based on a false, debunked, racist, eugenics theory that was used for all manner of horror, including Hitler's "Final Solution."

> "Vulgar it may have been, but to the race theorists of the nine-teenth and early twentieth centuries it was irresistible: if a per-son could attribute his virtues to this pedigree, he was beyond challenge. The obverse was an even more powerful notion, for without the proper pedigree a man was ipso facto inferior"

> ~ Daniel Okrent, *The Guarded Gate*

'Racehorse theory' has some ugly footprints. More from Seema Mehta, *LA Times*:

> "Initially used for horses, the theory was ultimately used to jus-tify selective breeding of people, including forced sterilization laws that were on the books in 32 states and used in some of them up through the 1970s.

> "'You can absolutely be taught things. Absolutely. You can get a lot better. But there is something. You know, the racehorse theory, there is something to the genes,' Trump told Larry King on CNN in 2007. 'And I mean, when I say something, I mean a lot.'"

And my Trump friends say he's not a white supremacist? How in the hell do you reconcile his embrace of the 'racehorse theory' and say he's not a white supremacist?

Can't wait for the retort, but please, please, let not your argument be:

"Well, Biden's a racist!"

Spare me that!

Three years later, he told CNN that his father was successful and it naturally followed that he would be too. "I have a certain gene. I'm a gene believer. Hey, when you connect two racehorses, you usually end up with a fast horse. And I really was—you know, I had a—a good gene pool from the standpoint of that."

And if you still don't believe that Trump embraces the racist eugenics gene theory, well, we have Don Jr. himself chiming in.

"Like him, I'm a big believer in racehorse theory. He's an incredibly accomplished guy, my mother's incredibly accomplished, she's an Olympian, so I'd like to believe genetically I'm predisposed to better-than-average," Trump Jr. told Michael D'Antonio in a 2014 interview, according to a transcript provided by the author.

Can we really call Don Jr. better than average? Can you? Really? One thing he did inherit from his father—the lack of an empathy gene.

Okay, to my Trump friends, are you still clinging to Trump not being a racist? A white supremacist? And if you don't feel he is a white supremacist, a racist, what is your line in the sand?

The Disinformation Pandemic

September 3, 2020

We are in the midst of a disinformation pandemic.

I often have these conversations with Trump supporters, but they aren't really conversations because there is never an equal exchange of viewpoints, ideas, or even debates. Their idea of a debate is to send me a link, oftentimes emanating from Russia. It sometimes feels as if I am talking to a robot, or someone who has been taken hostage. But what's confusing is that these people are smart, nobody's fool, but it's odd because they seemed to have suspended critical thinking, with no acknowledgment of Trump's past or his white supremacy embrace. I was always under the impression that my friends were not racist, and that they had good hearts. But here they are, today, supporting a dyed-in-the-wool racist.

> "By adulthood, researchers have found, most Americans have been exposed to a culture with enough negative messages about African Americans and other marginalized groups that as much as 80 percent of white Americans hold unconscious bias against black Americans, bias so automatic that it kicks in before a person can process it, according to the Harvard sociologist David Williams."
>
> ~ David Wilkerson, *Caste*, Page 186

I'm not sure if it's 80%, but the negative messages we've been exposed to are a fact. But I still don't get it. I can't reconcile the dichotomy of my friend's goodness and their embracing of a racist.

In the southern rural areas, Trump supporters embrace a man who is fighting tooth and nail to take away their healthcare, their lifeline. How do you support a man who wants to leave you naked, devoid of any medical security blanket?

I didn't get it.

But I think I do now.

As Jake, the State Farm guy says, "Here's the real deal." Let's open the discussion with some words from Hitler's information czar, Joseph Goebbels.

> "If you tell a lie big enough and keep repeating it, people will eventually come to believe it. The lie can be maintained only for such time as the State can shield the people from the political, economic and/or military consequences of the lie. It thus becomes vitally important for the State to use all of its powers to repress dissent, for the truth is the mortal enemy of the lie, and thus by extension, the truth is the greatest enemy of the State."

Our president has told over 20,000 lies since taking office. This IV of poisonous lies has been injected into the bloodstreams of his base. It is daily, relentless, and served up with a sweetener, and scapegoats, making it more palatable. And if the listener has buried seeds of racism, his lies nourish the soil.

Since January, he has used the word hoax over 250 times, with no specifics or names, just poisoning the airways with unspecified charges, leaving people confused, helpless, wallowing in a dangerous environment created by a baseless conspiracy theory where only a strong leader like Putin or Trump can save them. Propaganda is the lifeblood of a demigod, and Trump is following Goebbels playbook to a tee.

As Trump has recently made clear, "I alone can fix it."

George Orwell, *1984*, "Ignorance is strength."

"War is peace."

"Freedom is slavery."

Kelly Ann Conway, "There are alternate facts."

Mark Meadows, Trump's Chief of Staff, "Lack of evidence of mail-in voting fraud is the definition of fraud."

Huh?????????????

The horror that Orwell predicted is unfolding in plain sight.

> "A misogynistic demagogue contends that the existing political system is corrupt and broken (rightfully so) and promises, through the force of his personality, that he can fix the problems with a new vision for government. But he needs both a mob (of admirers and attackers of perceived enemies) and a propaganda machine that feeds this mob a continuous stream of lies to promote his message while disparaging other sources that might counter these deceptions. We can't disregard how important this propaganda machine is in swaying opinion. If people hear enough lies, many people begin to believe them. Repetition and timing are key."
>
> ~ Gabe Ortiz, *Daily KoS*

Fox News is the propaganda arm of the Trump organization. These enablers foster and amplify Trump's daily lies, validating the scam, and legitimizing baseless conspiracy theories. Trump even praises QAnon, a person or group the FBI has deemed a domestic terror threat.

Recently, a reporter challenged Trump on his lie (already told 150 times) that he got the Veterans Program passed. Trump stated, "They been trying to get that passed for decades and decades and no president's ever been able to do it, and it got done." But here's the real deal. President Obama signed the Choice program into law in 2014. It was championed by two Senators Trump hates—Bernie Saunders and John

McCain. When the reporter pressed him as to why he would lie, Trump just walked away.

This administration also utilizes the power of euphemisms. Euphemisms were used by the Nazis to cloud the full extent of their horror. Jews were sent to 'work camps,' not concentration camps. Today, we have kids in concentration camps at the border, but the press never calls it like it is. These are concentration camps for kids, and what makes it even more egregious is the fact that these kids are separated from their parents, an act of cruelty that doesn't even measure on the Richter Scale.

Anna Deavere Smith said that we are becoming "… and we have less and less awareness of the pain of the other."

And perhaps that sums up the tragic fault of my Trump friends: a lack of empathy for the pain of others. The lack of empathy helps my Trump friends condone this daily drumbeat of lies and cruelty.

They are the modern-day enablers, having surrendered their integrity to Trump's propaganda juggernaut, a movement that resonates with their racism, their misogyny, and their homophobia.

Is there not one with the courage to say, "The emperor has no clothes."

Cruelty and Evil Do Not Belong in Government

September 21, 2020

Evil is hard to confront.

> "A Trump administration lawyer has disputed in court whether detained migrant children are entitled to toothbrushes and soap."

This breaks my heart. This level of cruelty sends a chill up my spine.

I think of these kids, separated from their parents, traumatized, in cages, sleeping on concrete floors, and if that is not enough, the Trump administration sic their Justice Department lawyers to deny American-grown concentration camp children, soap and toothbrushes.

Yes, you got that right. Our government is using Justice Department lawyers, our taxpayer money, to do research, write briefs, go to court, all for the purpose of denying innocent, incarcerated children soap and toothbrushes. Imagine being a five-year-old kid, extracted from your parents, a traumatizing event in and of itself, made to sleep on concrete floors, susceptible to diseases, hunger, and if that wasn't enough, if that didn't break their spirit, they are denied soap and toothbrushes.

Have they no shame?

How degraded must one be to think up such cruelty? How degraded must one be to follow such directives? Silence is a special kind of violence.

And this evil has multiple layers.

"In a 218-page motion filed Tuesday in U.S. District Court in Southern California, ACLU attorneys contend the administration has removed numerous children, including babies, from their mothers and fathers based on offenses as minor as traffic violations and misdemeanor charges dating back more than two decades."

Do we really have to remove babies from their mothers?

Is this really necessary?

We used to embrace immigrants coming into this country—why: their work ethic, their rich cultural heritage, which in turn made America deeper, richer, and stronger; and their embrace of the American dream, which helped build America into a global leader. Except for native Native Americans, we all sprang from immigrants. It's the secret sauce that made America great.

"More than 200 people the US deported back to El Salvador have been killed or seriously abused, including sexually assaulted and tortured, a report from Human Rights Watch says."

I'll tell you a little secret, the immigrants who seek asylum, who risk their lives in order to come into this country, fleeing executions, fascist dictatorships, sexual assault and torture, escaping religious persecutions, these are some of the most courageous people on this planet. These are the people we want in this country. The stories of mothers carrying infants 400 miles to avoid death squads, fathers going days without food in order to give their kids what crumbs were left, this level of courage is humbling. You see, the people who stayed home, who didn't fight, who succumbed and fell in lockstep to the repression, are the weak ones. We are being offered the warriors, the 1%-ers in courage, the souls who would die if it meant a better life for their children. We shouldn't be sending these heroic people back to their countries to be executed, tortured, or raped. We should be embracing them because immigrants are what makes America great.

Who is so degraded that they would inflict this level of horror and trauma on innocent children? Who is the ultimate bully here? Who is the coward who comes up with the idea of denying innocent children soap and a toothbrush?

I give you Stephen Miller, Trump's main advisor, an avowed white nationalist. I think all you need to know about Mr. Miller is this: when in high school, he ran for class president on a platform that janitors should pick up trash left behind by students. In other words, Mr. Miller encouraged fellow students to leave their lunch trash behind for the janitors to pick up. Miller went so far as deliberating throwing his trash on the floor.

- "Am I the only one," Miller asked in a campaign for his high school class government, "who is sick and tired of being told to pick up my trash when we have plenty of janitors who are paid to do it for us?"

This is the guy who has fashioned America's immigration policy. Trump embraces it because it resonates with his racist, white supremacy worldview—gotta stop those four-year-old terrorists, no telling what they will do when they turn five.

As *New York Times* columnist Jamelle Bouie writes:

- **Miller praised Calvin Coolidge's 1921 Immigration Act:** Like his former boss Jeff Sessions, Miller is apparently a fan of Calvin Coolidge and the racially exclusionary Immigration Act of 1921 that the 30th president signed. The 1921 Act all but excluded immigrants from Asian nations and was praised by Hitler as the type of policy he sought to implement. In 2015, Miller wrote about Immigrant Heritage Month as, "a good opportunity to remind people about the heritage established by Calvin Coolidge."

- **Miller apparently was in communication with a leading Islamophobe:** Miller suggested that he was in contact with and pitching political stories to leading Islamophobe Pamela Geller. Geller once falsely claimed, "Muslim immigration is tied directly to Islamic terror."

A few more words from Miller:

"Continue to worship at the alter [sic] of multiculturalism and we may come to see that we are participating in the sacrifice of the one culture which binds us all."

"Miller has advocated for changes to 'public-charge' rules, possibly forcing some 18 million noncitizens and 9 million children who are U.S. citizens, to choose between basic nutritional and housing needs and a continued ability to stay in the U.S. Similarly, Miller has proposed to evict families with undocumented members from public housing, even though this might lead to homelessness for 55,000 U.S. citizen and legal resident children."

Miller also said:

"I would be happy if not a single refugee foot ever again touched American soil."

I will end with this abomination:

"The Trump administration is making immigrant parents pay $800 for DNA tests to get their kids back."

As Americans, are we really doing this? To children???? Are we going to continue to remain silent on this, as did the German people whose silence aided, and abetted atrocities committed by fellow citizens?

PART II

I have several grandkids. One is turning nine in a couple of months. What that means is that he will soon be studying history, specifically the history of our presidents, and probably our current president. Our current president is a man I don't want my grandson to admire, or look up to, or emulate in any way. Let me count the ways ...

1. He spews lies, instead of the truth.

2. He lacks a moral compass, and is devoid of integrity.

3. He belittles, instead of validates.

4. He creates chaos, instead of order.

5. He divides, instead of uniting.

6. He degrades women, instead of respecting them.

7. He promotes violence, instead of peace.

8. He lacks compassion, instead enacts cruelty.

9. He worships money, not the goodness in people.

Do we really want our kids emulating the values put forth by our current president?

PART III

Our president is now unhinged. Any rational voice has been purged from his administration. What's left is an army of sycophants and enablers, people who validate and parrot Trump's evil impulses.

In other words, the filters are all gone.

And guess who's back on the team. The convicted felon Roger Stone who we know has Trump's ear. Here's the latest from Stone:

> "Trump should use his powers to declare martial law, arrest anti-Trump public figures like Facebook CEO Mark Zuckerberg, Apple's Tim Cook, former Sen. Harry Reid, President Bill Clinton, and former Democratic presidential nominee Hillary Clinton, and 'seize' voter ballots."

~ Daily Kos

What's at stake in this election is whether democracy will survive.

Bringing Back Jim Crow: Georgia's Anti-Voting Bill

April 8, 2021

This post is in honor of my Trump acolytes, who are now on record saying institutional racism is a figment of my imagination. As a result, I'm doubling down on the Jim Crow revival erupting in Georgia.

Last week the Governor of Georgia signed the new anti-voting bill into existence, surrounded by six white guys

and a painting

wait for it

a painting of

wait for it

a painting of a plantation.

Their dog whistles to white supremacists have been thrown away and they are now using bull horns to call their base. Trump is smiling in his bunker at Mar-a-Lago, a man who spent four years cultivating and fertilizing and nourishing white supremacy, granting them legitimacy, transmitting and nurturing their hate that was brought to fruition at the attack on the Capitol.

A PAINTING OF A PLANTATION!

Since it was Georgia, I assumed the State House would be adorned with those acclaimed black-and-white photos of people marching for the right to vote. And since Martin Luther King Jr. is from Georgia, I thought there would at least be some photos of him, fighting for voting rights, civil rights. Or photographs of John Lewis, a Georgia representative, marching for voting rights at the Pettus Bridge, speaking truth to power. I thought the walls would be full of images of people asserting their most fundamental rights.

But nope, the best Georgia could do was to use a painting of a plantation as a backdrop! A plantation for God's sake. All that was missing were the white robes and hood, and maybe the Confederate flag. Maybe they could have borrowed the Confederate flag from that guy who paraded it in the Capitol during the insurrection. The ceremony of the bill signing presented the Governor's archaic vision of America, when people of color were expected to know their place, and everyone lived happily ever after on the plantation.

I guess we should be glad it wasn't a painting of a hangman's noose, a buried symbol resurrected during the insurrection, where the N-word was liberally spewed according to the court filings of Capitol Police, and ironically, was meant for an old white guy, Mike Pence. (Don't worry, Mike is alive and well, having done his penance by forwarding Trump's Big Lie that Trump won the election. Pence's racism and mendacity have been restored; credentials required in today's Republican Party.)

Here's the question: was this ceremony staged in front of the plantation painting just an innocent mistake, that maybe this was perhaps the only accessible room at the time? I mean, should we just give the boy a pass, that maybe he didn't mean anything by it? Well, after four months of the Trump's presidency, I started to realize that his subtle racism, his spreading of chaos, his scapegoating of minorities, weren't innocent slips, but were calculated stratagems to embolden white supremacy. Even at the end, his campaign manager, Corey Lewandowski, quoted the sign at the entrance to Auschwitz, "Work will set you free." Yes. To raise money for Trump's Big Lie, he's going all-in on an Auschwitz/Nazi slogan.

It ain't a coincidence.

The first step in setting you free is not to build concentration camps.

Just saying.

We will never be free until we are all free.

Racism Is the Great Con

August 7, 2021

We fell for it. White people fell for it starting the day slave ships landed on the shores of the colonies.

White people fell for the con that their ultimate survival, their prosperity, their happiness, depended on the enslavement and suppression of others.

This is our legacy. How could we be so dumb?

As our country evolved, enslavers perfected the con down to a precise science, meant to preserve an autocracy under the guise of a democracy. But we still fell for it. We aired our grievances, we endured the poverty, the illiteracy, the degradation that a slave economy produces. We were told that our miserable lives were not our fault, that the fault lay with people of color. They were the ones that were keeping us in poverty, disabled by illiteracy, and wallowing in our degradation.

So, the enslavers marshaled a scheme that pummeled poor whites with the propaganda they were not responsible for their miserable lot and that people of color were the cause. African Americans were the scapegoats served up, fortified and legitimized by Biblical references taken out of context. The formula was simple: keep whites poor, illiterate, hungry, and they will support slavery. Just tell poor whites that if the slaves were freed, competition for jobs would destroy the job market because freed slaves would work for peanuts, which was better than nothing.

Keeping poor whites poor had many machinations. Enslavers ensured there was no public education in the South because they controlled the legislature and would vote against public schooling. If everyone was educated, they just might figure out the hustle. As for African Americans, it was illegal to be educated, subject to hanging or imprisonment. Kinda hard to achieve the American dream when the most powerful weapon, education, is denied you, a hangman's noose swinging in the breeze as a reminder not to learn to read.

And to make sure poor whites remained puppets to the enslavers, the KKK was formed. Embraced by poor whites, taking pride in themselves for the first time in their life because they were doing God's work, they kept people of color in their place. And for the first time in their lives, they could look down on someone. The subterfuge that plantation owners had poor whites' backs was a sham. (We see that today with our former president—you think Trump cares about poor whites in West Virginia or Mississippi?) After the Civil War, the con evolved through sharecropping, as the prison industrial complex was hatched with the use of prison labor, think chain gangs, the destination for African Americans if arrested for vagrancy or loitering. In other words, hanging out while Black.

Walter Johnson, in his book *The Broken Heart of America*, touches on this phenomenon.

> "And importantly, thus it has been possible to make poor and working-class white people believe that their interests lie in making common cause with their political leaders and economic betters. Common cause in whiteness: the idea that they might eventually share in the spoils, and the understanding that the discomforts and anxieties of their own precarious lives were due to—are due to—those below them rather than those above them."

~ Walter Johnson, Page 7

Enslavers, who controlled the southern economy, didn't believe in our Constitution, especially the part about men being created equal. They were living in a democracy they didn't believe in. We see that today manifested on January 6th, where the former KKK has been sanitized and morphed into modern-day white supremacy hate groups, like the Proud Boys and the Promise Keepers. It was no accident the Confederate flag was prominently on display during the attack on the Capitol. The insurrectionists had the same mindset as the enslavers, and, according to police testimony, the N-word was alive and well with the insurrectionists.

Millions of white people vote for politicians who screw them, most specifically in the red states. Rather than voting for politicians who battle to provide them with affordable health care, who battle to provide them with decent schools, who battle to fight global warming because the effects of climate change impact white neighborhoods also. The politicians they vote for simply provide them with scapegoats, and offer a vehicle to vent their grievances. But they really do jack-shit for working-class whites, and they do even less for working-class Blacks, and women. Because, let's be clear, when they talk about all men being created equal (or not), they really only mean men; not all humans.

Recently, four states turned down expanded Medicaid. FREE HEALTHCARE and the states say no. They are perpetuating the lie that this money will go to people of color who are looking for a handout. In Texas, for example, most of this money would have gone to white people. Racism makes white people shoot themselves in the foot. Recently, 120 hospitals closed in Texas, a result of saying no to Medicaid expansion, which has not only devastated the healthcare for poor rural communities but has devastated the economy of these regions, jobs evaporating into thin air. Citizens are so brainwashed, so inculcated with racism, that these decisions meant to foster racism recoil against whites, but they can't see it.

The Republican strategy has always hinged on dividing races with disinformation. They campaign on propaganda and outright lies. Page 59 of McGhee's, *The Sum of Us*, lays this out perfectly.

"I think Republicans were pretty good at what they're always good at, right? Pitting communities against each other and using a lot of dog-whistle politics around, like, Medicaid equates to Black freeloading people ..."

Lee Atwater, the famous Republican strategist was captured on tape laying out the true intentions of the Republican Party. McGhee, *The Sum of Us*.

"You start out in 1954 by saying, 'Nigger, nigger, nigger.' By 1968 you can't say 'nigger'—that hurts you, backfires so you say stuff like uh, forced busing, states' rights, and all that stuff, and you're getting so abstract. Now, you're talking about cutting taxes, and all these things you're talking about are totally economic things and a byproduct of them is, blacks get hurt worse than whites ... 'We want to cut this,' is much more abstract than even the busing thing, uh, and a hell of a lot more abstract than 'Nigger, nigger.'"

Republican puppets believed they would receive the trickle-down rewards if they embraced and forwarded the racial agendas of the Lee Atwater ilk. Atwater's propaganda kept poor whites looking down, not up, as explanations for their miserable lot. They were able to convince working-class whites that working-class Blacks were the enemy, not their equals. It got politicians elected.

"As Professor Haney Lope points out, priming white voters with racist dog whistles was the means; the end was an economic agenda that was harmful to working and middle-class voters of all races, including white people."

~ McGhee, *The Sum of Us*, Page 34

In the 1950s, municipalities would often construct community pools, meant to alleviate the summer heat for their local communities. And then African Americans asserted their right to swim in the local community pool. Instead of welcoming the Black kids, the local leaders banned Blacks from swimming in the community pools. This initiative was banned in court and instead of complying with the court order, the pools were filled with dirt. No kids got to swim. Racism is a powerful motivator.

God could have made things so much easier by making everyone one color. Instead, He gave us free will, our greatest gift from Heaven, and He bestowed upon us different colors of the rainbow for us to revel in the manna of different spices, colors, and cultures. We are saturated by the magic, the enchantment of other cultures—we just need to inhale the beauty, as we are surrounded by this alchemy. This was a gift, not a curse.

> "'When you cut government services,' as Reagan strategist Lee Atwater said, 'blacks get hurt worse than whites. What's lost in that formulation is just how much white people get hurt, too.'"
>
> ~ McGee, *The Sum of Us*, Page 39

Racism makes us blind. It prevents people from seeing who is pulling the strings.

> "Racism, then, works against non-wealthy white Americans in two ways. First, it lowers their support for government actions that would help them economically, out of a zero-sum fear that it could help the racialized 'underserved' as well."
>
> ~ McGee, *The Sum of Us*, Page 38

We are still fighting the Civil War, which had been fueled by another lie that it was a battle for state's rights. It was actually a battle to save an economic system that relied on the debasement and enslavement of human beings.

White supremacists are calling for a new race war. The mentality of enslavers' fascism has resurfaced (it never really left), and it has become a rallying cry for white supremacy hate groups empowered by Trump, and it is the same con employed by enslavers hundreds of years ago and has been excavated by Republican enablers.

"In July, 2019, police officers responding to a racist graffiti incident in Baltimore County, Maryland, encountered swastikas, as well as a phrase new to them: 'Race War Now.' In New York, the DMV canceled a Queens resident's vanity license plate in November 2018; the plate read GTKRWN, an acronym for 'Gas the Kikes, Race War Now.' In Washington state, local authorities used the state's 'red flag' laws in October 2019 to temporarily seize the weapons of Kaleb Cole, a member of the white supremacist group Atomwaffen, whom prosecutors claimed was 'preparing for a race war.'"

~ Cody Boteler, *Arbutus Times*

"Some neo-Nazi groups, such as Atomwaffen and Feuerkrieg Division, claim their very purpose is to prepare for 'race war.' Other white supremacists repeatedly reference it on podcasts or on white supremacist discussion forums such as Stormfront. The latter has featured a variety of race war-themed topics in recent years, including 'They Want a Race War, Don't They?' 'Blacks won't win the race war,' and 'When the Race War is Escalating, What Side Will You Be On?'"

~ Cody Boteler, *Arbutus Times*

There are powerful forces that seek to divide us, that keep us fighting each other based on artificial barriers, who implant fear into our psyches as a way of securing or maintaining power. Donald Trump emboldened white supremacists to come out of the closet. He empowered and validated their hate, their scapegoating. January 6th was much more than a failed coup, it was the first skirmish, the first attempt to restore fascism and the good old days of the Confederacy.

Dixie

I wish I was in the land of cotton,

Old times there are not forgotten,

Look away, look away, look away Dixie Land.

In Dixie Land, where I was born in,

Early on one frosty morn',

Look away, look away, look away Dixie Land.

Oh, I wish I was in Dixie, Hooray! Hooray!

In Dixie Land I'll take my stand

To live and die in Dixie.

Away, away, away down south in Dixie

This is the culture Trump tried to sell, where he takes his stand, the KKK ecstatic over his agenda. If a terrorist group like the KKK is happy about your programs and policies, shouldn't that give one pause, especially if you're the leader of the Free World?

Whites still cling to the delusion and still believe in the con that Dixie-land was some kind of utopia. Perhaps you could say it was for the enslavers, but they were a very unhappy, paranoid lot, soaked in the blood of their terrorism.

Orwell and Trump's Brave New World

January 6, 2021

I often ask my Trump friends what is it about the guy that attracts them. And their reply is often centered around their paycheck—they take home more—and the fact that he is a bit rough around the edges, unconventional, meaning he voices attitudes and hate they don't have the guts to say out loud. It is all about them, not the less fortunate, the voiceless, the forgotten. And they validate Trump's hate-strewn rhetoric and policies with their silence.

> "A people that elect corrupt politicians, imposters, thieves and traitors are not victims, but accomplices."
>
> ~ George Orwell

There is something deeper, insidious, cancerous, that is swilling around our political landscape. Trump is seeking to institute fascism in this country, surrounded by a band of enablers. He lost the election, but he is creating a false reality that he won, that there was election fraud, a lie his cult embraces and advances. As Joseph Goebbels stated, "Accuse the other side of that which you are guilty."

From George Orwell's book, *1984,*

> "The party told you to reject the evidence of your eyes and ears. It was their final, most essential command."

During a speech in July 2018, Trump said,

> "What you're seeing and what you're reading is not what's happening."

George Orwell, *1984*,

> "The further a society drifts from the truth, the more it will hate those that speak it."

Dare I say the press—what Trump has labeled an 'enemy of the people,' the one institution that has the courage to speak truth to power.

And then there was Kellyanne Conway's coining of a new Orwellian phrase on January 22, 2017: "alternative facts".

In other words, *1984*,

> "The party told you to reject the evidence of your eyes and ears. It was their final, most essential command."

Donald Trump is seeking to be reinstated as president by positing an alternate, false reality.

The president also meets most of the criteria of Orwell's 1944 definition of fascism.

> "Something cruel, unscrupulous, arrogant, obscurantist, anti-liberal and anti-working-class … almost any English person would accept 'bully' as a synonym for 'fascist'."

As the last days of his presidency tick down, Trump has become unhinged, soaked in disinformation, surrounded by conspiracy theorists who validate his insanity. During his phone call last Sunday to Georgia's secretary of state, he commanded, "I just want to find 11,780 votes." He has no clue that this command breaks federal law, nor does he care, nor do his enablers care.

In a way, it was good that Hillary didn't win in 2016. It made us realize that democracy is not a given, that it needs to be fought for. Every day.

Many Americans really don't want a true democracy, as it threatens their favored nation status, their first-in-line prestige. The deck is stacked in their favor, and they are too fearful to embrace America's signature concept that all people are created equal.

We have come so far this year, but we need to close the deal. The amount of destruction Trump is capable of in the next 15 days should not be ignored. We need him out yesterday so our democratic institutions can be fortified.

1984,

> "The Party seeks power entirely for its own sake. We are not interested in the good of others; we are interested solely in power—pure power."

Intentional Cruelty:
A Tale of Two Meetings

January 23, 2021

On January 20th, 1942, senior government officials of Nazi Germany met in Wannsee, a suburb of Germany, to work out the final logistics of the Final Solution, the extermination of every Jew within German-controlled real estate.

They were tasked with a simple directive: the execution of the Final Solution. Various blueprints emerged, including mass sterilization, and deportation to the island of Madagascar. Heydrich proposed transporting all Jews to concentration camps in Poland and simply working them to death, but that draft was squashed as simply being too time-consuming.

There was an urgency to the Final Solution, and time-consuming logistical plans were quickly eliminated.

They finally settled on the gas chambers as the most efficient mechanism to execute the mission. When implemented, a thousand Jews a day were murdered, which met with Hitler's expectations.

Absent from the conference was any qualms of conscience, or moral misgivings. It was a cold, calculated strategy conference, like a PTA meeting where they discuss the logistics of a fund-raising bake sale.

Morality played no part in the discussions.

In early May 2018, eleven senior advisers of the Trump administration were called to the White House Situation Room. A month earlier, the Trump administration had launched the 'zero tolerance' immigration policy, affecting parents with small children. Thus far, US border agents had failed to separate parents from children (including infants) and Stephen Miller wanted to know why. He was especially angry at Kirstien

Nielsen, the Homeland Security Secretary, who seemed reluctant to embrace children being separated from their parents.

When a Federal Judge eventually ordered kids to be returned to their parents, it was revealed that the administration had no mechanism established that would reunite kids with their mothers and fathers. By that time, over 2800 children were separated from their families. (It was revealed afterward that the administration had phone numbers for the parents but hid that fact from the authorities at the border.)

But just think about that for a second. The Trump administration actually had meetings on the logistics of child separations. And it was debated and voted on, with Kristen Neilson, Secretary of DHS, being the lone dissenter. Anyone not voting for child separation, warehousing kids in cages, was denounced by Stephen Miller as "being a lawbreaker, an un-American." He also stated, "If we don't enforce this, it is the end of our country as we know it."

A bit of an overreaction to the power of five-year-olds, but that wasn't all. The administration actually went to court to prevent children from having toothbrushes and soap. Yes, Trump lawyers, using taxpayer's money, actually wrote legal briefs to deny innocent children soap and toothbrushes. This level of cruelty makes me ashamed for our country.

In both meetings, any ethical or moral considerations were deemed nuisances, betrayals of some higher purpose. The proposed logistics for each meeting were different, but what linked the conferences was the inhumanity, the absence of compassion and empathy. This level of cruelty, evil unshackled, enabled each group to implement their atrocities by deleting the humanity of their victims, Jews and children.

I am often criticized for pointing out these Hitler-Trump comparisons. I don't seek these stories, but they become impossible to ignore, and they keep emerging without any dedicated research. They are staring at us, we just have to look. Evil, if not confronted, becomes contagious, and spreads like cancer.

A country can never heal unless it confronts its complicity for its sins. Until it opens the cupboards and releases all of its secrets. Confronting its secrets and sins enables a nation to flourish. Our nation, our democratic institutions, have been poisoned by the Trump administration. He has emboldened white supremacists while fanning the flame of racial discord, culminating with the assault on our Capitol on the 6th. The cruelty dealt to children at the border was the tip of the iceberg of the cruelty that Trump and his enablers exacted upon citizens of the United States, especially the poor and people of color.

As a nation, we need a reckoning, an accounting of the level of cruelty and criminality that ran amok these last four years. We need to repent.

Voter Suppression Bills

March 30, 2021

It's the cruelty that still gets to me.

After Agent Orange lost the presidential election, I thought that a wave of empathy and compassion would waft over the land, disinfecting the populace of hate, disinformation, and scapegoats.

But then the Republicans introduced more than 250 voter suppression bills, mostly aimed at communities of color, making me realize that the disease Trump infected this nation with was still simmering, waiting for the next demigod to roll our open wounds in the cesspool. Trump didn't create the racism boiling beneath the surface; he exploited it to get elected, massage his ego, and to further the big grift. He gave white supremacy their long sought-after legitimacy, coaxing the venom out of the sewers with his dog whistles which evolved into direct appeals for an insurrection.

With their around 250 voter suppression bills, Republicans are exhuming the Jim Crow playbook, but this time their shoes are shined, and they wear tailored suits and prescription sunglasses.

But the constant remains—Republican cruelty.

If the Republican voter suppression bill in Georgia passes, people will be forbidden to deliver water to someone waiting in line to vote. Yes, they actually thought of that. Let's say you have a 90-year-old grandmother who has been voting since the 1940s, never having missed a vote, and she starts withering from the heat, dehydration setting in because of waiting in the long lines created by Georgia Republicans who have shuttered voting locations, mostly in communities of color. And out of compassion, you offer your grandmother water. WATER! You offer her water. Well, you could get arrested and your grandmother would lose her right to vote.

Is this what our Founding Fathers intended?

And the Republicans thought of this, but even worse, they wrote it down, and even worse than that, they are trying to put it into law.

Cruelty and hate have not been extinguished with the removal of Agent Orange and his co-co-conspirator Stephen Miller.

And they say with a straight face that this is all about election integrity, that it's not about race. It's like when Southerners propagate the falsehood that the Civil War was all about state rights, not slavery.

The least they can do is to be honest with their bigotry. I have a lot more respect for an honest bigot than a dishonest bigot. But hey, that's just me.

Republican leaders have finally said out loud that they believe the only way they will win elections is to restrict the voting pools. Truth be told, they don't believe in or want a democracy, with the more radical sect promoting a race war.

> "A Republican lawyer arguing before the Supreme Court on Tuesday admitted that his party needed voter suppression laws that disproportionately impact voters of color in order to compete with Democrats.

> "Republicans admitting that they can't win without voter suppression laws is nothing new, but it's shocking to see them put this before the Supreme Court as if it's a valid legal argument. And it's scary to think that the court's 6-3 Right-wing supermajority might agree with them.

> "Democrats in Congress are already working on a major bill that would greatly expand voter access, but the fight to stop

voter suppression isn't limited to Washington. Republican-controlled state legislatures are the front lines of voter suppression laws."

~ CNN

"My dream is to meet my father."

~ Immigrant boy at the border

Back in 2016 when immigrant families arrived at the border seeking asylum, the Trump administration gave parents a choice: stay with your children while they are incarcerated, or abandon your children to the whims of DHS, perhaps never to see them again. They all elected to stay with their children in the incarceration camps. And to twist the knife a little more, the Trump Administration went to court to deny kids soap and toothbrushes. I can't help but think back to a time when children were locked in cages, sans soap, toothbrushes, toilet paper, food, clothing, heat, and medical treatment. You know, what that so-called master race was able to conjure and implement back in the 1930s and 40s.

It's hard to comprehend this level of cruelty created by an American administration, but it is alive and well as symbolized by the voter suppression laws exploding across the land. I thought we were better than that.

These refugee children are now being labeled by Lindsey Graham as future terrorists. Apparently, he can look into the eyes of a three-year-old and see the makings of a future 9-11 terrorist. This repressive immigration policy by the Trump Administration harkens back to the Nazi camps, where mothers were often given a choice as to which one of their kids would die and which one would be assigned to forced labor camps.

Trump is exiled, but his legacy of evil continues to poison the body politic. He has spent the last four years empowering white, extremist hate groups such as the Proud Boys and QAnon, unleashing an avalanche of disinformation, including the Big Lie: that Trump won the election. Armed with the Big Lie, with a merry band of enablers, Trump has followed Joseph Goebbels's playbook to a tee.

"If you tell a lie big enough and keep repeating it, people will eventually come to believe it. The lie can be maintained only for such time as the State can shield the people from the political, economic and/or military consequences of the lie. It thus becomes vitally important for the State to use all of its powers to repress dissent, for the truth is the mortal enemy of the lie, and thus by extension, the truth is the greatest enemy of the State."

And boy, did he ever repeat it.

The Big Lie is alive and well, soiling our democratic institutions, despite Republican statements to the contrary. And for now, the man who ignited the insurrection remains free, despite overwhelming evidence that he cultivated the riot for months. But don't believe me; believe Republican leader Mitch McConnell's words,

> "This was an intensifying crescendo of conspiracy theories orchestrated by an outgoing president who seemed determined to either overturn the voters' decision or else torch our institutions on the way out.

> "'There is no question, none, that President Trump is practically and morally responsible for provoking the events of the day,' he said, and added that Mr. Trump watched the events unfold on television. 'A mob was assaulting the Capitol in his name,' he said. 'These criminals were carrying his banners, hanging his flags and screaming their loyalty to him.'"

McConnell said the people who stormed the Capitol believed they were acting on the wishes and instructions of Mr. Trump.

"Having that belief was a foreseeable consequence of the growing crescendo of false statements, conspiracy theories and reckless hyperbole which the defeated president kept shouting into the largest megaphone on planet earth."

Who am I to contradict the wisdom of Moscow Mitch?

According to the latest intelligence reports, Trump invited and solicited Russia to interfere in the 2016 and 2020 elections, with Russia using Rudy Giuliani to funnel disinformation to the Trump campaign.

But here's the thing, the battle for the hearts and minds, the soul of America has just begun. If Stacy Abrams didn't get the vote out in Georgia, the ability of the Biden administration to rebuild America would have been sabotaged. We need a Stacy Abrams in every state, fighting off the Republican voter suppression machinations. The Democrats won the House, the Senate, and the Presidency, but that doesn't mean the battle is won. The battle has just begun to restore our democracy—it's an ongoing battle. As demonstrated over the past four years, most Republicans have relinquished any morsel of integrity or ethics. Many Republicans continue to kiss the ring of Agent Orange, repeating and doubling down on the disinformation that continues to spew forth from Mar-a-Largo.

Back in the 1970s, the Koch Brothers, currently the most egregious polluters in this country, had an epiphany: every year, they would pour millions into Republican candidate's coffers who would do their bidding in their respective legislatures. After doing that for a decade or so, they realized they needed to create a grassroots movement in order to get their repressive and cruel legislative agenda implemented. So, they started with state legislatures around the country, grooming their candidates to take over legislatures. Today, Republicans control 85% of the legislature. The Koch brothers also funded think tanks in order to propagate their ideas, which led to funding colleges and universities that agreed to teach their programs and agendas in exchange for funding. Today there is a graduate school of business at George Mason University titled Koch Business School, the curriculum closely shaped and monitored by the Kochs.

Despite last fall's victories, progressives have their work cut out for them. We need a grassroots juggernaut to combat the disinformation and cruelty sure to be unleashed by the Republican Party propaganda machine. Tucker Carlson just said,

> "There's no evidence that white supremacists were responsible for what happened on Jan. 6. That's a lie."

It's abundantly clear they have no shame, and we can't have people running the country who are shameless ... and most importantly, we can't have people running the country who are CRUEL.

Voter Suppression, No Food or Water

March 30, 2021

No food or water in the voting lines.

When the Founding Fathers wrote our Constitution, enslaved people were deemed to be three-fifths of a person. Since they were enslaved, they were unable to vote, but slave states had more governmental representation due to these additional numbers.

No food or water in the voting lines.

Once the enslaved were emancipated, African American men could vote, theoretically, and if they attempted to vote, they would probably be hanged.

No food or water in the voting lines.

Moving to the 19th century, voter suppression of African Americans morphed into a different form—poll taxes and literacy tests, the threat of murder hovering like a dark cloud. And hangings were still a part of the infrastructure of racial terror. There were 4400 hangings between Reconstruction and World War II.

No food or water in the voting lines.

And despite the KKK's reign of terror, African Americans continued to march, and continued to insist on America's sacred promise—the right to vote. There were heroes: Robert Moses risked life and limb registering voters in Mississippi; Ida B Wells, John Lewis, Martin Luther King Jr., Chaney, Goodman, and Schwerner. All (and many more) put their life on the line to fight for the right to vote.

No food or water in the voting lines.

And they marched, crossing Edmond Pettus bridge, where they were shot at, beaten, and tear gassed. But they continued to march, culminating in the passage of the Voting Rights Act in 1964, which has since been gutted.

No food or water in the voting lines.

And then voter suppression morphed into a more sinister, Teflon-coated sheen in the form of gerrymandering. Voter suppressants now have tailored suits, shined shoes, speak in unctuous tongues, and communicate with dog whistles to their base. Like the KKK, the intention is the same: suppress, squash, and disenfranchise the powerless, the voiceless, the discarded. Mostly people of color.

No food or water in the voting lines.

And then the prison industrial complex was hatched, devastating communities of color and guaranteeing low voter turnout—Black males were incarcerated at an alarming rate. Can't vote from a jail cell. Eligible voters in poor communities were systematically disenfranchised.

No food or water in the voting lines.

And then the Russians got involved in voter suppression during the 2016 election, creating faux BLM websites exhorting African Americans to stay home and not vote, that their vote didn't matter.

No food or water in the voting lines.

And speaking of lines, why are there 8-hour, 11-hour waiting voting lines in communities of color? I am a white guy living in the suburbs. When voting, I wait an average of five minutes. And Governor Kemp has the gall to say his voting bill isn't racist. How dumb does he think people are?

No food or water in the voting lines.

This isn't just an African American problem. Both whites and Blacks should be outraged by the latest construction of systemic racism. If the people in power can sabotage the right to vote for one group, they can do it to anyone. We are all in this together. No one is free until we are all free. Freedom only comes about through taking responsibility. The abomination that has occurred in Georgia with the passage of the suppressive voting law needs to be fought tooth and nail.

The soul of America is at stake.

Book Burning

November 21, 2021

It's only a matter of time before they start burning books.

Texas State Representative Matt Krause has compiled a list of 850 books that he wants banned. Books like *The Confessions of Nat Turner* by William Styron, and *Between the World and Me* by Ta-Nehisi Coates. And he wants to target LGBTQ+ books that portray anything other than heterosexuality as normal. Virginia gubernatorial candidate Glenn Youngkin has also boasted that he wants to ban books, including the Pulitzer Prize winning novel *Beloved*, by Toni Morrison.

There now appears to be a tsunami of states lining up in lockstep to arbitrarily ban books: Texas, Virginia, Ohio, Kansas, and New Jersey. And they all seem terrified of LGBTQ+ books like award-winning *Gender Queer: A Memoir*, which chronicles a journey to self-identity. Books by women, and people of color are in their scopes. In Virginia, some officials have even broached the idea of holding a book burning, oblivious and insensitive to the history of book burning. Here are just some of the books being banned in Kansas:

1. *The Hate U Give* by Ange Thomas, which is a critically acclaimed young adult novel.

2. *Fences* by August Wilson, one of America's most decorated and impactful playwrights.

3. *The Absolutely True Diary of a Part-Time Indian* by Sherman Alexie, which won the 2007 National Book Award for Young People's Literature.

4. *All Boys Aren't Blue* by George Johnson, that was named best books of 2020 by Kirkus Reviews, the New York Public Library, and others.

5. *The Handmaid's Tale* by Margaret Atwood, which is simply a classic.

6. *The Bluest Eye* by Toni Morrison, the Nobel Prize winner.

7. *They Call Themselves the KKK: The Birth of an American Terrorist Group* by Susan Campbell Bertoletti, winner of the American Library Association's 2011 award for excellence in nonfiction for young adults.

You see a pattern here?

I can see that critical race theory is gonna have a hell of a fight to be implemented in these and other states. By the way, another name for *critical race theory* is history. That's all CRT is; it's history, real history! Without the whitewash.

Fascism has a playbook, handed down from generations of dictators, all of whom ascended to power using this easy-to-follow checklist. I'm listing here a few of their top hits:

1. Attacking the press, labeling them an enemy of the people.

2. Purge from the government whistleblowers, or anyone who attempts to expose their criminality.

3. Attack labor unions as enemies of capitalism, all the while enriching far-right industrialists.

4. Cater to white nationalists, targeting racial, religious, and ethnic minorities in incendiary, violence-provoking speeches.

5. Attacking science. As Hitler stated so eloquently: "To conquer a nation, first replace science with Christianity." Michael Flynn, former convict, former Trump's National Security Advisor,

wants the US to be under one religion, and I'm betting it ain't the Jewish religion. Just a hunch. But how the hell would one implement this? Will he follow Hitler's blueprint?

6. Confiscation of history and culture, which leads to number seven.

7. Book burning.

"Where books are burned, in the end, people will be burned."

~ Heinrich Heine, 1821

In Nazi Germany, they banned such authors as Hemingway, Jack London, Helen Keller—wait, what? They banned Helen Keller? They sure did. On the other hand, we are banning Nobel prize winners like Toni Morrison.

The sheer fact that book burning is on the table in the United States trips multiple alarms. But this slow erosion of our democracy has been brewing for the past five years. Our former president, after Charlottesville, informed us that neo-Nazis had some very fine people. But hadn't we as a nation concluded that Nazis were not very fine people.

Hadn't we at least agreed to that?

I guess not.

It has become abundantly clear that Trump and his minions want to install fascism in this country, with Trump as the supreme leader.

When the press is vilified,

when election integrity is questioned,

when there isn't a peaceful transfer of power,

when a bi-partisan commission is established to ferret out the truth of the failed coup, when the vice president is pressured to ignore our Constitution and deny the will of the people,

when there is a deliberate disinformation campaign waged by Russia hoping to install a puppet President in the United States,

when the truth is no longer the truth,

when there are alternate facts and we can't trust what our eyes see,

and finally,

when the idea of holding a book burning is suggested,

well, these are all symptoms of fascism.

> "In retrospect, the barbaric destruction of cultural and intellectual treasures has often been interpreted as a precursor of the Holocaust."

> ~ Holocaust Museum

The Texas Anti-Abortion Bill

October 7, 2021

Texas recently passed a draconian anti-abortion bill, seeking to sabotage a woman's right to choose. I'm always amazed at the hypocrisy of pro-lifers who won't lift a finger in protest when deranged gunslingers execute our children in places like Parkland and Sandy Hook, or San Jose, and Colorado Springs, or the Indianapolis FedEx shooting, or the Santa Fe shooting, and the Boulder shooting, and the Muskogee shooting, or the spa shootings in Atlanta. And don't forget the Emanuel African American Methodist Church shooting, or the Carthage nursing home shooting. It goes on and on, the body counts climbing as gun manufacturers soak gun magazines in steroids. Where were the pro-lifers then, when children, when our fellow citizens, were being gunned down?

Where was their moral outrage when we bombed innocent women and children in places like Iraq, Vietnam, and Afghanistan?

Never saw them on the picket lines.

Where was their outrage? Where were the protests, as we offered up our kids to be slaughtered, sacrificial lambs, as the pro-lifers cowardly stood silent to the evil propaganda that spewed forth from the NRA?

Pro-life? No, this is pro-fascism, an ism our former president has been reigniting these last 5 years.

But what about the men? Did this new Texas law address the culpability of men in abortions? Where was the men's punishment in this bill, given the fact that men are co-conspirators in pregnancies? Make no mistake about what this battle is really about: power, patriarchal thugs planting their flag, asserting their power over women, in perhaps their most vulnerable state.

If you can control the body, you can control the mind.

One of the more disturbing aspects of the new law is granting citizens the power, anonymously—yes, anonymously—to turn people who get an abortion in to authorities. And there is a $10,000 payout for their efforts. The law also applies to anyone who aids and abets an abortion, say the Uber driver who drives a woman to an abortion clinic out of state.

This fascist doctrine has precedent: East Germany's reign of terror was sustained through a network of citizens spying on citizens during the Cold War era and extending into the 1980s. At one point in East Germany, there were 173,081 citizens spies, a vital instrument in maintaining fascism.

Hitler's ascension to power was fueled by citizen spies who turned in Jews who were hiding from the SS. Citizen spying is a vital element in the longevity of fascism.

This is the pedigree of the new Texas law. It makes you wonder if they studied the Third Reich playbook in writing this law.

Ya gotta wonder.

But this assault on a woman's rights has deeper roots. A woman taking control of her body is an assault on the patriarchal infrastructure that has been raging against women for centuries. Evangelicals have traditionally been on the forefront of subverting women's rights, sabotaging a woman's right to choose, frequently galvanized by the misinterpretation of scripture. In Kristin Kobes Du Mez's book *Jesus and John Wayne*, we read,

> "Christian homeschooling remained an effective mechanism for instilling and reinforcing biblical patriarchy."

> ~ Page 189

Megachurch pastor Jack Hyles commanded women to,

> "...be in complete and total submission to their husbands and to male leadership. Whereas boys must be trained to be leaders, girls should be trained to submit."

~ Page 33

In Marabel Morgan's *The Total Woman*, we read on page 61 that,

> "The Biblical remedy for marital conflict was the submission of wives to husbands."

Then on page 69, we learn,

> "Only in time, as abortion became more closely linked to feminism and the sexual revolution, did Evangelicals begin to frame it not as a difficult moral choice, but rather as an assault on women's God-given role, on the family, and on Christian America itself."

For Tim LaHaye, women's subordination was theological, social, and sexual.

> "The very nature of the act of marriage involves feminine surrender."

There is no other word for this than fascism—the tyrannical control of another human being, emanating from fear and insecurity. This anti-abortion law reeks with the stench of patriarchism, misogyny, and Texas has been simmering in this rot for more than a century, a deliberate misreading of scriptures fueling the tyranny. White power patriarchism depends on the subjugation of others. They live in fear of a level playing field and their disinformation-fueled psychosis extends beyond women: African Americans, Muslims, LGBTQ+, and Hispanics. Doug Wilson, another prominent evangelical wrote the following in his book *Southern Slavery: As it Was*.

"He questioned the supposed 'brutalities, immoralities, and cruelties of slavery.' The slave trade might have been unbiblical, he allowed, but slavery most certainly was not. To the contrary, the radical abolitionists were the ones 'driven by a zealous hatred of the Word of God.' Horrific descriptions of slavery were nothing more than abolitionist propaganda. The life of a slave had been a life of plenty, of ample food, good medical care, and simple pleasures, marked by 'a degree of mutual affection between the races' that could never be achieved by coercive federal legislation."

A "life of plenty"? Really???

Critical race theory ain't gonna have an easy time in Texas.

The same forces, the same dynamics, that seek to control a woman's body, seek to control and oppress 'others.' Racism is a form of fascism. It is undergirded by fear, and it uses the same fascist playbook. This Texas anti-abortion law is just another step in the fight to install fascism in this country. Trump primed the pump and the Texas anti-abortion law emerged from the slime. Trump didn't come up with the idea of an anti-abortion law, but he emboldened the agents of suppression by priming the pump with hatred and scapegoats. Trump has been seeking to install fascism for the last five years. Let's count the ways.

1. Moved to isolate the US from other democratic nations ... —CHECK

2. Sought to cancel treaties and agreements that promoted harmony with democratic nations—CHECK

3. Expressed deep respect for totalitarian leaders and their methods of governance. Dare I say Vladimir Putin, Kim Jung-un—CHECK

4. Moved to forge alliances with totalitarian dictatorships—CHECK

5. Attacked the media as an enemy of the people—DOUBLE CHECK

6. Sought support from white nationalists, and white supremacists, by targeting racial, religious, and ethnic minorities in incendiary speeches and oppressive policies—CHECK

7. Urged police to assault peaceful protesters—CHECK

8. Attacked labor unions and sought to enrich far-right billionaires, including himself—CHECK

9. Postured as a military strongman while ordering arms build-ups that served no defensive purpose—CHECK

10. Purged government officials and whistleblowers who attempted to expose the corruption—CHECK

11. And then there is January 6ᵗʰ—TRIPLE CHECK

Our country is soaking in disinformation, fertilizing the Delta variant of misogyny and racism, and watering the fields producing hatred, generated by fear. Trump was a master at this, tossing the raw meat of people of color to the white hoards seeking explanations for their misery.

Democracy is on the brink. The Texas anti-abortion law is a symptom of a larger cancer that is pumping through the bloodstream of our republic. We need to confront and eradicate this legacy of hate.

As Charlton recognized, "submission theology protects the privileges of the Powerful." ~ Kristin Kobes Du Mez, Page 281

Doug Wilson, a prominent evangelical in the 1990s wrote, immodest women were "responsible for men's actions," and women who refused masculine protection were "really women who tacitly agree on the propriety of rape."

Agree on the propriety of rape? Well, we got work to do as this cruel, hateful, misogynist disinformation is carousing through Republican blood.

It is part of their DNA, always has been, keeping women under their boot.

The Cult

September 7, 2021

A friend of mine recently shared a text she received from her brother.

"I'd rather receive false information and keep my conservative views than receive true information and follow a socialist agenda."

A Trump supporter posted,

"They shouldn't be fact-checking anything. They should allow people to have a voice."

Mike Lindell, the pillow guy, said,

"You need to stop fact-checking this and start reporting this."

How did we get here?

Joseph Goebbels:

"If you tell a lie big enough and keep repeating it, people will eventually come to believe it."

George Orwell:

"And if all others accepted the lie which the Party imposed—if all records told the same tale—then the lie passed into history and became truth. 'Who controls the past,' ran the Party slogan, 'controls the future: who controls the present controls the past.'"

Bill Moyer:

"Trump has resurrected the Big Lie. But, pathetically, he also resorts to the Little Lie."

"Trump's strategy is to flood the zone—to proliferate so many lies that by the time one lie is rebutted, he has put out several more, and he seems to believe even the lies that contradict previous lies. Ignorance really is Trump's strength."

OUR NATION'S FRACTURE IS NOT BY COINCIDENCE. THERE IS A CAUSE.

When the Third Reich was storming through Europe, in the beginning stages of the Final Solution, the SS would roll into town with the purpose of exterminating all Jews. The SS did not possess the manpower to execute this battle plan, so they had to solicit townspeople to engage in the genocide. There would be a town meeting beforehand where the SS would deputize citizens to participate in brutal first-degree murder. They even gave the citizens an out, saying, if killing women and children is too much, then stay home. The local baker, the printer, the policemen, the truck driver, etc., all willingly participated in the execution of the towns' Jews. They would spend the day executing men, women, and children and afterward settled down to a nice family meal.

Most of the townspeople willingly participated. Just ordinary citizens, your next-door neighbor type.

The German and Polish people didn't wake up one day hating Jews. There is no hate-Jews gene. Their willingness to personally participate in a Holocaust was implanted by a propaganda machine from the previous two hundred years, often led by pastors who decried the evilness of the infidels. The German soil was fertilized with hateful disinformation and antisemitism; Hitler simply exploited and harvested the hate, which had festered and metastasized for decades. The citizenry had been primed and pumped, fertile ground for a despot to exploit.

"If you tell a lie big enough and keep repeating it, people will eventually come to believe it."

~ Joseph Goebbels

Last week Trump held a rally in Alabama, attended by an unmasked crowd, COVID-19 raging in the state, a state with one of the lowest vaccination rates in the country. These attendees are playing Russian Roulette with their lives, but perhaps more importantly, their loved ones' lives. Do they not comprehend the risk, or are they unable to see the risks that are staring them right in the face?

Why would they attend this rally, putting themselves, and their loved ones at risk?

"If you say it enough and keep saying it, they'll start to believe you."

~ Donald Trump, July 5, 2021

Louisiana has one of the worst environmental records of any state in the union. Their cancer rate is off the charts, their fish and wildlife have been devastated, water is contaminated in whole swaths of the state—especially in the petrochemical regions along the coast. In those areas you can't fish, you can't swim, nor can you eat any fish poisoned by the chemicals leaking into the waterways. And you can't move as the pollution raining down has wiped out the value of your home. So, the residents endure the chemical rains that fall from the plants causing multiple forms of cancer and birth defects. And they try not to drink the water. Whole families die of cancer, often in their 40s and 50s. They are imprisoned in some chemical nightmare which they stoically endure, fueled by disinformation about regulations and government agencies like the EPA.

So, who do they vote for? They vote for Republicans who promise to shut down the EPA.

"'Environmentalists want to stop the American Dream, to protect the endangered toad,' Madonna Massey says, 'but if I had to choose between the American Dream and a toad, hey, I'll take the American Dream.'

"But word from the pulpit also seems to turn concern, away from social problems in Louisiana—poverty, poor schools, pollution-related illnesses—away from government help, and away from the Great Paradox."

~ Arlie Russell Hochschild, *Strangers In Their Own Land*

As in Germany, the pulpit was a source for the injection of propaganda. And you could say Fox News is its own pulpit. They certainly like to repeat certain things … over and over and over. Dare I say Trump's Big Lie?

A few of Fox's greatest hits:

- Business anchor Eric Boiling referred to the EPA as "job terrorists" who are "strangling America."

- Lou Dobbs commented in 2011 that "as it's being run now, (the EPA) could be part of the apparat of the Soviet Union."

- Charles Krauthammer compared the rise in EPA air quality standards to an "enemy attack" on America.

~ Arlie Russell Hochschild, *Strangers In Their Own Land*

This is a sampling of the drumbeat of disinformation that spews out of Fox daily. And they repeat and repeat and repeat their propaganda, which ignites the prejudice and racism simmering beneath the surface.

Meanwhile, the good people in Louisiana are dying from cancer while in their forties, never questioning or fighting the cause, made impotent by the bile that Fox News spews daily.

"And if all others accepted the lie which the Party imposed—if all records told the same tale—then the lie passed into history and became truth. 'Who controls the past' ran the Party slogan, 'controls the future: who controls the present controls the past.'"

~ George Orwell

In Georgia this past weekend, a vaccination event was shut down by anti-vax protesters. This was fueled by the disinformation propaganda spewed out 24/7 by Fox News and their disinformation puppets of Tucker Carlson, Sean Hannity, and Donald Trump—all three have been vaccinated.

The irony and hypocrisy are chilling, and laughable, if not for the fact that people die from this lethal disinformation. Right now, in my hometown, there is a family of four girls, all vaccinated, including their mother. Their father, who refused to get vaccinated, is in the hospital hooked up to a respirator. It's not looking good for him. The disinformation he ingested about the vaccine could literally kill him. Someone should be held responsible. His wife could become a widow and his daughters could grow up without a father.

DISINFORMATION HAS CONSEQUENCES, INCLUDING DEATH.

"If you tell a lie big enough and keep repeating it, people will eventually come to believe it."

~ Joseph Goebbels

After the Civil War, as plantation owners started to regain their power, a propaganda campaign was launched against the recently freed African Americans. They were labeled animals, shiftless, lazy, dumb, poised to take a white man's job, but perhaps their biggest sin, the biggest lie propagated, was a supposed desire to rape white women. Poor degenerate white men embraced the propaganda, giving them pride and a mission, while shielding them from the true cause of their degradation. Instead of aligning with Black people, as they were both suppressed by the white power structure, plantation owners kept the races fighting each other, which created a smokescreen to hide the real source of their suppression.

"The lie can be maintained only for such time as the State can shield the people from the political, economic and/or military consequences of the lie. It thus becomes vitally important for the State to use all of its powers to repress dissent, for the truth is the mortal enemy of the lie, and thus by extension, the truth is the greatest enemy of the State."

~ Joseph Goebbels

Texas is one of the states that turned down Expanded Medicaid, a lifeline for citizens across the state, especially citizens living in poverty. The reason: they considered Expanded Medicaid a handout for people of color. There is this ongoing disinformation campaign that people of color are always looking for handouts, a theme pushed for hundreds of years. But it's a lie and the consequence of that lie is that in Texas, poor people no longer have healthcare, affecting more white people than Black. This disinformation propagated by white people literally sabotages white people. And not only do poor people in Texas not have healthcare, but 120 hospitals and clinics have closed because the state turned away federal money for Medicaid.

"If you say it enough and keep saying it, they'll start to believe you."

~ Donald Trump, July 5, 2021

We have entered a new era where truth can be manipulated, denied, and changed. Lies are a lazy vehicle to power, as displayed by Donald Trump in his Big Lie campaign. Trump does not believe in Democracy; he lusts for power, and will do anything to get and maintain that power, which he will use to exact vengeance on his enemies, both real and imagined.

Our democracy hangs in the balance. Like Hitler, Trump didn't create the racism, the hatred; he simply exploited it by using the technology developed by Goebbels.

We must continually assault disinformation with truth. It's our only salvation.

Putin, Kanye West, Genius, and Pedophilia

April 13, 2022

Three Republican Senators—Susan Collins, Lisa Murkowski, and Mitt Romney—recently voted to affirm Ketanji Brown Jackson's nomination to the Supreme Court. Ketanji Brown Jackson is the most qualified candidate to be nominated to the Supreme Court in the past fifty years. For this treasonous, egregious act, Marjorie Taylor Green labeled the three "pro-pedophilia."

Joseph Goebbels once wrote, "Accuse the other side of that which you are guilty."

I never thought I would hear myself saying this, but Joseph Goebbels nailed it.

In the article, *Republican Sexual Predators, Abusers and Enablers* Pt. 23, author Cajsa Lilliehook exposes Republican pedophiles by listing their crimes. She has close to 700, with no end in sight.

- #627 "T. Elliott Welch, anti-gay, anti-COVID lockdown, rightwing conservative pastor has resigned after his arrest for child pornography."

It is universally agreed upon that Putin is a war criminal; there is no wiggle room on this fact, but that doesn't stop our former president from calling him a genius. Can a war criminal be considered for genius status? Is the number of people you kill, execute, maim, or disable, the criteria for determining your place in the genius pantheon? Hitler killed six million Jews and millions of others, does that make him a genius? How about Stalin? He is reported to have killed up to sixteen million

Russians during his reign—does that make him, in Trump's eyes, more of a genius than Hitler, who in comparison had such paltry numbers?

- #630 "Trump Commerce Dept. official Adam Hageman—child pornography."

And then we have Trump, who is forever declaring himself a genius. But is he? Can you really call yourself a genius after declaring bankruptcy six times? I'd call that a chink in the armor. Can you call a guy a genius who stated there are very fine people in the neo-Nazi movement? Doesn't that speak to an inability to judge character, which could be perceived as a character flaw, therefore not a genius, which in turn taints his whole genius status, assuming we all agree that Nazis are bad guys. OK, I know what you're gonna say, that issue is still in flux among some people, including Fox News.

- #632 "NH Republican Rep. Kyle Tasker plead guilty to sexual solicitation from a 14-year-old girl."

Then we have Kanye West, who has also declared himself a genius. As far as I can tell, Kanye doesn't have the body counts Hitler and Stalin possess, although someone should give Pete Davidson a heads-up. But we haven't talked about Trump's body counts: remember all those rallies he gave before the election? It's been estimated that he is responsible for over 75,000 covid deaths during the last weeks of his campaign, due to all those unvaccinated, unmasked, close-quarter rallies. Now these aren't Hitler or Stalin numbers, but it should give us pause.

- #639 "Insurrectionist Sean McHugh, who on Jan 6th accused Capitol Police of protecting pedophiles, was convicted of raping a 14-year-old girl. 240 days in jail."

Maybe, just maybe, we don't need body counts to be declared a genius. Gandhi brought the English Empire to its knees with non-violence, no shots fired. Ya gotta admit, that's kinda genius. Not one freakin' shot. So maybe Putin isn't a genius. Maybe he should try the non-violent route in his attempted conquest of Ukraine. God knows his rockets, bombs, and atrocities aren't closing the deal, not to mention the slew of bad press it is generating, despite the fact he declared it fake news—I wonder where he got that idea from. (As an aside, Hitler, Stalin, and Trump all declared the press an enemy of the people. Just saying—I'm unclear as to Kanye's stance on all this, probably not good.) Nobody told Putin that people dislike having to leave their homeland, or have their children murdered, or have their cities bombed. It tends to piss people off, and motivates them to fight back. I think Putin views this war as some video game, with no real consequences.

- #642 "Matthew Palmer, a former COO of MD Dept of Commerce and a former aide to Republican Gov. Hogan pleaded guilty of sharing and having pictures and video of children being sexually abused."

For years, Republicans have been labeling Democrats as communists, a scarlet letter they utilize for the purpose of getting elected, and in lieu of developing policies and programs designed to enhance their constituents' lives. They have now added pedophile to their name-calling arsenal, along with their new term, groomer. Remember when the Republicans accused President Biden and Hillary of running a pedophile ring? Let's be honest here, that would be a time management feat of unparalleled proportions: running the country while secretly running a pedophile ring.

And here we go again: "Accuse the other side of that which you are guilty." I can't believe I'm saying this, but Goebbels nailed it again.

- #648 "Republican Sheriff candidate Doug Litwhiler stepping down from the race due to being accused of preying on young girls in a Facebook post. It included screenshots he sent to underage girls and was not anonymous."

If anyone is a communist, it's gotta be the people who lavished praise on the Republican's favorite communist, Putin, the genius. We know a lot of Republicans are pro-Putin, as they share similar values, Tucker Carlson being their pro-Putin mouthpiece. (Tucker Carlson now appears on Russian TV with his pro-Putin stance featured prominently in their propaganda.)

On *Daily Kos*, there's an enormous list of Republican sexual predators. Here's just a small number of over 1,000 currently named:

- #628 "US House candidate Anthony Bouchard impregnated a 14-year-old girl. He was 18. He married her. She killed herself. This is a tragedy for everyone, but a 4-year difference is too much at that age. She was only 14."

- #629 "Conservative evangelical pastor Mack Charles Andrews raped and tortured multiple children, including one girl he raped on her father's grave when she was nine. Released after serving only 5 years."

- #631 "PA Republican Schuylkill County Commissioner George Halcovage—sexual harassment."

- #633 "Chad Perkins, a Missouri Republican state representative, abused his power as a cop to solicit sexual favors from a drunk teenager when she was in his custody."

- #634 "Insurrectionist Ryan Samsel has a history of violence and sexual assault."

- #635 "Athens, TX Mayor James Montgomery, who credited his 2017 victory to being the most conservative candidate, was arrested during a sting operation for online solicitation of a minor."

- #626 "Kansas State Rep. Mark Samsel ranted about masturbation, sex, and one of his student's genitals. He kneed the student in the crotch in class and suggested girls in the class check his balls, a physical assault for which he was arrested."

And then we have the former Speaker of the House, Republican Dennis Hastert, who left in disgrace after settling a sexual abuse scandal and is currently serving time in prison for fraud. He sexually abused boys as young as 14.

But it keeps goin. On Thursday Ruben Verastigui was arrested on a federal charge of receipt of child pornography. Verastigui was an aide to the Trump re-election campaign and was a digital strategist for the Senate Republican Conference and the Republican National Committee.

"Accuse the other side of that which you are guilty."

So it continues, Republicans accusing Democrats of that which they are guilty, with pedophilia becoming the one issue Republican politicians are running on: not their solutions to healthcare, global climate change, institutional racism, rebuilding our infrastructure, closing the wealth gap, etc., etc. At the last Republican convention, the Republicans presented no party platform; in other words, they stand for nothing. The platform they came up with was loyalty to their cult leader, Trump. Now, with the mid-terms looming, they were forced to come up with a platform, and wiping out pedophilia became their go-to issue. This is the communist hysteria from the 1950s all over again where people like Joe McCarthy and Nixon tried to root out communists in every crevice of society, and the hysteria and fear they generated got them elected to office.

Pedophilia is our modern-day red baiting.

When Republicans are not accusing Democrats of pedophilia, they spend their time embracing Putin's reign of terror.

Listed here are some of the ties that bind Putin and our right-wing friends. Tom Hartmann: *Why is the GOP Siding with Putin?* Daily Kos:

- "Putin runs rigged elections and the GOP is openly working to rig elections in over 20 states."

- "Putin trash-talks LGBTQ people and the GOP has put homophobia at the center of their 2022 electoral strategy."

- "Putin embraces white nationalism in Russia, just as the GOP does here."

- "Putin has 'actively cultivated neo-Nazism' both in Russia and 'in the United States' while the GOP lionizes Kyle Rittenhouse and embraces American neo-Nazi movements."

- "Putin has contempt for the rule of law while the GOP embraces people who tried to overthrow the government of the United States."

- "Putin put so much money into the NRA that they'd become, as NPR described the result of the Senate investigation, a 'Foreign Asset to Russia Ahead of 2016,' shoveling cash and support to Republican candidates."

- "Putin frequently lies to his people about things that are easily disproven…the same as Trumpy Republicans do on an almost daily basis."

- "Putin shuts down independent news media, while Trump and some Republicans call media in the US 'the enemy of the people.'"

- "Putin attack science in Russia as Republicans do here in the US."

- "Putin promotes a muscular 'Christianity' through corrupt preachers who openly defy the teachings of Jesus, as does the GOP."

- "Putin's politicians are funded by rightwing oligarchs, just like Republican politicians are here."

- "Putin hates 'liberals' and civil rights protestors, just like the GOP (which has gone so far as to legalize running them down with cars)."

One final shout-out to perhaps Goebbels' greatest hit:

> "If you tell a lie big enough and keep repeating it, people will eventually come to believe it."

The execution of this maxim by Donald Trump in his promotion of his Big Lie would bring mist to Goebbels' eyes, perhaps even a fully formed tear, or at the very least, a warm smile.

Book Burning II

February 14, 2022

Once book banning was rekindled, it was only a matter of time.

Last week, Pastor Locke of Tennessee hosted a book-burning event. Yes, we now have book-burning events in the land of the free and the home of the brave. Are we parroting Nazi Germany now? FYI, if you live in Tennessee, you might consider getting rid of your Harry Potter and Twilight books, just in case the brown shirts pay you a little visit, courtesy of an anonymous tip.

Just saying.

The racist seeds planted by Republicans decades ago have taken root, nourished by Trump and his enablers for the past five years. This insidious assault on our democracy is real, well-funded, and violent.

Last weekend the neo-Nazis demonstrated in Orlando and the Florida Governor couldn't find it in his heart to denounce the violent, racist, antisemitic hate group. I lived under the illusion that the Nazi issue was settled. Nazis are bad, right? They put people in ovens, right? That's a bad thing, right? Is there wiggle room on this issue now? How about the Holocaust? Too many people are promoting the lie that it didn't happen. Is there now wiggle room on the Holocaust? Alex Jones said Sandy Hook never happened, that it was some government sleight of hand.

I'm starting to see a trend. And the number 1984 always pops up when I go get my lottery ticket … can't explain it.

Trump has resurrected the technology of the Big Lie as pioneered by Hitler's propaganda minister, Joseph Goebbels. "If you tell a lie big enough and keep repeating it, people will eventually come to believe it."

Trump has been beating the voter fraud drumbeat for two years and it has proved to be an effective fund-raising tool.

History, the lifeblood of a democracy is under assault, evidenced by the vicious attacks on critical race theory. *The 1619 Project* is simply history, filling in the gaps in America's timeline, excavating the truth about our country's past. Republicans are looking to suppress our history, trying to protect white kids from feeling uncomfortable about the past, promoted by senators like Josh Hawley. And there is a pending bill in the Florida legislature that is truly chilling:

> "The Republican bill—called 'Individual Freedom'—would prohibit private businesses and public schools from training staff or students about racism in U.S. history in a way that makes them feel 'discomfort, guilt, anguish, or any other form of psychological distress on account of his or her race.'"

Let's say your kid is in an AP English class and while studying *To Kill a Mockingbird*, he starts to feel uncomfortable. Does he then turn his teacher in to the police to be incarcerated? As the prison industrial complex is being dismantled, (hopefully), with fewer and fewer clients to fill the beds, perhaps teachers will be the new bed-fillers, a salve to a struggling industry.

You laugh, but in Virginia the Governor has set up a tip line where parents can call in and report teachers who dare teach critical race theory. Didn't the Nazis have a tip line to report on Jews who were in hiding?

Josh Hawley weighed in with the following,

> "We heard that we are systemically racist. You heard that once or twice? We heard that the real founding of the country wasn't in 1776, it was in 1619 or whatever. We heard that America is founded in lies and evil. That's what we've been told. All of that is false. All of that is a lie."

No, Hawley is lying.

In reading *The 1619 Project*, created by Nikole Hannah-Jones, (I'm a white guy by the way) I haven't felt discomfort, guilt, or anguish. What I did feel was a profound sadness, born out of the knowledge that a human being could exact such cruelty, hatred, and violence on another human being. And what makes it doubly heart-rending, is that it was done to children, kids wailing for their mothers. There's the story of a five-year-old girl, her mother sold by the plantation owner, who would walk to the gate every morning and wait for her mother to come back. Well, she never returned. I can't imagine the hole in that child's heart, made more poignant when I think of my kids and grandkids.

By telling the truth about our past, it helps illuminate and understand the present. It serves to remove the barriers, the rhetoric erected to divide us. It launches a cleansing, paving the way for a refortification of democracy's infrastructure, which has been chiseled away by disinformation termites. A true recounting of our past will unleash a resurrection, resulting in an embrace of our shared humanity.

The 1619 Project isn't a doom and gloom tale. It is a history of triumph, achievement, endurance, incremental victories against impossible odds, and courage. They are stories about empowerment, persistence, creativity, survival, and glory, counterpointed with acts of cruelty that makes the flesh crawl. These are inspiring American stories and should serve future generations as inspiration in our eternal quest for a more perfect union.

Ken Burns once said, "Stories liberate us from the tyrannies of the past."

The legacy of enslavers' DNA continues to infect our culture with hate and structural racism. It is the mold that eats away at our democratic foundation, dividing us, offering up scapegoats for our grievances, readily offered up by former President Trump. Our nation has never shed its financial addiction to structural racism.

This is important.

Russia has never been shy about broadcasting their intention to divide America, specifically along racial lines. There's nothing they would relish more than if America erupted in Civil War. That's their goal, their single-minded purpose.

Previously, our battlefield with Russia occurred with the construction of nuclear arsenals capable of annihilating each country a hundred times over. Spying was an integral weapon in the war between the *superpowers*, but Russia has developed and implemented a new strategic weapon— disinformation.

"It probably cost Clinton the election," said Frank Figliuzz, former FBI official. He reported that, "an analysis of the tweets from the trial of Kyle Rittenhouse came largely from outside the United States." Figliuzzi noted that Putin's approach is more of the "divide and conquer" style that Americans saw around the Black Lives Matter movement to pit different races against each other."

During the 2016 election, multiple Black Lives Matter websites materialized, created by the Russian troll factory in St. Petersburg. The predominant message of these insidious websites was for African Americans to stay home on election day, that their vote didn't matter.

And it worked.

The fact that over 70% of the tweets during the Rittenhouse trial came from outside of the United States underscores the fact that Russian and foreign disinformation has continued to chisel fissures into our democracy.

Democracy is a 24/7 battle. It's a living, breathing entity that must be fought for daily because fascism lies in wait. Letting our guard down invites the tentacles of fascism to squirm its way into the body politic.

The forces of fascism have been empowered by our former president who sought a coup on January 6th, now described by Republicans as "legitimate political discourse." Are you freaking kidding me? "Legitimate political discourse."

The Republican party has now entered the twilight zone by calling the insurrection "legitimate political discourse."

This is Orwellian on steroids. If January 6th was "legitimate political discourse," I wonder what the hell illegitimate political discourse would look like.

People often tell me these are dark times. I disagree. These are great times because the rot in our society is surfacing, being confronted, a result of the light shining on our buried history of racism, sexism, etc. There are seismic changes occurring in our society: people fighting for voting rights, people confronting the wealth gap, people confronting the pharmaceutical industrial complex, people confronting the prison industrial complex, people confronting misogyny, police brutality, systemic poverty, and systemic racism.

These are glorious times.

Bill Gates once said of the busted tech bubble of the late 1990s that it was one of the most innovative times in world history because of the amount of pure research, and pure innovation that was percolating. That turbulent time is what spearheaded the tech revolution, forever changing society.

This is a similar time. We have discovered that democracy is a fragile thing, to be fought for in the trenches daily. We took it for granted before. There is more work to be done to combat the assault of fascism and the demigod on this grand experiment to achieve a more perfect union.

I'm betting on us.

Karma

July 6, 2022

Karma is a bitch. It will bite you in the ass eventually.

Now, unless you are a blood relative of Sean Hannity, there's no more debate. Trump orchestrated a failed coup, a failed insurrection. His intent was to institute a fascist state, with Trump as King, very similar to his buddy Putin's government.

Democracy held strong. Only the criminal trials remain.

Here's my prediction:

Trump is arrested for treason, which, per US Code Title 18, is punishable by death. Trump, a resident of Florida, will be on Florida's death row, anxiously waiting for DeSantis to pardon him.

Only one problem: DeSantis won't pardon him because he is afraid Trump would run against him in the Republican Primary. In a battle of nastiness, hate, innuendo, lies, disinformation, misogyny, racism, and homophobia, DeSantis knows Trump would emerge victorious from that mosh pit. By the way, there is precedent here: in 1904, James Curley won the Boston Democratic primary while still in jail.

It's hard to out-Trump Trump.

In response to this, Trump and Rudy (yes, he's back and in the next cell) collaborate on a new social media platform titled *Prison Central*. Kanye West and Vanilla Ice provide the theme music. While Trump's lawyers file appeal after appeal, Trump decides he's gonna run for President in 2024, becoming the first-ever death row presidential candidate. Trump's campaign message is simple: he will put the libs in the electric chair. Trump's base is over the moon about this new platform and readily contributes to Trump's new fund-raising con. Trump states that when he is president, he will televise the executions. The networks see dollar signs with this new reality show concept, and Trump starts entertaining offers for the new show, tentatively titled *Kill of the Week*.

He promises to start with Mike Pence, kickstarting the fall line-up.

Fox News wins the bidding war and Sean Hannity, a fellow prisoner, will provide the play-by-play while the Pillow Man, another fellow prisoner, brings color commentary. One side note, after a couple of years, Trump is moved to the psych ward when his ranting about a stolen election becomes unbearable to the prison personnel. As one prison guard stated, "He won't shut the f… up about it."

After 20 years, when Trump loses his final appeal, he comes up with his last con: Trump asks the world, "What would you eat for your last meal?" McDonald's, Burger King, Subway, Mike's Subs, the Soup Nazi, KFC, etc., all bid for the right to serve his last meal, which Trump insists be televised.

The bidding becomes intense, but McDonald's wins. In the contract, McDonald's insists that the deal was off if it was found later that there was ketchup on the wall.

Involuntary Relocation

July 25, 2022

Words have power. They can change the course of history, but they can also serve as an agent of suppression and enslavement.

A group of Texas educators has proposed to the Texas State Board of Education a new term for slavery: Involuntary relocation. As a friend of mine likes to say, "That's some bullshit." Involuntary relocation refers to the transport of African Americans on slave ships, with the deadly stacking of human bodies in the cargo holds.

So if they define involuntary relocation as the transportation of humans for the purpose of enslaving them, what will they call the actual enslavement? The working in the fields, flanked by overseers with guns and whips, working from sunup to sundown, and for no pay. (I can see the Involuntary relocation workers opening up their paycheck, seeing 0.00, and saying WTF).

I wonder what their label is for forced labor: involuntary field hands? In my mind, the word *slavery* pretty much nails it.

> "This summer, the board will consider updates to social studies instruction a year after lawmakers passed a law to keep topics that make students 'feel discomfort' out of Texas classrooms."
>
> ~ Brain Lopez, Texas Tribune

Okay, I guess Texas won't be interested in history any longer, probably will wipe it from the curriculum—I mean, how important could it be, and God forbid they make anyone uncomfortable. History will be written and performed by the Hallmark Channel, a happy ending guaranteed for all. I'm guessing the AIDS plague won't be addressed; the Civil Rights Movement won't be touched; the origins of structural racism won't be discussed; that the Civil War wasn't about slavery but was all about state rights; that the South won the Civil War because there was some kind of fraud; slavery was a benign arrangement between 'happy Negroes' and their 'owners,' a win-win; and of course, Donald Trump really won the 2020 election.

If the Texas Board of Education has its way, a generation of ignorant, uninformed, reactive students who lack basic thinking skills will grow up easily manipulated by politicians who offer up racism, homophobia, misogyny, etc., etc., in order to get elected. The students will be devoid of critical thinking, a necessary ingredient for a demigod's assent.

Why are they so afraid of these words: *slavery, slaves, critical race theory, gay,* etc.? They are simply words; they don't bite. You're not allowed to say gay in Florida schools now.

Words have power.

Okay, it does bear repeating that involuntary relocation is the term the Texas Board of Education wants to use instead of slavery.

> "Every record has been destroyed or falsified, every book rewritten, every picture has been repainted, every statue and street building has been renamed, every date has been altered. And the process is continuing day by day and minute by minute. History has stopped. Nothing exists except an endless present in which the Party is always right."
>
> ~ George Orwell, *1984*

George Orwell, in his prophetic book, *1984*, documented the evolution and mechanisms of fascism. The Texas Board's statement about slavery pushes America down a slippery slope, a descent Orwell warned us about—insertion of fascism into our democracy.

"The most effective way to destroy people is to deny and obliterate their own understanding of their history."

~ George Orwell

There has been a four-hundred-year-old plot to entomb African American history. And it's not just African American history: Harold Zinn's groundbreaking treatise, *People's History of the United States*, has been banned and vilified.

History is simply truth, and truth is the salve that can heal a nation. And truth is the weapon that can bridge the artificial racial divide that is choking our country.

But truth, in America, is under siege.

There has been a concerted, intentional effort to bury our real history, with the purpose of hiding crimes and acts of horror, brutality, and torture. It's unfortunate because embedded in the tales of violence and repression resides stories of triumph, persistence, courage, and love. Inspirational stories that celebrate the American character, the American soul. They are stories about Americans striving to achieve a more perfect union. These are stories that can inspire future generations of children, celebrating our nation's glory.

The Texas board isn't the only one to chisel away at democracy's infrastructure. It is happening all across the country. And it's subtle, step by step, county by county, state by state by state. And it starts with words.

In Tennessee, Paster Locke ignited a book-burning party last spring. Every day, more and more books are banned, including books by Pulitzer Prize winner Toni Morrison. Here's a partial list of banned books:

- *The Great Gatsby*, by F. Scott Fitzgerald.

- *The Catcher in the Rye*, by JD Salinger.

- *The Grapes of Wrath*, by John Steinbeck.

- *To Kill a Mockingbird*, by Harper Lee.

- *The Color Purple*, by Alice Walker.

- *Ulysses*, by James Joyce.

- *Beloved*, by Toni Morrison.

- *The Lord of the Flies*, by William Golding.

Can't help but think of this quote from George Orwell's *1984*:

"Ignorance is strength."

Nikole Hannah-Jones recently published a tome titled *The 1619 Project*, excavating history that has been buried. Almost immediately, the book was challenged in numerous counties throughout the United States, in addition to the author being vilified.

The 1619 Project is a brilliantly documented treatise that simply tells our history, US history.

Republicans are banning abortions, banning books, banning trans rights, gay rights, voter's rights, all the while seeking to ban gay marriage and interracial marriage. There is a proposed law in Virginia that would prohibit a woman from divorcing her husband while pregnant.

I kid you not.

Republicans don't seem to stand for anything, except banning.

"A people that elect corrupt politicians, imposters, thieves and traitors are not victims... but accomplices."

~ George Orwell

During his four years in office, Donald Trump told over 30,000 lies. There is a special Orwellian quote for such a herculean milestone:

"And if all others accepted the lie which the Party imposed—if all records told the same tale—then the lie passed into history and became truth."

~ George Orwell, *1984*

Trump did his best in trumpeting his Big Lie, trying to embed it into our history.

"If you tell a lie big enough and keep repeating it, people will eventually come to believe it."

~ Joseph Goebbels

The use of disinformation, outright lying, has been elevated to an art form by the Republican Party, spearheaded by the former president. Disinformation and lying are the main ingredients of fascism. Democracy has the weapon of truth and is flexing its muscles through the January 6th committee. The January 6th hearings have become America's truth and reconciliation hearings, laying bare the cesspool of the last administration, given life by the band of enablers.

Shakespeare prophetically wrote about Trump in his play, *Richard III*, and not only did it not end well for Richard, but his band of enablers met a gruesome fate, as will Trump's minions: Bannon, Rudy, Powell, Eastman, the Pillow Guy, etc.

The Republican Party has known the power of words, as well as the power of dog whistles. They use words to bury the truth, distort the truth, and manipulate the truth. They embody Orwellian principles, as well as Joseph Goebbels' playbook.

Lee Atwater, the famous Republican strategist, who had a special talent in the utility of words, was captured on tape laying out the true intentions of the Republican party. McGhee, *The Sum of Us*.

"You start out in 1954 by saying, 'Nigger, nigger, nigger.' By 1968 you can't say 'nigger'—that hurts you, backfires so you say stuff like uh, forced busing, states' rights, and all that stuff, and you're getting so abstract. Now, you're talking about cutting taxes, and all these things you're talking about are totally economic things and a byproduct of them is, blacks get hurt worse than whites ... 'We want to cut this,' is much more abstract than even the busing thing, uh, and a hell of a lot more abstract than 'Nigger, nigger.'"

There you have it, the fascist Republican blueprint said out loud.

Orwell is shaking in his grave right now.

"In a time of deceit telling the truth is a revolutionary act."

~ George Orwell

Thoughts and Prayers

June 3, 2022

In an previous essay, I asked how many murdered children would it take for Republican lawmakers to pass common-sense gun legislation.

After the Uvalde carnage, I finally have my answer. INFINITY!

They ain't budging. I was assuming they had a modicum of empathy and compassion. I was assuming deep in the recesses of their soul, there was a moral strain that just needed to be rekindled. I was assuming kids' lives trumped campaign contributions.

Boy, was I wrong.

Republican lawmakers, imagine your children, your grandchildren, locked in a classroom, a locked-and-loaded deranged gunman executing them one by one. Put yourself in the room, witnessing the horror, your 5-year-old in line for execution along with their friends. Take a moment to imagine selecting a small casket for your tiny loved one, or being unable to identify them without dental records.

Now imagine the trauma ingrained on a kid's soul who survived the executions. Occupy the body of a five-year-old who is screaming in horror as their friends are executed, knowing they are next, with no parent or grandparent there to save them, their last moments on earth, alone, filled with horror, in stark terror.

This can't happen anymore. It needs to stop.

Republican lawmakers need to imagine the horror by putting themselves in their loved one's shoes. If they are incapable of imagining the horror, the carnage, unwilling to put themselves in their kid's or grandkid's shoes, they need to be voted out. Their soul is beyond redemption.

New York Times Sunday Review: 05/29/2002

- Authorities said the gunman was able to obtain the weapons legally. Uvaldi, Texas, 2022, 21 killed

- Authorities said the gunman was able to obtain the weapons legally. Buffalo N.Y., 2022, 10 killed

- Authorities said the gunman was able to obtain the weapons legally. Boulder, Colo., 10 killed

- Authorities said the gunman was able to obtain the weapons legally. Atlanta, Ga., 2021, 8 killed

- Authorities said the gunman was able to obtain the weapons legally. Dayton, Ohio, 2019, 10 killed

- Authorities said the gunman was able to obtain the weapons legally. El Paso, Texas, 2019, 23 killed

- Authorities said the gunman was able to obtain the weapons legally. Virginia Beach, Va. 2019, 12 killed

- Authorities said the gunman was able to obtain the weapons legally. Thousand Oaks, Cal., 2018, 12 killed

- Authorities said the gunman was able to obtain the weapons legally. Pittsburgh, Pa., 2018, 12 killed

- Authorities said the gunman was able to obtain the weapons legally. Parkland, Florida, 2018, 17 killed

- Authorities said the gunman was able to obtain the weapons legally. Sutherland Springs, Texas, 2017, 26 killed

- Authorities said the gunman was able to obtain the weapons legally. Las, Vegas, Nevada, 2017, 60 killed

- Authorities said the gunman was able to obtain the weapons legally. Orlando, Florida, 2016, 49 killed

- Authorities said the gunman was able to obtain the weapons legally. Roseburg, Ore., 2015, 9 killed

- Authorities said the gunman was able to obtain the weapons legally. Oak Creek, Wis., 2012, 7 killed

What follows is the Republican mantra of "thoughts and prayers," the Republican lawmaker's boilerplate, cold-hearted response.

Senate Majority Leader Mitch McConnell (R-Ky.) said, "The entire country is praying for the children, families, teachers, and staff and the first responders on the scene."

"Horrified and heartbroken to learn of the significant loss of life in the shooting in Uvalde, Texas," wrote Sen. Marsha Blackburn (R-Tenn.), "please join me in lifting their loved ones up in prayer."

"There are no adequate words to express the horror at Robb Elementary," Sen. Ron Johnston (R-Wisc.). "My sincere condolences to these families. Something this horrific, children being slaughtered in their school."

Sen. Ted Cruz (R-Texas) outdid all of them, though, writing that he and his wife are fervently praying for the families of the victims of the, you guessed it, "horrific" shooting. Daily Kos.

Mitt Romney said, "Grief overwhelms the soul. Children slaughtered. Lives extinguished. Parents' hearts wrenched. Incomprehensible. I offer prayer and condolence but know that it is grossly inadequate. We must find answers."

We have answers. They are called gun control laws. Gun control works. It's been proven time and time again that gun control works. And around 87% of Americans back the gun control legislation.

"After Bill Clinton banned assault weapons in 1994, mass shooting deaths dropped by 43%. After the Republican Congress let the ban expire in 2004, they shot up by 239%. We don't need to arm teachers; we need to BAN assault weapons again," said Lee Turner, Congressional candidate for South Carolina District 4.

The top ten traceable donations from the NRA:

- Mitt Romney $13,637,676

- Richard Burr $6,987,380

- Roy Blunt $4,555,752

- Thom Tillis $4,421,333

- Cory Gardner $3,939,199

- Marco Rubio $3,303,355

- Joni Ernst $3,124,773

- Rob Portman $3,063,327

- Todd C Young $2,897,582

- Bill Cassidy $2,867,074

Key word—traceable.

OK, I see that Mitt Romney has over thirteen million reasons not to do anything about mass shootings. Sorry kids. He won't do anything about assault weapons, but he stands ready with his thoughts and prayers.

As a side note, but a major one, Russia funneled huge amounts of money to the NRA during the 2016 election … just saying.

The Republican 'thoughts and prayers' platitude continues to be voiced because they willingly sacrifice our children's lives to the altar of the NRA.

They have no shame; they have no soul.

Look, I recognize that sometimes thoughts and prayers is all we can do. I know this. I have felt this level of helplessness at times in my own life. But this is not the same thing. WE CAN STOP THIS! We can fix this! We just need our politicians to worry more about children's lives than large donations.

Their 'thoughts and prayers' should be addressed to their own souls, as their souls are soaked in the blood of American children.

The Best of Times

June 17, 2022

Many people lament about how divisive, stringent, and confrontational these times are, about how it has never been this bad.

Au contraire.

These are remarkable times, cataclysmic times, a time of hope, of change, of triumph. In America, these are times for achieving a more perfect union, a time of connection, a time to recognize our shared humanity, a time to repair the tears in our souls. And, most of all, it is a time for peace.

And all this is happening before our very eyes.

In America, the buried cesspool of hate, misogyny, homophobia, and structural racism, has finally been excavated; a virus that has infected America since 1619, when the first shackled humans landed on our shores. But now, empowered by Donald Trump, trumpeted by Fox News, this slime has crawled out of the sewers, revealing their ugly, naked intent.

This naked slime, absent the dog whistles, enables us to confront and handle the cesspool. It's hard to confront and battle forces you can't see. Now, it's out in the open, and that's a good thing.

So why do I call these the best of times? Let me count the ways.

1. The battle to vote in states throughout the land was simply inspiring during the 2020 election. The right to vote forms the bedrock of our democracy. We have this curious phenomenon in this country of politicians blocking people from voting ... in a democracy. How odd? I always found it hard to wrap my head

around that. But in 2020, some waited in line for eight hours, insisting on their constitutional right to vote; some went to different polling stations because the one they always voted at was closed; some fought the new Voter ID rule tooth and nail to cast their vote. The yeoman work by Stacy Abrams to get people to vote rekindled our faith in civic engagement. Our nation, on the brink of fascism, fought for democracy.

2. The LGBTQ+ community is standing up and asserting their dignity and their rights.

3. The marginalized, the ignored citizens, and the underclass are insisting on their dignity and their rights, and there is no stopping them as they 'fight the power.'

4. With Roe vs. Wade on the chopping block, women are marching and lobbying to preserve their right to control their own bodies.

5. A wannabe fascist was voted out of office. (How pathetic, a failure as a fascist, which aligns with his failure as a businessman—six bankruptcies, and his failure as a president.)

6. Structural racism became part of the conversation. People started to confront the fabricated structures that spewed out racism, fascism, and intolerance. It's all related.

7. The January 6th committee, in full throttle, is peeling off the layers of lies and obstruction, laying bare the plot to sabotage our democracy, Trump at its helm, pulling the levers. This big reveal is all good.

8. In a way, it's good Hillary didn't win. If she had, we would have drifted back into our complacency. The election of Trump forced us to realize democracy is fragile, that it needs to be fought for every day. This was a realization that had profound effects, mobilizing massive groups to retake our democracy.

9. Our full history is now being excavated, and is now being taught throughout the land, all despite the book bans, and book burnings. Books like *The 1619 Project: A New Origin Story*, by Nikole Hannah-Jones, are seeping into our classrooms, libraries, our consciousness, despite the attacks to suppress them. You can't suppress truth. To achieve a more perfect union, the truth about our history must be told, as only the truth can start to heal the fissures of this nation.

10. It's becoming harder and harder for dictators to triumph. One of the weapons against fascism is social media, exposing crimes of dictators, as evidenced by Putin's imbroglio in Ukraine. He doesn't realize it yet, but Ukraine's democracy will ultimately prevail, no matter how many Ukrainians are murdered or jailed. It's hard to bury or arrest the ideas of freedom. You can't put these ideas in jail, the force is too strong. You can't suppress the notion of freedom, as it is part of the fabric of our souls.

11. Taiwan is presently in a battle with the repressive regime of China, asserting its right to be an independent democracy. China operates under the delusion they can halt the idea of freedom, but unfortunately, that genie is out of the bottle. Taiwan will prevail.

Fascism requires scapegoats, enemies, and secrets. Democracy requires connections, dialogue, and transparency. Democracy always wins because its weapon is truth, and truth is the salve that will heal the world.

So, these are all good things, and it's happening now, all over the world. People are taking a stand and won't be denied. Complacency is being shattered, and the seeds of democracy and freedom are taking root. And there are thousands of other groups and movements, fighting for a more perfect union, breaking down the barriers that prevent us from embracing our common humanity. More and more, light is being shed on corruption, lies, structural inequities, and suppression.

These are the best of times. Humanity is swelling up as we realize that to conquer suppression, we must trust each other, connect with each other, and by connecting, we empower both ourselves and others. It's an eternal quest that can now come to fruition.

The dawn of peace is near.

It truly is the best of times, and now is the time to be our best.

Pro-Life, Anti-Children

June 3, 2022

I'm confused. So, you are anti-vax, not wanting the government to tell you what to do with your body.

But you are anti-abortion, allowing the government to tell you what to do with your body.

And you call yourself pro-life, but you are really anti-children.

Where was your voice when we dropped bombs and Agent Orange on innocent children in Vietnam?

Where was your voice when we dropped bombs on innocent children in Iraq?

Where was your voice against the NRA when weekly executions of children occur in schools across the nation?

Where was your voice when Republican states fought to deny children healthcare, neonatal care, daycare, rights that every child should have?

Where was your voice when preschool funds were slashed, knowing that preschooling is a large facilitator in future achievement? In Missouri, that money was used to give billionaires tax cuts. Where was your outrage?

Where was your voice when funding was cut in Medicaid, the only lifeline marginalized children have?

You're not pro-life. You're pro-cruelty. You support candidates who block any effort to remove AK-47s from deranged gunmen who execute children. The hollow thoughts and prayers you serve up after every shooting reek of hypocrisy. You enable this abomination and my heart cries as I read the latest: 19 children and two teachers were shot dead in Texas by an eighteen-year-old gunman, locked and loaded to the gills.

19 CHILDREN!!!!!!!!!!!!!!!!!

Have you no shame?

You don't realize you are soaking in disinformation, a significant portion of it emanating from Russia's St. Petersburg troll factory.
So, please don't insult me or yourself by saying you are pro-life.

And you call yourself a patriot? And you're all about preserving the Constitution? Preserve this: work to stop voter suppression, which is running rampant throughout the land. As much as you want to deny it, fight it, people have a right to vote regardless of the amount of melanin in their skin.

Our democracy's foundation is built on preserving the right to vote—for all citizens!

Let me repeat that: FOR ALL CITIZENS.

You may call yourself pro-life, but the truth of the matter is you are anti-children.

Putin and Family Values

March 23, 2022

It's been interesting to watch Republicans backpedal on their bromance with Putin. Before the Ukrainian War, they fawned all over him, despite the fact he is a documented fascist, psychotic dictator who fights democracy with draconian, violent measures, including the murder and torture of dissidents. Putin's presidential opponent, Alexei Navalny, was poisoned, and then imprisoned.

How could any American support such a despot? Trump called him a genius for invading Ukraine. In other words, Trump supports the fact that Putin is seeking to obliterate a democracy in the interest of taking more land. Wait, what? Yes, Trump chose the side of the dictator, not the democratic state of Ukraine.

But how could this be? What is the tie that binds?

Putin said,

> "Properly speaking, the attempts to use us in their own interests never ceased until quite recently: they sought to destroy our traditional values and force on us their false values that would erode us, our people from within, the attitudes they have been aggressively imposing on their countries, attitudes that are directly leading to degradation and degeneration, because they are contrary to human nature. This is not going to happen. No one has ever succeeded in doing this, nor will they succeed now."

Traditional values. Where have I heard that term before? Oh yeah, the religious right. They are all about traditional values. Won't shut up about traditional values. For the religious right, traditional values is their euphemism for sexism and homophobia.

LONDON (Thomson Reuters Foundation)—"Right-wing U.S. groups have put more than $280 million into campaigns against LGBT+ rights and abortion worldwide since 2007, almost $90 million of which focused on Europe, according to a report on Tuesday."

That's a lot of freakin' money dedicated to suppressing the basic rights of another human being. Aren't we all children of God? Didn't our Constitution mention something about being created equal? Where does this hate and fear spring from?

For years, Trump's part of the American right has viewed Russia as a 'white Christian bastion' of traditional values. The Russian leadership plays into this narrative, too. Sergei Naryshkin, Russia's intelligence chief, said this month that the West was trying to "cancel" his country. If you see Russia merely as an extension of yourself and your political project is the United States, then it is difficult to part with it.

White Christian bastion. The key word being 'white'. To put it simply, for Republicans, stamping out homosexuality trumps democracy. It is why they can embrace Putin, who fathered an espionage campaign designed to obliterate homosexuality in Russia, a crusade that includes the murder and incarceration of LGBTQ+ Russians.

Madison Cawthorn has declared Zelenskyy a thug; Marjorie Taylor Greene has labeled Zelenskyy a dictator while also parroting Russian propaganda and disinformation. Trump has called Putin a genius while Tucker Carlson's disinformation is now posted on Russian propaganda news outlets.

But why? Why this embrace of a violent, paranoid fascist? What is Putin and the religious right afraid of?

The United States has a history of gay politicians, hiding in the closet, who, ironically, work to suppress legislation designed to grant basic civil rights to LGBTQ+ citizens. It's a subterfuge they adopt to camouflage their sexual orientation, a cover-up our patriarchal society demands of LGBTQ+ people in the public domain.

To name a few:

> "Sen, Carl Kruger who voted against marriage equality in New York State." (*Daily Mail*)

> "Troy King, the Alabama Attorney General who was reportedly caught by his wife in bed with a male assistant, had made anti-gay rhetoric part of his political mantra." (*Advocate*)

> "Curtis, who served as a Republican member of the Washington State House of Representatives from 2005 to 2007 and voted against a domestic partnership bill and a bill that would have out-lawed discrimination based on sexual orientation." (*Advocate*)

> "In Congress, Bauman established a reputation as a staunch conservative, often criticizing the state of morality in the United States. He was a founding member of several conservative activist groups including the Young Americans for Freedom (YAF) and the American Conservative Union (ACU), where he served both as national chairman. In 1980, while running for re-election, his own morality was questioned when he was charged for attempting to solicit sex from a 16-year-old male prostitute." (*Washington Post*)

> "In 2011, it was revealed that Puerto Rican Senator Roberto Arango, who was a vocal enemy against gay marriage and rights in San Juan, had posted shirtless photos of himself on the gay dating mobile app Grindr. Amidst the ensuing controversy, Arango resigned." (*Advocate*)

In America, the patriarchal infrastructure requires subjugation of one's true nature to anyone who seeks entrance into the halls of power. Our racist, homophobic power structure stems from the dissemination of fear, prejudice, and disinformation. African Americans know this force firsthand. During Reconstruction, there were measures and laws designed to suppress their very existence, including public hangings. It was illegal for them to read, meet in groups, and vote. They lived under the repressive terrorism of the KKK, which sought to deny their very existence. And the list goes on. The toxicity bred by the anti-gay movement has continually sought to castrate fellow citizens, dehumanizing them, which opens the door to violence against them. It is a logical progression from racism.

> "Two years after reports of a 'gay purge' sent shockwaves worldwide, it's clear that the perpetrators have gone unpunished because of state-sponsored homophobia and impunity for human rights violations in Chechnya."

> ~ Amnesty International

Big lie, there was another big lie: gays are all pedophiles, lying in wait, ready to snatch your kids and indoctrinate them into the gay lifestyle. This rhetoric got people elected, and the dog whistle of anti-gay rhetoric continues today by appealing to our most base instincts. Gays are dehumanized, and blamed, both requisite in scapegoating a whole swath of the population. Labeling helps to condone violence and discrimination.

For African Americans, our country labeled them animals, which the law codified, the pastors justified, resulting in suppression and violence:

> "While the early Christian right groups were motivated primarily by antisemitism, anticommunism, and the defense of racial segregation, they also expressed fear about changes in the nuclear family and the relationship between the sexes. By the 1970s, when open espousals of antisemitism and racism were no longer socially acceptable, Blacks and Jews were largely replaced by gays and feminists."

> ~ John Gallagher and Chris Bull, *Washington Post*

The advocacy of family values by Trump and his acolytes reveals the hypocrisy of the movement. Under Trump, the separation of babies from their parents or guardians ruffled no feathers in their conscience, the incarceration of toddlers ruffled no feathers in their conscience, the placement of grade school children in shelters with histories of sexual and physical abuse ruffled no feathers in their conscience, and the fact they had no plan to reunite 2342 children with their parents. Well, if that is family values then ...

Family values is simply a license to hate. Putin knows this. Back in the day, the right-wing movement was saturated with racism, Blacks being the faggots, with a Bible thumping pastor finding Biblical references to justify the terrorism.

The paranoid fear of the LGBTQ+ community is the connective tissue between a maniacal despot and the far right. And speaking of paranoia, Putin recently laid off a thousand workers because of a fear of being poisoned. That is next-level paranoia, paranoia on steroids. Like all dictators, he has someone taste his food before he eats it. I wonder what that job pays.

Hang in there as I'm coming to the point. You've all seen those pictures of Putin on horseback, shirtless, right? Some people describe him in those pictures as masculine and sexy. But some people would describe those pictures as 'pretty damn gay', a lonely man trapped in the closet. There are other signs. Have you ever seen a picture of Putin with a woman? Perhaps if he could reveal his true self, he might find it in his heart not to bomb maternity hospitals, children, or civilians. As those American, closeted gay, self-loathing politicians who campaigned and voted against gay rights; perhaps Putin, a prisoner in the closet, wallowing in self-loathing, could break free and no longer feel compelled to assert his manhood by bombing children.

To answer my question: it is the paranoid fear of gays and lesbians that is the connective tissue between a maniacal despot and the far right.

Let us pray.

Let us pray for the 'others', for they are we.

Amen.

Emasculation

May 18, 2022

People like Tucker Carlson of Fox News and Senator Josh Hawley have been decrying the emasculation of the white male. (You didn't think they would be concerned about the well-being of men of color now, did you??) There are multiple causes for this neutering, but a direct consequence of this emasculation is the breeding of a tsunami of locked-and-loaded white guys: insecure, grievance-stricken, undereducated, miseducated, dis and misinformed, seething with hate and conspiracy theories. Because of their force-fed indoctrination, they embrace guns, racism, and hate. They decry scholarship and education, all tinged with a false patriotism, and infused with the racist Replacement Theory mantra. (The "great replacement" theory, in simple terms, states that welcoming immigration policies—particularly those impacting nonwhite immigrants—are part of a plot designed to undermine or "replace" the political power and culture of white people living in Western countries.)

In other words, they embrace ideas/things that will further emasculate them. In the process, they become instruments of violence, of divisiveness, seeking to fill the void in their lives left there by their arrested development of character, integrity, and education.

They are a seething mass of disinformation who feel marginalized, abandoned by politicians, looked down upon, and powerless—prime beef for a demagog.

When you don't instill in your son a sense of honor, values, a sense of integrity, morality, empathy, kindness, the void left becomes a magnet for weapons and hate, which serve to bestow a false sense of manhood, and masculinity. Our nation has become saturated with armed white males who are causalities of the propaganda that assaults them 24/7, including the Russian disinformation onslaught. The lack of character development, the sabotaging of education, disinformation saturation, history denying, are causing the emasculation. They ingest the delusion that guns make a man, that their most treasured asset is the size of their gun, rather than the content of their character.

The consequence of this indoctrination is the breeding of cowards, believing a gun infuses you with testosterone and courage. Dare I mention Kyle Rittenhouse, or the recent Buffalo shooter who was a big advocate of Replacement Theory, as promoted by Tucker to millions of viewers on Fox News?

This false masculinity has fostered the idea that 'the others' are the problem, soldered in by disinformation, their lack of education and their subsequent inability to engage in critical thinking, makes them a magnet for conspiracy theories. And we have a new problem that further exacerbates the contamination: books are being banned, denying white guys access to our history, our culture, making them a sponge for propaganda and disinformation, further cemented by an anti-intellectual, anti-educational mindset, further emasculating them, consigning them to the bottom tier of society.

These locked-and-loaded eunuchs, evolve, or should I say, devolve, into Trump acolytes.

Now, one of Tucker's solutions to white male emasculation is to have your testicles blasted with red-light therapy. I ain't no oncology doctor, but I wouldn't touch that with a ten-foot pole. That reminds me of Trump's Clorox solution to COVID-19. One man actually took his advice and died.

So, when Tucker and Hawley whine about white males' emasculation, what they are really talking about is the absence of character, an absence they perpetuated and enabled. It gets right-wing candidates elected because this absence prevents their constituency from doing any critical thinking about the real issues. Instead, they devour the scapegoats the disinformation right-wing politicians nourish them with.

Here's the problem Tucker and Josh don't seem to understand: character is fortified and built through education, moral and ethical enlightenment, absorption in the richness of other cultures, the study of history with all its stories of triumph and tragedy. Tucker and Hawley are lazy, offering up scapegoats (usually people of color), denying history, suppressing history, fighting common sense gun laws, as if taking away a person's AR-15 renders them impotent.

I am reminded of Martin Luther King Jr. marching, knowing that a sniper bullet could kill him at any moment, but he kept marching, unarmed. I am reminded of the Berlin Wall coming down without one shot being fired. I am reminded of Gandhi, bringing the whole British empire down without one bullet being fired. That's courage, not some guy flaunting an open-carry weapon, who lives with the delusion that the gun gives him stature, power, which is simply a cloud illusion of strength.

And here's a big secret I'm revealing to Tucker and Josh: manhood is constructed from taking responsibility, not embracing scapegoats, parroting grievances, and seeking causes other than oneself for one's grievances and discontent.

Yes, for white males, in 'the winter of their discontent', the ones packing heat seek the source of their discontent by looking below them, rather than looking above them. And that strategy has never brought peace or salvation. The essence of irresponsibility is believing that some other person, group, race, or government is responsible for one's condition. Embracing scapegoats as THE cause of one's condition is a prescription for disability and embracing weapons ain't never gonna bring you to the promised land.

To further disable the armed white male, right-wing leadership has decided that teaching the truth about American history will no longer be tolerated. *The 1619 Project: A New Origin Story* by Nikole Hannah-Jones, is simply history, American history, with an open desire to nourish and enhance our culture by speaking the truth about America. The more uneducated the white male becomes, the more susceptible he is to propaganda, and a big slice of that propaganda is to have the white male blame people below him, the powerless, the voiceless, and need I say, people of color, rather than the people above them. Thus, the white male falls for the eternal con.

"And importantly, thus has it been possible to make poor and working-class white people believe that their interests lie in making common cause with their political leaders and economic betters. Common cause in whiteness: the idea that they might eventually share in the spoils, and the understanding that the discomforts and anxieties of their own precarious lives were due to—are due to those below them rather than those above them."

~ Walter Johnson, *The Broken Heart of America*

Well, I'm glad that Josh and Tucker think that the white male needs some help. Unfortunately, they embrace a culture that breeds disinformation (actually, let's call it for what it is—lies), and lies won't raise one out of the darkness. The foundation of character is truth, and only by embracing truth can masculinity be restored.

"There's much talk these days of what being a man entails. I'm more of a man than someone like Tucker Carlson will ever be because I have experienced grave injustice yet chosen the path of compassion, truth and forgiveness."

~ George Takei

Amen!

The Big Lie

November 4, 2022

> "If you tell a lie big enough, and keep repeating it, people will eventually come to believe it."
>
> ~ Joseph Goebbels

> "If you tell a lie big enough, and keep repeating it, people will eventually come to believe it."
>
> ~ Joseph Goebbels

> "If you tell a lie big enough, and keep repeating it, people will eventually come to believe it."
>
> ~ Joseph Goebbels

Right now, our democracy is in peril, under assault from Trump's Big Lie. It's been well documented that Trump knew he lost the election, that his Big Lie campaign was a money-making con, designed to swindle money from his base in a last-ditch effort to regain power. The principle laid down by Goebbels acts as his guiding principle. The only question that remains is, will the principles of our democratic institutions weather this frontal assault?

Trump at times has appeared to admit to losing the election. In June, he told Fox News Sean Hannity that he "didn't win" (Kelsey Carolan 4/5/22).

"Former White House aide says she heard Trump in private blurt out 'Can you believe I lost to this guy?' while watching Biden on TV" (Alyssa Farah Griffin).

HE KNEW!

"If you tell a lie big enough, and keep repeating it, people will eventually come to believe it."

~ Joseph Goebbels

Trump lost the election, but he has a history of FAILURES: six bankruptcies, his charity foundation being shut down by the state for fraud, his Atlantic City hotel being fined ten million dollars for money laundering, his conviction of racial discrimination for denying people of color access to his apartments, his near bankruptcy before Russian Oligarchs bailed him out. Currently, he is fighting numerous lawsuits ranging from business fraud, to sexual assault, to stealing highly classified government documents.

His insecure, fragile ego can't take losing, partly because he cheats, cons, commits fraud, and he is a compulsive liar. He lacks character, a sense of responsibility, and empathy. As his former chief of staff, John Kelly noted, "everything is transactional for him."

"If you tell a lie big enough, and keep repeating it, people will eventually come to believe it."

~ Joseph Goebbels

Trump is the Johnny Appleseed of the Big Lie, his minions robotically channeling Trump's Big Lie, injecting a disabling serum into the bedrock of our democracy—voting.

Trump lost sixty-five court cases regarding the election. His Attorney General stated emphatically there was no election fraud; his Election Security Director stated there was no election fraud.

"If you tell a lie big enough, and keep repeating it, people will eventually come to believe it."

~ Joseph Goebbels

Despite overwhelming evidence of his deception, he compulsively chants the Big Lie, sucking minions into his vortex of disinformation, robots who act as carrier waves, spreading the torch of the Big Lie.

> "A people that elect corrupt politicians, imposters, thieves and traitors are not victims, but accomplices. A society becomes totalitarian when its structure becomes flagrantly artificial: that is when its ruling class has lost its function but succeeds in clinging to power by force or fraud."

> ~ George Orwell

Brief list of the current carrier waves:
Kari Lake: Arizona gubernatorial nominee
Blake Master: Arizona Senate nominee
Tudor Dixon: Michigan gubernatorial nominee
Ted Budd: North Carolina Senate nominee
D. Vance: Ohio Senate nominee

The list goes on and on, including the Senators and Congressmen who not only pushed the Big Lie, but who supported the insurrection, which was based on the Big Lie.

> "If you tell a lie big enough, and keep repeating it, people will eventually come to believe it."

> ~ Joseph Goebbels

Democracy flourishes in truth. Fascism takes hold and infiltrates through lies and disinformation. Hitler himself didn't kill six million Jews and millions of others, he needed enablers, cruel-hearted robots to carry out the genocide. Trump created the Big Lie, with help from Rudy, and, like Hitler, created his robots and enablers to carry out his assault on democracy.

Before Hitler seized power, he had the backing of only about 30% of Germans. With that base, he was able to seize power through violence, intimidation, and brandishing scapegoats.

Trump's base is around 30%, and we are starting to see the consequence of his violent rhetoric, as his enablers spread disinformation, fermenting grievances, labeling and offering up scapegoats. We saw this call to violence on January 6th, and last week we saw the attack on Nancy Pelosi's husband.

Trump has been fanning the flames of race conflict for the past six years, and from that conflict, that chaos he created, he intends to seize power.

> "If you tell a lie big enough, and keep repeating it, people will eventually come to believe it."
>
> ~ Joseph Goebbels

The parallels between Trump and Hitler's ascent are too striking to ignore. He is seeking to dismantle our democracy and he is doing it in plain sight. Hitler had his Storm Troopers and we saw Trump's police force in Portland covering their badges and identities. Today, on his social media platform Truth Social, Trump broached the idea of executing Biden. Mass shooters have already been motivated by Trump's hate speech. And in Florida, we see DeSantis created his own million-dollar, private police force that is supposed to stop election fraud. I believe there were 20 individuals charged with voter fraud in Florida's last election—guess you can never be too careful. As Trump stated, "It's not how many votes that are counted, it's who counts the votes." Putin knows this stratagem as he got around 90% of the votes in the last election.

We are in the next phase of fascism—the inciting of violence. Already, disinformation about the attack on Paul Pelosi is coursing through social media outlets, despite the police debunking the disinformation.

"If you tell a lie big enough, and keep repeating it, people will eventually come to believe it."

~ Joseph Goebbels

We let the fox into the henhouse, and by so doing we learned that democracy is not a static principle, but an idea that needs watering and nourishing to keep it breathing. It needs to be created every day.

Democracy flourishes through the moral spine of its leaders. Its foundation rests on the integrity of its leaders.

Republicans no longer stand for anything. They have sold their souls to a false prophet who lacks any sense of morality, empathy, and compassion. They have abandoned democracy and depend on disinformation and lies to get elected. There is no sewer they will not climb into if they think it will help them get elected, just witness Marco Rubio's racist ads against Val Demings.

Our most potent weapon to save democracy is the lever in the voting booth.

Thirty million Democrats didn't vote in our last election. That can't happen. This is our chance to restore democracy and vote all those racist, misogynistic, wannabe fascists out, and when this happens, we will once again bask in the brilliance of our Founding Fathers whose character was powerful enough to fend off an attack from within.

"If you tell a lie big enough, and keep repeating it, people will eventually come to believe it."

~ Joseph Goebbels

Fascism

October 16, 2022

When the Nazis herded women and children into concentration camps, they separated children from their mothers by telling the kids their mothers were just taking a shower and would rejoin them shortly. And it's true, they did take a shower of sorts.

When Ron DeSantis herded petrified immigrant families onto planes destined for Martha's Vineyard, they were told they were going to Boston where a job, housing, and food awaited them.

Am I comparing the Nazi death camps to Ron DeSantis' stunt? No. What I am saying is both of these leaders had the same mindset, which is an inhumane level of cruelty.

The eternal battle between democracy and fascism is being waged in this country now, and for fascism, its DNA is soaked in cruelty. Cruelty is the point.

Trump's campaign to install fascism, while knee-capping democracy, has deep roots, guiding principles, and mentors. Enslavers, the Third Reich, and Donald Trump all embraced and executed these principles in their relentless, maniacal quest for power and money.

The prominent DNA strand of a fascist is cruelty. Cruelty is the mask that camouflages their cowardice, their deep-seated hidden fear of others. They have no shame, no moral compass, and are incapable of empathy. You can't argue with them, or appeal to their conscience. Their insecurity, their lack of self, breeds their cruelty.

In this essay, I will examine the machinations of fascism and its fundamentals, its instruments of implementation, and its frontal assault on democracy, which we are fending off now. It will show the parallels between enslavers, the Third Reich, and our former president.

The foundation of fascism's infrastructure is propped up with lies. Lies and disinformation serve as weapons to divide and secure power, using scapegoats to tenderize their lies.

> "By means of shrewd lies, unremittingly repeated, it is possible to make people believe that heaven is hell and hell heaven. The greater the lie, the more readily it will be believed."

> ~ Adolf Hitler

Enslavers in the South saturated the land with lies about African Americans, as well as poor whites. The basic lie was that African Americans weren't human, and therefore naturally suited for slave labor. This belief has deep roots. Thomas Jefferson weighed in, stating that separation from loved ones mattered little to African Americans.

Destitute whites were included in this broadside propaganda. Preachers, as dictated by enslavers, promulgated this false concept, and even cherry-picked out-of-context Bible passages, to justify the bondage and cruelty.

> "White ministers eagerly promised that they would henceforth work harder than ever to make Christianity into a toll that would help enslavers govern their society.

> "But he should not suffer. God had created some people unfit for freedom. Slavery was God's will. To worry about slavery was to doubt God. To oppose it was hearsay."

> ~ Edward Baptist,
> *The Half Has Never Been Told*, Page 210

To keep the lie aflame, and slavery viable, enslavers manipulated poor whites into thinking that their degradation, ignorance, and poverty sprouted from African Americans.

> "By predicting that poor whites would be massacred by the 'black plague,' masters tried to scare white laborers into supporting the

institution of slavery—regardless of what it did to their jobs or wages."

~ Kari Leigh Merritt, *Masterless Men*, Page 83

We see this played out today. Poor whites elect politicians who vote against programs designed to help their communities: infrastructure, healthcare, global warming, and voting rights. They sabotage their quality of life because they fall prey to the disinformation that assaults their newsfeeds.

"When asked to vote on a specific issue, Missourians chose the most progressive options. But when asked to vote for a politician, over half of Missourians chose Republicans who sought to strike down the very ballot initiatives for which they had voted."

~ Sarah Kendior, *Hiding in Plain Sight*, Page 46

Degraded and suppressed by enslavers, poor whites took the bait that their degradation stemmed from their partners in decadence. To maintain their tyranny, enslavers kept both races ignorant. It was a crime for enslaved people to read, punishable with hanging. Enslavers also forbade public education for both poor Black and white people; schools were only available for the offspring of white landowners. Keeping whites ignorant and illiterate enabled the elite to keep a chokehold on Black and white workers. Destitute whites were kept in line with threats of slave labor, and later on the wealthy played Black and white laborers off each other, disabling their power, thus constructing a wedge between two groups who had common ground.

"Meanwhile, the Northern press and Republicans in Congress charged that Democrats had adopted the idea that "the subjugation of white freemen may be necessary that African slavery may succeed in Kansas."

~ Edward Baptist, *The Half Has Never Been Told*, Page 374

Despite the manipulation of poor whites and Blacks, they often connected and shared resources, despite threats to maintain the racial divide. During the years of slavery, there were many stories of the enslaved sneaking food to starving whites, who had no way of competing with forced labor, and therefore remained destitute with no job prospects.

The source of poor Blacks' and whites' degradation was not each other but the enslavers, and later, the landowners, who evolved another stratagem—sharecropping, a different shade of enslaving people, and convict leasing, a more sinister shade of free labor.

"There is but one way for the oligarchy to perpetuate slavery in the Southern States and that is by perpetuating absolute ignorance among the non-slaveholding whites."

~ Kari Leigh Merritt, *Masterless Men*, Page 143

Enslavers, and later, landowners, kept industry out of the Deep South. They were making so much money with forced free labor that manufacturing posed a threat to their monopoly. Manufacturing in the South would have proven to be a boon to the Southern economy, an alternative to plantation work, and would have benefitted both poor Black and white laborers.

"For virtually all white Americans were now interested, almost all profiting in some way—financially, psychologically, or both—from slavery's growing empire."

~ Edward Baptist, *The Half Has Never Been Told*, Page 137

Assaulted with the propaganda that Blacks were the source of their degraded condition, poor whites carried the torch of racism, a false doctrine meant to exploit the working class.

"And importantly, thus has it been possible to make poor and working-class white people believe that their interests lie in making common cause with their political leaders and economic betters. Common cause in whiteness, the idea that they might eventually share in the spoils, and the understanding that the discomforts and anxieties of their own precarious lives were due to-are due to-those below them rather than those above them."

~ Walter Johnson, *The Broken Heart of America*, Page 6

The Third Reich was constructed on lies and disinformation, mimicking the enslavers' business plan. Hitler and his enablers studied America's suppression of African Americans, marveled at American Jim Crow laws, how it kept African Americans shackled and powerless. They even sent a delegation to America to study America's blueprint for the suppression of a race. The lessons learned were applied in their genocide of Jews.

We begin to see the stark reality of fascism, the maniacal cruelty that coursed through the bloodstream of the Nazis as they systematically sought to exterminate an entire race. Here are some of the fundamentals the Nazis sought to implement:

1. Cancelled treaties with other nations that promoted harmony. But wait, didn't Trump pull us out of NATO, cancel the Iran Nuclear treaty, etc.?

2. Attacked the free press, and all opposition voices were silenced. But wait, didn't Trump rant that the press was an enemy of the people?

3. Purged the government of officials who tried to expose the corruption. But wait, didn't Trump continually purge his administration of people he deemed disloyal to him: Comey, John Bolton, Dan Coats, Rod Rosenstein, James Mattis, John Kelly, Jeff Sessions, Nikki Healey, Scott Pruitt, Rex Tillerson, Andrew McCabe; and this is just a tip of the iceberg. There's not enough bandwidth to absorb the names. Let's just say it was a lot.

4. Prodded police to attack peaceful protesters. But wait, didn't Trump attack peaceful protesters in Portland, and then there was the incident where his henchmen cleared a path through peaceful protesters, including the minister, so he could hold up a Bible upside down?

5. Hitler courted white nationalists and targeted racial, religious, and ethnic minorities for persecution, and, especially in the case of Jews, execution. But wait, didn't Trump align himself with white supremacists and not only attacked minorities, but incited violence against the marginalized? And lest I forget, his famous quote from Charlottesville that there are "very fine people on both sides."

6. Hitler attacked labor unions, accusing them to be an enemy of capitalism while enriching far-right industrialists. But wait, didn't Trump fight for that massive tax break for his rich friends? And Trump himself was a beneficiary of that tax cut. How fortuitous.

Hitler, relying on his big lie, was able to convince Germans that the reason for their World War I defeat, their economic devastation, was the Jews. Hitler didn't invent antisemitism; he exploited it. The landscape of antisemitism had been nourished and tilled for over a hundred years by pastors throughout Europe. Germans, having been groomed from the pulpit for over a century, readily embraced the cruelty, the disinformation, and the conspiracy theories of the Nazi party. Ordinary citizens, your baker, butcher, cabinet maker. Your civil servant, schoolteacher, engineer, etc. all participated in the genocide.

The Nazis would roll into Polish towns, call a town meeting for the entire town, and then ask for volunteers to aid in killing all the Jews in the town. And except for a few squeamish citizens, all would participate in the pogroms, having been infected with disinformation all their lives. One police chief made this statement about the executions,

"I would also like to say that it did not at all occur to me that these orders could be unjust. It is true that I know that it is also the duty of the police to protect the innocent, but I was then of the conviction that the Jews were not innocent but guilty. I believed the propaganda that all Jews were criminals and sub-humans and that they were the cause of Germany's decline after the First World War. The thought that one should disobey or evade the order to participate in the extermination of the Jews did not therefore enter my mind at all."

~ Kurt Mobius, Police Battalion

Disinformation is a powerful tool of fascism. Disinformation is so powerful that it can make one execute children or storm the Capitol.

And this brings us to the reign of Trump, who uncorked the full arsenal of fascism: lies, inciting violence, misdirection, racism, scapegoats, etc.—fascism's greatest hits.

When caught with his hand in the cookie jar regarding confidential secret documents, the propaganda juggernaut went into full misdirection mode. Joseph Goebbels: "Accuse the other side of that which you are guilty."

Our former President is a Zen master at the smokescreen. He first claimed they were planted, then blamed the FBI for Gestapo tactics. Then he claimed that he reclassified them as non-confidential just by thinking the thought. Then he had his enablers offer even more bizarre explanations like Mark Rubio who stated it was just a storage issue. It's hard to keep up with the misdirection.

And of course—of course—he pulled the GOP's favorite weapons from its holster: whataboutism, and false equivalents. And you knew this had to come: what about Hillary's emails?

All these sleights of hand were designed to take the focus off the fact he stole highly classified, confidential documents, including nuclear documents.

And the question looms: why?

Fueling the insurrection was the Big Lie, a lie he knew to be a lie.

"Trump at times has appeared to admit to losing the election. In June, he told Fox News's Sean Hannity that he 'didn't win'."

~ Kelsey Carolan, 4/5/22

"Former White House aide says she heard Trump in private blurt out 'Can you believe I lost to this guy?' while watching Biden on TV."

~ Alyssa Farah

By promoting the Big Lie, a lie he knew to be a lie, Trump commenced his assault on democracy, adhering to Goebbels playbook:

"If you repeat a lie often enough, people will believe it, and you will even come to believe it yourself… The bigger the lie, the more it will be believed."

~ Joseph Goebbels

I really believe, at this point, Trump believes his Big Lie. He has repeated it so often that it has seeped into his bloodstream. It has served as an excuse to fundraise and hold rallies with his cult followers who lavish him with adoration. He lives for these rallies, as did Hitler.

While in office, Trump told over thirty thousand lies; adopting the Big Lie proved seamless.

"And if all others accepted the lie which the Party imposed—if all records told the same tale—then the lie passed into history and became truth. 'Who controls the past,' ran the Party slogan, 'controls the future: who controls the present controls the past.'"

~ George Orwell, *1984*

As a nation, we find ourselves at a tipping point. Our former president intends to pile drive the bedrock of democracy—voting rights. Sixty-five courts, many manned with Trump judicial appointees, have ruled there was no election fraud. His attorney general, Bill Barr, stated there was no election fraud and he was fired. Chris Krebs, the Director of the Cybersecurity and Infrastructure Security Agency, was fired after stating the 2020 election was the most secure in our history.

There is no question who won the 2020 Presidential election, and despite that truth, Trump has unleashed a tsunami of voter suppression barriers, blatantly targeting communities of color and the disenfranchised. They never hide their intent. Voter suppression was a staple for enslavers and the Third Reich. It's how they consolidated their power. As Trump stated, "it's not how many votes that are counted, it's who counts the votes," which has always been his insidious intent, laid bare during the January 6th hearings.

Let's review the sobering similarities between Hitler and Trump:

1. Both labeled the press an enemy of the people.

2. Hitler vowed to make Germany great again. Trump vowed to make America great again.

3. Both used racist rhetoric to rise to power.

4. Hitler was anti-Jew; Trump is anti-Muslimism, anti-Hispanic, anti-anyone who isn't male and white.

5. Hitler had his secret police that arrested anyone who opposed the regime. Trump sicced cops, their identities hidden, on peaceful Portland protesters. And you could say that the Proud Boys and the Oath Keepers were Trump's Storm Troopers—they certainly demonstrated quality on January 6th.

6. Hitler packed the court with extremist judges. Trump packed the court with extremist enablers, resulting in the overturn of Roe vs. Wade. And here is what Hitler had to say about abortion:

"I'll put an end to the idea that a woman's body belonged to her … Nazi ideals demand that the practice of abortion shall be exterminated with a strong hand."

~ Adolf Hitler

So there you have it.

We are fighting the eternal battle, but we are armed with invisible, powerful weapons, time tested, ready to be unleashed upon the merchants of disinformation. These weapons are truth, kindness, love, a moral imperative, and courage.

Democracy is on the ropes, but history has shown that when a country flexes its invisible muscles, change occurs. Look no further than Martin Luther King Jr. and Gandhi.

Truth trumps lies seven days a week. Or should I say, truth trumps Trump.

Please!

Vote!!!

Deniers

August 4, 2023

Lordy, Lordy, Lordy, this nation is presently infected with Holocaust deniers. (I'm not sure how they explain away those photographs of the camps.) But this week, we were treated to a new breed of deniers—slavery deniers. Not sure who is spawning this new ecosystem, but the rot, the hate, the cowardice, the disinformation, as usual, spews out of Republicans' mouths.

Yes people, Ron DeSantis and the Florida Education Board are disseminating the idea that slavery wasn't so bad after all. It was just one big job-training initiative, preparing African Americans for life after their bucolic existence in paradisical plantations. In Texas, the term slavery is being changed to 'involuntary relocation.' Can't help but think of a George Orwell quote:

> "The most effective way to destroy people is to deny and obliterate their own understanding of their history."
>
> ~ George Orwell

> "Libs, you're on notice. The Mommies are now in charge. 'Liberty' now means what we say it means. History is what we say it is."
>
> ~ Ron DeSantis

Further underpinning this attack on truth is Florida's wildfire of banned books. Make no mistake, we are in a battle with fascism. What's at stake is the very soul of this nation, the very soul of our democracy.

Our former president laid the groundwork to implement fascism, copying Hitler's fascism manual: attack the press, seek support from white nationalists and white supremacists, urge police to assault peaceful protesters, cancel treaties and agreements meant to promote harmony with democratic nations, offer love to totalitarian leaders. And the list goes on and on.

In order for fascism to take root, history must be rewritten, entombed, and education white-washed. Presently, we are dealing with Trump's Big Lie. Hitler: "If you tell a lie big enough and keep repeating it, people will eventually come to believe it." And people actually believe his lie despite the factual evidence thoroughly debunking his daily dose of lies.

I mean, come on: he lost sixty-five court cases. His own Attorney General said there was no election fraud. His chief election cyber chief said there was no election fraud. The Dominion verdict lays bare the conspiracy behind the Big Lie.

But people still believe there was election fraud. Repeating a big lie over and over again does work.

It's no surprise that the history of slavery is being rewritten—rewritten history is part of America's DNA. There is ample precedent in America's past. There was the famous Wilmington, North Carolina Black slaughter that was waged in 1898 by white supremacists, wiping out a whole city of middle-class Blacks, execution style. It was a riot, reminiscent of the January 6th riot, ignited by months of disinformation from the media and the pulpit. 300 back residents were executed. It is estimated that 2,000 Black Americans were displaced, and the Black newspaper building was torched. No arrests were made and there were no prosecutions.

So what did our history books say about this riot?

Wilmington's Lie by David Zucchini, page 335 states,

> "The state's school textbooks, presided over by white supremacists, ensured that the enduring myths of 1898 were passed

down to each new generation of white pupils. A 1933 textbook placed the blame for the killing on elected black officials."

They were the victims, not the perpetrators. This atrocity will never appear in DeSantis's educational curriculum. Nor will the Tulsa race massacre of 1921, another event where a Black middle-class was erased, including what was then called Black Wall Street.

These acts are all part of the Fascist playbook. The parallels to the Third Reich's ascension are staring us right in the face.

So how do you fight this evil? I used to try to have conversations with Trump Republicans, but they were incapable of having a rational exchange of ideas. They loved to send me links, but because they were members of a cult, critical thinking was no longer in their wheelhouse. Like their leader, they are shameless, and absent of integrity. Pointing out the truth or attempting an exchange of ideas can't penetrate the epidermis of their disinformation bubble.

So what can you do?

You keep exposing the lies, all day, every day, because the lies never stop. We all have to fill the vacuum in the wake of disinformation and lies. We can't depend on another person to do it; it must be done by ourselves, daily. That's the only way we save democracy. The lies are the fuel that Republicans hope will hoist them into office. The January 6th committee simply exposed the Trump lies, and each Trump trial will expose more lies, acting as a cleansing agent for our democracy.

Democracy is a living, breathing organism and its oxygen is truth. Democracy will wither on the vine if citizens turn away from the fight, their apathy condoning fascism, extinguishing the light.

Democracy in Peril

December 30, 2023

The story of our teetering democracy is not the tale of the machinations of Donald Trump. At its core, it's a chronicle of the cowardliness of enablers, and how they fertilized the terrains so that Trump can plant his messages of hate, racism, and violence.

Without his enablers, Trump would be an insignificant blip in history, a con man with a reality TV show where contestants debased themselves in front of their deity, Donald Trump. Without enablers, Hitler, Mussolini, Stalin, and Franco would have perished in obscurity.

> "The world will not be destroyed by those who do evil, but by those who watch them without doing anything."
>
> ~ Albert Einstein

> "In the end, we will remember not the words of our enemies, but the silence of our friends."
>
> ~ Martin Luther King Jr.

> "Our lives begin to end the day we become silent about things that matter."
>
> ~ Martin Luther King Jr.

There is a racial aspect to the blind faith of enablers. Despots like Trump force-feed scapegoats to their acolytes. The scapegoats serve as explanations as to why their lives are miserable. It relieves them of responsibility for their condition. Scapegoats are the secret sauce of fascists. Hitler served up the Jews as to why the Germans lost World War I. For Mussolini, it was the Jews and the immigrants. For Trump, it was the Muslims, the Hispanics, the immigrants, the people of color, the liberals, the leftists, the Black Lives Matter, the Washington Post, the New York Times, CNN, etc. I could keep going, but I don't have that kind of time.

There are no mirrors in the MAGA movement. Self-examination is not a thing in the alternate reality that is the MAGA entity, just as global warming, institutional racism, and solar power are not a thing in the MAGA orbit.

So why does propaganda stick and dictate behavior? Joseph Goebbels answered that question:

> "Propaganda helped us to power ... propaganda kept us in power. Propaganda will help us conquer the world."

And what's the motivation behind a person enabling evil? Walter Johnson touched upon the reason in his book, *The Broken Heart of America*.

> "And importantly, thus has it been possible to make poor and working-class white people believe that their interests lie in making common cause with their political leaders and economic betters. Common cause in whiteness, the idea that they might eventually share in the spoils, the understanding that the discomforts and anxieties of their own precarious lives were due to—are due to—those below them rather than those above them."

"Due to those below them rather than those above them." This leads to the next question: why would anyone debase themselves and genuflect to a false prophet?

Why? They lack character, integrity, and the ability to think critically. And where does that condition come from? Republicans are systematically sabotaging education, the teaching of history. Books are being banned in droves, and Black and LGBTQ+ history is being whitewashed and buried. Science is under attack and critical thinking is on the endangered species list.

Despots, like Trump, gained their power from acolytes devoid of an ability to think critically. Fascists depend on their blind faith followers, blaming everything on those below them. Lack of education and lack of integrity enable them to be manipulated and programmed.

We can't blame the boogie man, or Donald Trump, for taking away our democracy. Our silence, our apathy, our cynicism, our attack on truth and education will serve as a welcome mat for dictators to seize power.

Sara Huckabee Sanders, the Governor of Arkansas, says that teaching AP African American History is a "propaganda leftist agenda" designed to teach kids to "hate America."

A governor said this.

A governor of a state in the United States of America said this.

A Governor. Not a filing clerk, a Governor.

George Orwell said this:

> "The most effective way to destroy people is to deny and obliterate their own understanding of their history."

This is the Republican's reincarnation of the Jim Crow laws. Their racism is like a chameleon, constantly changing colors and fabrications, forever reinforcing institutional racism, education being a major target.

Presently, Arkansas ranks 47 out of 51 states in quality of education. In other words, Ms. Sanders is advocating to make Arkansas students even dumber, less able to engage in critical thinking, and therefore more susceptible to propaganda. This dumbing down of the electors is Republican's long-term strategy to achieve and maintain power. The debating of ideas and the proposals of policy have been flung overboard. All that matters is loyalty, or more precisely, obedience. To be obedient takes no critical thinking.

> "The philosopher Theodore Adorno's assertion that television could continue fascist tyranny by fostering 'intellectual passivity, and gullibility' was good news to postwar autocrats, who knew that discouraging critical thinking was key to maintaining themselves in power."

> ~ Ruth Ben-Ghiat,
> *Strongmen Mussolini to the Present*, Page 106

Whitewashing our history, sabotaging learning institutions, denying science in order to restrict critical thinking, is a Republican fundamental. This dumbing down of the electors enables a former President to claim he won an election when he didn't, to claim global warming is a hoax, to claim the way to keep our children safe is to have more guns, to claim there are good people on both sides when referring to neo-Nazis, to claim, as stated by Kellyann Conway, that there are alternative facts.

> "Political language ... is designed to make lies sound truthful and murder respectable, and to give an appearance of solidity to pure wind."

> ~ George Orwell

Orwell's prophesies continue to be reenacted by the Republican Party, a party surging toward fascism, one banned book at a time. Governor De-Santis, a Republican candidate for President, said,

> "Libs, you're on notice. The Mommies are now in charge. 'Liberty' now means what we say it means. History is what we say it means."

In other words, there is a direct attack on history, a fundamental of fascism. It is reminiscent of slavery, where the power structure sought to keep poor whites and Blacks illiterate, the better able to control and terrorize them.

Republicans no longer use code words. They are very overt about their march toward fascism. Simmering in the fascism gumbo is racism, homophobia, Islamic phobia, misogyny, white supremacy, anti-immigrant, etc. They say it out loud now.

"Laziness is a trait in blacks. It really is, I believe that."

~ Donald Trump

Meanwhile, a fifth chairperson, Harris County GOP chair-elect Keith Nielsen, announced Saturday he will not take office as planned after coming under fire for posting the following Martin Luther King Jr. quote, "Injustice anywhere is a threat to justice everywhere," on a background with a banana. This was reported by Naomi Andu, Clare Proctor, and Miguel Gutierrez Jr. of *The Texas Tribune*.

America has a history of falling for red herrings, a practice that is a building block for fascism. Fascism is in the blame game. Don't believe me, just listen to a speech by Donald Trump and his foghorn of disinformation. He accepts no responsibility for anything. He simply feeds scapegoats to the manufactured grievances of his base.

"Now the Depression had thrown them to the ground. Not understanding how and why those above them were responsible for the crisis that threatened them, they blamed most of it on the enemy lurking below: the Negroes, Jews, Catholics, Mexicans, anarchists, socialists, and, of course, the Communists—all enemies of True Americanism."

~ Michael Joseph Roberto, *The Coming of the American Behemoth*, Page 292-3

Donald Trump needs to be defeated, and every citizen needs to play a part. You can't brush it off with a flippant "doesn't matter who's in office, they are all corrupt." They aren't all corrupt, and it does matter who's in office. Eighty million people didn't vote in 2020, and it is this disengagement that ushers in fascism. There is a weakness in Democracy that Trump exploited.

> "… in the career of Huey Long epitomized the essential weakness of Democracy—the pathetic willingness of the electorate to trust a glib tongue and a dramatic personality. Quite justified, he was called a forerunner to American Fascism."

> ~ *Washington Post* editorial after the death of Huey Long

Trump was elected because we all thought his enablers would stop him, the Constitution would stop him, our friends and neighbors would stop him, but his enablers had neither the character nor the integrity to say no. Given their lack of critical thinking, they believed him when he said that only he could fix things.

If Trump is reelected, we can't blame the boogie man; we can only blame ourselves for looking away, our silence paving the way for American fascism.

> "When fascism comes to America, it will be wrapped in the flag and carrying a cross."

> ~ James Waterman Wise

Our country is divided at a level unprecedented. So what's the cause? Is this just a random occurrence, or is there a causal agent secretly working behind the scenes?

> "The revanchist Kremlin has to paralyze and inflame US politics. Russian state media, bots, trolls and online proxies exploit disagreements in the US over social issues like abortion, gun control, ethnic groups and police behavior.

> "Putin has also allocated increased resources to troll farms, such as the notorious Internet Research Agency (IRA); the IRA uses fake social media accounts to foment division

abroad. These efforts are part of the Kremlin's coordinated, heavily financed effort to undermine democracy."

~ Ivana Stradner

"Yevgeny Prigozhin, the Russian minister, openly stated in early November, 'Gentlemen, we interfered, we are interfering and we will interfere. The goal is not to promote one political side over another. It's to keep the United States as divided as possible.'"

~ Rachael Maddow, *Prequel*

Mission accomplished.

This overlapped with its desire to "provoke and amplify political and social discord in the United States" (in the words of special counsel Robert S. Mueller III), leading it to weigh in not only on electoral politics but cultural fights—investing in amplifying and exacerbating contentious social debates.

This strategy of divisiveness has deep roots going back to Nazi Germany, was adopted by Putin, and is now being reenacted by Trump and his minions, divisiveness being the thread that courses through all three bloodlines.

"Germany's agents were tasked with finding these fissures in American society and then prying them further apart, exploiting them to make Americans hate and suspect each other, and maybe even wish for a new kind of country altogether. A partisan, bickering, demoralized America, The Nazis believed, would be incapable of mounting a successful war effort in Europe. It might even soften us up for an eventual takeover."

~ Ivana Stradner

Valentine's Day: The Look of Love

February 22, 2023

Three years ago, I had a double lung transplant. It was successful, and three years later, I feel healthy and blessed. I received my new lungs on Valentine's Day, which gave that day a special meaning for my wife and me. I was on my deathbed, waiting for a miracle, when I got the call from the hospital informing me that they had a new set of lungs, an exact blood and size match. In addition to saving my life, my transplant not only forced me to reflect on my mortality, but also on the love and beauty that surrounded me.

One of the things that happens when you receive a transplant is you visit a lot of doctors, both before and after the operation. Before the operation, as my breathing capacity deteriorated, I became eligible to receive a handicap parking tag, which was a godsend at the time, as a walk of over twenty yards drained my body of oxygen. Now that I am healthy, my wife refuses to let me use the sticker, rightly asserting I don't need it and others need it more.

But when I was using my handicap sticker, I began to observe couples who parked in the handicap spaces. And it was always one spouse who was helping their partner into a wheelchair, or a walker, usually the wife helping the husband. As I continued to observe this ritual, I realized I was bearing witness to deep and profound acts of love. I was witnessing the embodiment of "till death do us part." Parking in handicap spaces granted me access to lifelong devotions, a sacred pledge that these couples would be there for each other during the good times and bad. It was a quiet courage. The handicap parking spaces were populated by couples who had not bailed on their partners during their time of vulnerability, and I was blessed to bear witness to these quiet, tender acts of devotion, acts of tender mercies.

I then realized we are all surrounded by these quiet, silent moments of love, of kindness, of courage. It is what sustains and nourishes our souls, makes us human, and connects us. We just have to look; the beauty is right in front of our noses. And as I observed these partners in the hand-icap spaces, I realized what a gift my lung handicap bestowed upon me. It opened me up to the glory and the grace that was all around me. I just had to look.

Race

January 9, 2023

Race has a chokehold on the soul of America.

It is a cancer we refuse to treat, its deadly serum coursing through our nation's bloodstream, often through social media. It was our nation's original sin, and its virulent and variant viruses continue to infect and divide our nation. Americans, unwilling to apply the cure, raise the question—what are the antibodies to racism?

As with election deniers, there are racism deniers, convinced America has shed itself of the cloak of bigotry. After all, didn't we elect a Black president and a Black vice president? For some, those two elections cleansed the slate—no racism here.

> "People who perceive that the social system discriminates against racial minorities are more likely to support policies to reduce that discrimination. Racists know this. That's why denial of racism is a time-honored tactic."
>
> ~ James Loewen, *Sundown Towns*, Page 422

Turns out our nation is still knee-deep in bigotry, despite electing a Black president. His presence simply poked the bear. Conversely, Trump excavated the cesspool of festering hate, no longer needing racist Republican dog whistles, unleashing a groundswell of hate and venom. Trump provided a safe harbor and legitimacy for the ascension of white supremacists. Just last week, he dined with a racist, Holocaust denier, Nick Fuentes, further normalizing and legitimizing hate and racism. The Southern Strategy, as articulated by Lee Atwater, the famous Republican strategist, no longer requires filters. Bigotry and vitriol is aired out loud, no subterfuge required. Trump elevated and legitimized racism in the mainstream. Incendiary bigotry, long buried, spewed out in a cauldron of hate and disinformation, boiling over into our politics and culture. Lee Atwater:

> "You start out in 1954 by saying, 'Nigger, nigger, nigger.' By 1968 you can't say 'nigger'—that hurts you, backfires so you say stuff like uh, forced busing, states' rights, and all that stuff, and you're getting so abstract. Now, you're talking about cutting taxes, and all these things you're talking about are totally economic things and a byproduct of them is, blacks get hurt worse than whites... 'We want to cut this,' is much more abstract than even the busing thing, uh, and a hell of a lot more abstract than 'Nigger, nigger.'"

The full glory and promise of America can never be achieved till we root out this malignancy. James Baldwin nailed it with these words,

> "White people in this country will have quite enough to do in learning how to accept and love themselves and each other, and when they have achieved this—which will not be tomorrow and may very well be never—the Negro problem will no longer exist, for it will no longer be needed."

> ~ James Baldwin

So, what is the antibody? Can America afford to wait for white people to "learn how to accept and love themselves and each other?"

I see more urgency.

I have friends, good people, who insist they are not racist, but who support Trump, an avowed white supremacist. And I know if they worked with or lived near any person of color, they would treat everyone with dignity and respect. I've seen this. And they wouldn't have a problem if someone with a different racial background wanted to marry their daughter or son. One-on-one, these people have no problem with people of color. And they insist they aren't racist, but they still support a white supremacist.

So, what gives?

I do attempt to engage in conversations with these people, trying to pry open their reasons for their blind faith. But they withdraw, get uncomfortable with any mention of Trump, as if they are ashamed of their allegiance. The hardcore Trumpites love to send me links in place of dialogue, links that are brimming with disinformation and conspiracy theories.

A common theme emerged when I asked about Trump, wondering how they could support a compulsive liar, a man accused of twenty-four sexual assaults, a man with Russian mob connections that laundered money through Trump Towers, who stole top secret government documents, etc.: the most I got out of them was that he was a strong leader, good for the economy. But it simply isn't true. Among other metrics, under the Trump Administration, the deficit went up every single year. Under President Biden, the deficit has fallen sharply—to the tune of $1.4 TRILLION this year alone.

Morality was never part of the equation. Of the last seven presidents, Trump was last in GNP growth. And then there is the impression that Trump was a great businessman: you can't call yourself a great businessman if you declared bankruptcy six times. Their support seemed to hinge on "what's in it for me." His supporters were convinced he had their backs, especially poor whites whose healthcare was constantly on the chopping block with no replacement on the horizon. They were not concerned about the wealth gap, children living in poverty, or global warming. It was all about what was in it for them.

But we still haven't answered the question: why do non-racists support racists? The easy answer is, well, they're racist and that's why. But I think it goes deeper.

We have institutional racism in this country and this infrastructure breeds bigotry, divisiveness, and poverty. The maniacal mortar used to build these structures is designed to hide the true nature of their carnage on a community, on a country. If there is any pushback or protest, people of color are deemed the problem. The propaganda machine points fingers at people of color for any negative consequences. Structural racism is constructed so white people can live in a cocoon of irresponsibility and privilege, denying their gut that whispers, "We are all our brother's keepers."

I grew up in Maryland, in a town of working-class, middle-class residents, mostly white. Most of the people I knew grew up in a two-parent family, although who knows what occurred behind closed doors. In my family, my father's alcoholism left scars on the entire family, and in every family I knew, drinking was part of the zeitgeist. We all went to decent schools, and most of us got a decent education. I personally was a horrible student, but I was exposed to books and became a voracious reader. George Wallace, an ardent segregationist received 14.7% of the Maryland vote in the 1968 Presidential election. There were a few Black students in my school. If you recall from a previous chapter, one Black student, was well-liked by the student body. He was personable, smart, engaging, and was generally part of the in-crowd. One day, he was seen walking arm in arm with a white girl and he went from being 'a great guy', 'one of the boys', to 'a ni…r'. And the girl was labeled with other degrading words.

Behind closed doors in my town, there was raging bigotry, easily ignited. It turned out that at the end of the day, they weren't their brother's keepers, unless your brother was white.

Being a member of the basketball team, we would sometimes play inner-city D.C. schools, and I saw the contrast between my school and the D.C. schools. First, the facilities were old and run down, badly needing repairs and care. The libraries were sub-par, and you felt an overwhelming feeling of decay. It felt like some of the schools had been abandoned, that they were just a warehouse for kids, and learning was an after-thought.

I realized later this was an example of systemic racism. This was a segregated school, in a segregated city, created by decisions based on race, bigotry, and hate. Segregated cities aren't created by chance. In his book, *Sundown Towns, A Hidden Dimension of American Racism*, James Loewen documented over a thousand towns that were intentionally kept white, segregated, some with explicit signs like, "Don't let the sun set on you in this town, nigger."

In his book, *An American Dilemma*, written as World War II wound down, Gunnar Myrdal noted that residential segregation has been a key factor accounting for the subordinate status of African Americans. Separating people geographically makes it much easier to provide better city services to some than to others, to give some children better opportunities than others, and to label some people as better than others. In Roosevelt, the Black township in Long Island, "as tax money dried up, the schools withered." Page 370

The underfunded city schools handicap their students from day one, releasing them into the world saddled with the imprint of inferior, segregated education, attendant with its psychological assault on their self-esteem. This structure is systemic and institutional. As the famous 1954 ruling in Brown vs. Board of Education, the Supreme Court ruling documented that segregated education produces psychologically damaged kids, whose self-esteem is trampled.

Dr. King also challenged the tendency to cast Black behavior as the problem, rather than investigating the structures of racism in the North.

> "Many whites who oppose open housing would deny that they are racists. They turn to sociological arguments... [without realizing] that criminal responses are environmental, not racial."
>
> ~ Martin Luther King Jr.

Despite the ruling, schools continued to remain segregated as mobs threatened violence if school integration was implemented.

Segregated housing is another racist infrastructure. White people were fed the propaganda that having people of color move into their neighborhood would destroy housing values, home ownership being the lever, the steppingstone for middle-class wealth. Non-white Americans purchasing a house in all white neighborhoods were subjected to multiple forms of violence, including murder and firebombing.

This is structural racism, and it persists today. This is an issue my white friends are oblivious to, often purposely. The playing field regarding education is not level, saturated in inequities, purposely designed. With my racist/non-racist white friends, this issue never enters into their consciousness as they cast their votes for politicians who not only perpetuate the inequities, but widen them. Systemic racism wasn't talked about in school, especially now, where critical race theory (CRT) is often banned from being taught. Critical race theory is simply history, and history is under attack. CRT is being banned in many school districts across the US. Systemic, racist infrastructures, once built, engage in a dizzying array of insidious maintenance to preserve their privilege.

Gaslighting history is a major instrument in keeping our citizens ignorant, which dilutes their power, and their identity. Politicians rail that if white students were to study CRT, they might feel upset, feel bad about themselves. Here's what history does: it empowers us because the study of history breeds understanding, which, in turn, breeds character; it brings one to understand the world, and oneself, on a deeper, richer level. Denying, altering, or whitewashing history, sabotages our growth, and our humanity. Understanding ourselves and the world around us promotes connections. You start to realize there is a common humanity, that we are related, with similar hopes and dreams. But because we can't legislate morality, how do we get good people to care, to abdicate their privilege, to be participants in equality, in justice? How do I get my friends to have systemic racism enter their consciousness? Because if I could figure that out, I believe they would no longer support a politician like Trump.

> "… most people still do not turn first to history and social structure to explain why African Americans have less wealth, lower test scores, and are concentrated in inner cities and a few suburbs."

> ~ James Loewen, *Sundown Towns*, Page 416

Housing segregation and discrimination is another systemic racist structure, many years in fabrication. Segregated neighborhoods are a direct consequence of 'Red Lining', a process whereby a circle is drawn on a map by bankers who then deny mortgages to people of color in that red-lined area, which in turn denies the one sure-fire route to generational wealth. If that wasn't enough, unscrupulous speculators descended on these neighborhoods and financed homes for residents. This con got residents to pay finance companies to secure a house. The only problem was, they had no equity until the house was fully paid for. And if they missed a payment, the finance company had the right to seize the house, leaving the potential homeowners bereft.

Predators prey upon poor communities, extracting blood money, symbolized by check-cashing facilities and pay-day loan stores. There were also the drive-by inspections where a family would buy a house for ten thousand dollars, and after they moved in, they would discover the house required another ten thousand dollars in repairs, which they couldn't afford, and ultimately were forced to abandon their house, leaving the finance company with another house to double-dip on.

This corruption, this predatory assault on red-lined, vulnerable, communities, gutted these neighborhoods. This depressed not only the property values—property that most of the residents couldn't own given the red lining that ran rampant throughout the cities—but this purposeful segregation, predatory assault, doubled up as a psychological assault on the soul of a community. This is another structure of institutional racism, a structure with far-reaching consequences for people of color.

> "Focusing on black crime, he said, was a way to avoid looking at the much greater crime of ghettoizing people in communities with insufficient schools, jobs and city services."
>
> ~ Martin Luther King Jr.

Should I go on? Yes! The prison industrial complex, is a money-making structure using people of color as fodder for the money-making pillaging. We've all seen the statistics:

> "African Americans represent 12.7% of the US population, 15% of US drug users (72% of all users are white), 36.8% of those arrested for a drug-related crime, 48.2% of American adults in state, and federal prisons and local jails and 42.5% of prisoners under sentence of death."
>
> ~ Statistical Abstract of the United States (1999), Sourcebook of Criminal Justice Statistics, (1998), National Household Survey of Drug Abuse (1998) and Bureau of Justice Statistics Bulletin: Prisoners and Jail Inmates at Midyear 1999

Private industry entered the incarceration business in the early 1970s. In order for this fledgling enterprise to be profitable, beds needed to be filled with inmates. States would contract with these companies, guaranteeing inmates in order to fulfill their contractual obligations.

> "One in three black men between the ages of 20 and 29 live under some form of correctional supervision or control."
>
> ~ Maurer, M. & Hurling, T., Young Black Americans and the Criminal Justice System: Five Years Later (Washington DC: The Sentencing Project, 1995)

The prison industrial complex is a ravenous beast that needs to be fed so it can produce its blood money, usually on the backs of people of color and the powerless.

President's Johnson War on Poverty, morphed into the War on Drugs, which was the smokescreen for the War on the Powerless and Voiceless. This out-of-control juggernaut devastated disenfranchised communities, taking dead aim at the family structure by incarcerating a disproportional number of Black males.

These are just three institutional racist structures. There are many more, including voter suppression. But having established these structures, how are they maintained?

> "The most effective way to destroy people is to deny and obliterate their own understanding of their history."

> ~ George Orwell

How do you maintain systemic, racist structures? One way is to deny history, deny these structures exist. Books are being banned—70% of them seem to be by authors of color. There was even a book burning in Tennessee. School boards flip out on CRT.

Knowing one's history is empowering, transformative, and that lever of power is under attack. Systemic racism would collapse under the glare of our true history, which isn't often pleasant, but it is inspirational. Our history of people of color is saturated with unspeakable horrors, but is coupled with stories of triumph, courage, and resistance.

Let's get back to my racist-but-not-racist friends. Like I said, most would treat people of color with dignity and respect on an individual basis, but they have no clue about the systemic racist structures that exist and where they came from. Why is that important? Knowing one's history, knowing American history, humanizes one; it breeds empathy. Unless you are evil, learning about other cultures, their histories, makes us realize our common humanity. It cultivates connections and understanding. My friends are not invested in our true American story, and that's the problem.

> "He who controls the past controls the future. He who controls the present, controls the past."

> ~ George Orwell

America is great because of its diversity. The beauty, the culture, the heroes, and the history that have emerged from our unique gumbo is the envy of the world. On my Instagram account there are these very young, female Japanese dancers, probably teenagers, dressed in what looks like Japanese kimonos, dancing to a James Brown song, "Get Up". It is mesmerizing—the creative choreography, the rhythm, a sacred tribute to a giant on the opposite side of the globe. The genius of James Brown could only happen in America. It's why a Guatemalan woman, with two small children, will walk 400 miles to the American border, all for the sacred promise of a new life in America.

But immigrants arrive here and they quickly find out it is not a meritocracy, that hard work is not necessarily rewarded, and that they are easily given scapegoat status by politicians who seek office by demonizing people of color and immigrants.

Despite the scapegoating, this country breeds greatness and innovation.

Book burning, book banning, history denial, racism, homophobia, misogyny, antisemitism, anti-Muslim sentiment, are all cut from the same cloth and serve to sabotage the glory and honor of America. This fear stems from a hidden fear of others, flamed by politicians and right-wing media. These are the mechanisms that solidify and maintain systemic racist structures. Trump's Big Lie is part of the mechanism used to divide us, to denigrate others, to offer up scapegoats for manufactured grievances.

Back to my Trump acolytes. Here's an insight as to why they embrace a white supremacist. In Walter Johnson's book, *The Broken Heart of America*, we read,

> "And importantly, thus has it been possible to make poor and working-class white people believe that their interest lie in making common cause with their political leaders and economic betters, common cause in whiteness: the idea that they might eventually share in the spoils, and the understanding that the discomforts and anxieties of their own precarious lives were due to—are due to—those below them, rather than those above them."

The "idea that they might eventually share in the spoils" is a sure sign they are victims, lacking character, unable to navigate life to achieve a future, and waiting for the spoils to rain down from their masters.

Addressing systemic racism is the opposite of hoping to share in the spoils. Systemic racism is locked in, perpetuated by disinformation, the use of scapegoats, denial of history, and by intentional segregation. Systemic racism is built to last, but it can be unraveled. I believe that if my friends understood the true history of this country, its horrors and its ascension, that would be a first step in dismantling the insidious structures of infrastructure racism. I believe this act alone would start to chisel away their heartlessness, and help to reboot their humanity.

The truth of the matter is, we are our brother's keepers. We can never be free until we are all free.

But, how do you create empathy, understanding? Unless you are part of the 2.5% who are truly evil, truthful history would be a first step in restoring empathy and humanity in our citizens. Here's the deal, if you deny that institutional racism exists, then it makes sense you would support a white supremacist. Denying that fact enables you to blame the victim and not the system, and enables you to deny that the system even exists. It also constructs a wall which prevents you from being your brother's keeper.

So, I think James Baldwin was onto something. "White people in this country will have quite enough to do in learning how to accept and love themselves and each other ..." In other words, white people have work to do. White people are the ones storming the capital, brandishing Confederate flags or wearing Auschwitz tee shirts, all symbols of hate and suppression.

Our children don't need to be protected from the truth, they relish the truth because it empowers them and builds character. Truth is empowering; it breeds empathy, compassion, and courage.

The second thing that needs to be done is for the systemic racist architecture to be revealed and dismantled. Taking down statues is symbolic but does nothing about the infrastructure.

And third, we must keep the dialogue flowing, no matter how difficult these conversations can become. We can't afford to retreat to our bunkers, lobbing grievances, because our democracy is built upon the full participation of its citizens. It won't work any other way.

> "Being taught to avoid talking about politics and religion has led to a lack of understanding of politics and religion. What we should have been taught was how to have a civil conversation about a difficult topic."
>
> ~ Ryan Fournier

If my white friends understood systemic racism, and all its machinations, I believe their innate goodness, their humanity, would manifest itself; but right now, there persists an intentional effort that has endured for over four hundred years to bury the truth, to ensure the electors remain ignorant, (a vital ingredient for the implementation of fascism), to

263

unleash disinformation that only serves to separate Americans, to bury history, and in the more egregious cases, to alter history.

All these efforts are designed to divide and separate us, but connections are America's superpower. Our breaking down the barriers to connections will save the union.

As I mentioned before, three years ago, I underwent a double-lung transplant. Among other things, the operation forces you to confront your mortality, and as part of that process; you realize you are all alone, even while surrounded by the love of family and friends. It was a chilling realization, and I wasn't sure how to process it.

And I wondered, what is the antibody to this gut punch? And then it struck me: the antibody was to connect, to recognize our common humanity. Connections are what keep at bay the feelings of stark loneliness that impending mortality injects into your consciousness.

But then I realized there's a superpower that is even more powerful than connections, that slays loneliness. It is HELP.

We are at our best when we help. Helping people takes us out of ourselves. And the ironic truth is that the helper often benefits more than the ones being helped. Years ago, Ann Devere Smith, the famous actor and writer known for her one-woman shows, had a student come in and tell her he was suicidal. Instead of sending him to a counselor, she sent him to work in a homeless shelter. Guess what? No longer suicidal.

Helping is one of the most powerful tools we have. It can restore our being, our pride, in addition to dissipating our loneliness. And yet, structural racism endeavors to sever connections by labeling people as 'other', they are different from us, or dangerous, etc.

Racism is an artificial construct used to maintain power by offering up scapegoats to suppress and separate people. Racism would melt if we started really connecting with each other. Removing structural racism would be a giant step in ushering in a new era of peace, reconciliation, and hope. My white friends could finally realize James Baldwin's prayer:

> "White people in this country will have quite enough to do in learning how to accept and love themselves and each other, and when they have achieved this—which will not be tomorrow and may very well be never—the Negro problem will no longer exist, for it will no longer be needed."

And the promise of our Founding Fathers can finally be realized.

In the end, goodness always wins out.

> "The arc of the moral universe is long, but it bends towards justice."

> ~ Martin Luther King Jr.

> "The fundamental litmus test for American democracy—its economy, government, criminal justice system, education, mass media, and culture—remains: how broad and intense are the arbitrary powers used and deployed against black people. In this sense, the problem of the twenty-first century remains the problem of the color line."

> ~ Cornell West

America's New Ni...rs

June 18, 2023

I start with the famous quote from Lee Atwater, the Republican strategist whose cancer was imprinted onto Republican machinations for decades, and unfortunately, his insidious racism continues to course through the veins of the Republican Party.

> "You start out in 1954 by saying, 'Nigger, nigger, nigger.' By 1968, you can't say 'nigger'—that hurts you, backfires. So you say stuff like, uh, forced busing, states' rights, and all that stuff, and you're getting so abstract. Now, you're talking about cutting taxes, and all these things you're talking about are totally economic things and a byproduct of them is, blacks get hurt worse than whites ... 'We want to cut this,' is much more abstract than even the busing thing, uh, and a hell of a lot more abstract than 'Nigger, nigger.'"

> "LGBTQ people are nine times more likely than non-LGBTQ people to be victims of violent hate crimes."

> ~ UCLA, Williams Institute

> "LGBTQ youth are *more than four times as likely* to attempt suicide than their peers"

> ~ Johns et al., 2019; Johns et al., 2020

> "The Trevor Project's on LGBTQ Youth Mental Health found that *45% of LGBTQ youth* seriously considered attempting suicide in the past year, including *more than half of transgender and nonbinary youth.*"

These alarming statistics aren't created in a vacuum; there are causal agents planting seeds of prejudice, and manufacturing hate, followed by its inevitable violence. Republican politicians spew homophobia fear-mongering, pumping venom into hate groups who in turn terrorize and bully their latest scapegoat—people in the LGBTQ+ community.

These are human beings, they don't deserve to be bullied, terrorized. People show up at LGBTQ+ events, armed to the gills, striking fear and horror into the protesters. In the eighties and nineties, often the most strident critics of the 'gay lifestyle' were later revealed to be gay.

Another terrorist group, the KKK, were also soldiers of anti-grooming. They used violence in an attempt to preserve a white Protestant world, absent Jews, Christians, and certainly Blacks. It's the old story: targeting 'others' through the demonization of 'others.' But aren't we all God's children?

"Pure womanhood. Our Little Girls Must be Protected."

~ Timothy Egan, KKK banner,
1923: A Fever in the Heartland

"Anyone who can make you believe absurdities can make you commit atrocities."

~ Voltaire

And boy, do we have some absurdities, especially in Florida where we have the mini-me fascist DeSantis calling the plays. He is using tax-payer money to fund a lawsuit against Disney, accusing them of infect-ing kids with LGBTQ+ propaganda. Really?

There have been over 500 books banned in Florida. Access to Amanda Gorman's poem, *The Hill We Climb*, is now restricted in Florida. It is a poem of hope, redemption, and ascension.

Amanda Gorman:

"'I'm gutted. One parent could get my poetry banned from classrooms. And yet one country can't ban assault rifles from massacring children.'

"At least 525 anti-LGBTQ bills were introduced this year in forty-one states, HRC found, including more than 220 pieces of legislation that explicitly target transgender people."

~ *The Hill*, 6/8/2023

What are they afraid of? Drag queens aren't marching into schools and gunning down children with AR-15s. Aren't they avoiding the real problem?

The school children of Florida will no longer be taught Black history, and critical race theory is being treated like a plague. Large swaths of history, including the Gay Rights Movement, the Women's Movement, Civil Rights Movement are all on the chopping block. Black history is hanging by a thread. Instead, students will be taught that enslaved people lived the good life, free room and board, and only a few enslavers were cruel, the rest were benevolent plantation owners with kindly overseers, providing a utopian work environment. A county in Texas wants to call slavery "involuntary relocation," a not-so-subtle attempt to bury America's original sin.

And talking about grooming!!!! Students in some schools will be taught Biblical passages that, when interpreted in a very specific way, proclaim homosexuals are abominations.

When Ed Jackson, a member of the KKK, became governor of Indiana in 1922, he pledged to "fire all Jewish and Catholic professors". (*A Fever in the Heartland*, Timothy Eagan.) Sounds like Florida's present agenda of weeding out educators who appear to be woke, whatever the hell that means. The KKK is not dead, and continues to infect our culture through the medium of the Republican Party. Even Trump couldn't bring himself to denounce David Duke, the former Grand Wizard of the KKK, during the 2016 political campaign.

For fascism to take root, the first target is always education, and we are witnessing this offensive in Florida. Hitler piloted massive book-burning events, and last year, a pastor in Tennessee ignited a book-burning event. Teachers are resigning in droves because they are no longer allowed to teach the truth about American history.

History is uncomfortable, but confronting our uncomfortable truths is how we achieve a more perfect union.

> "This summer, the board will consider updates to social studies instruction a year after lawmakers passed a law to keep topics that make students 'feel discomfort' out of Texas classrooms."
>
> ~ Brain Lopez, *Texas Tribune*

The absurdities rampant in Florida are the ignition for the subsequent violence against LGBTQ+ citizens.

Republican presidential candidates are running on platforms that spew hate toward the LGBTQ+ community. These are the new ni...rs. With people of color, the assault has become more subtle, abstract, like the voter suppression subterfuge, and the election integrity con. Three million dollars of tax-payer money was used in Florida to finance DeSantis's special police force under the guise of election integrity. Oh, and they found four violators, a couple of them felt they were eligible to vote, and two more who tried to vote twice for Trump. Talk about no bang for your buck—three million dollars!!!!!!!!! Where have I seen this movie before? Oh yeah, Hitler's brown shirts, but how about an American precedent? In 1922, DC Stephenson, the Grand Dragon of the Ku Klux Clan "... was backed by his own private police force, some 30,000 men legally deputized to harass violators of Klan-certified virtue." Egan. They were the precursors to the brown shirts. Hitler actually admired the way we suppressed and terrorized Black Americans, which inspired him when he began laying groundwork for the Holocaust. He admired America's homegrown terrorist group, the KKK.

If Hitler is an admirer of your group's ideology, as an American, shouldn't that give you pause????

There's nothing that a fascist likes better than their own personal police force.

For Black Americans, the road to equality continues to be blocked. A friend of mine recently said to me that we have made strides in regards to progress toward Black people in our society. We had a Black president, we have all kinds of Black executives, and Black people in prominent positions in sports, but the wealth gap between Black and white people keeps widening, which indicates that the systemic racial infrastructures continue to endure. The systemic racist educational structures are perhaps the most entrenched, damaging, breeding inequity in every graduating class, strengthening the power structure.

Republicans don't overtly say they don't want people of color to vote, they just set up legal labyrinths to sabotage their inalienable right to vote. Republicans whitewash the suppression by selling it as maintaining election integrity.

The Republican Party has no vision and no policy initiatives that would benefit their constituents. Instead, they seek to take away healthcare and voting rights, a stratagem that disproportionally targets communities of color. They never realize that their policies knee-cap poor white communities also. Poor whites vote for politicians who undermine their standard of living by taking away their healthcare, by ignoring global warming, which impacts poorer communities more than anyone. You ever see a billionaire live within a mile of a coal processing factory?

But why do poor whites fall for the grift?

"And importantly, thus it has been possible to make poor and working-class white people believe that their interests lie in making common cause with their political leaders and economic betters. Common cause in whiteness: the idea that they might eventually share in the spoils, and the understanding that the discomforts and anxieties of their own precarious lives were due to—are due to—those below them rather than those above them."

~ Walter Johnson, *The Broken Heart of America*, Page 7

Back in the day, it was enslavers who fought to keep poor whites and poor Blacks separated. They knew the two groups had common ground—both being exploited by enslavers and power structures—so they had to be kept at war. And we see this today, the races pitted against each other, the Republican lawmakers being the puppet masters, and who are puppets to organizations like the NRA.

"By predicting that poor whites would be massacred by the 'black plague,' masters tried to scare white laborers into supporting the institution of slavery—regardless of what it did to their jobs or wages."

~ Kari Leigh Merritt, *Masterless Men*, Page 83

While this sleight of hand is performed by Republican politicians in manufacturing LGBTQ+ demons, Republican politicians bury the lead, like eighteen-year-olds marching into schools with their legally purchased AR-15s, gunning down innocent children. Having sold their souls to the NRA, Republican lawmakers seek to change the dialogue to manufactured issues.

People in the LGBTQ+ community are the collateral damage of this subterfuge.

"The most effective way to destroy people is to deny and obliterate their own understanding of their history."

~ George Orwell

So why do I bring this up? LGBTQ+ people are the new ni...rs. Republican leadership needed a new demon because demonizing African Americans no longer wins elections on its own. You can't put out any more Willie Horton ads—a political ad during Ronald Reagan's campaign carrying the message that a big Black man was coming to rape your wife or daughter so vote for me and I will protect you from this Black incursion.

Here's the thing, scapegoats are used to camouflage the real issues. Correct me if I'm wrong: no drag queen has shown up at an elementary school and gunned down twenty-three innocent children. Our kids are being gunned down by psychotics, armed to the gills, and Republican politicians engage in LGBTQ+ fearmongering. In the 150 days that have passed this year, there have been 263 mass shootings, and Republicans are hyper-focused on drag queens. And it's not just the hundreds of dead children, it's also the survivors who will forever be traumatized, forever strapped with horrific images of their friends being gunned down.

"If arming more people meant that we would be safer, we would be the safest country on earth."

~ Shannon Watts

Republican policies seek to enrich and empower a tiny section of the population and harm everyone else. So how do you pull this off—scapegoats!

Cruelty

March 18, 2024

Cruelty is the point.

Last month two children and their mother died trying to cross the border at the Rio Grande in Eagle Pass. The Border Patrol silently watched, the children and mother slowly drowned, choking and begging for help, the agents paralyzed by Governor Abbott's inhumane and deadly policy.

The agents who bore witness to a child's slow and horrific death prompt the question: what does that do to a person's humanity, to their core, their integrity, knowing they are witnessing a gruesome murder, a child's murder, and they remain frozen, silent. A stain gets imprinted on these agent's souls, on their humanity, which in turn facilitates their willingness to commit the next atrocity.

> "There is no flag large enough to cover the shame of killing innocent people."
>
> ~ Howard Finn

Cruelty is the point.

As the Third Reich spread its terror across Europe, the SS would arrive in towns and announce they would be executing all the Jews in the town: men, women, and children. The SS didn't have the personnel to execute this pogrom, so they solicited the town's citizens to carry out the genocide. Most volunteered, eager to engage in the next days' brutality, having been saturated for two hundred years with antisemitism, a good portion of which came from the pulpits all across Europe.

You gotta ask, in executing a pogrom, what does that do to a person's soul and humanity? What is the damage, the trauma, to a soul that participates in unimaginable barbarity? Do they become dead inside, easily pliable when called upon to perform the next atrocity?

Cruelty is the point.

After the Civil War, as Jim Crow was being re-established in the South, the sheriff would often conduct hangings of African Americans in the town's square, the community bearing witness, including women and children. It was treated as a festival, entertainment for the whole town.

You gotta wonder what kind of cruel implant is pasted onto those children's souls, witnessing horror that is treated as entertainment. And what becomes of those children, infected with hateful propaganda embedded into their hearts and minds, passed down from generation to generation, their souls hardened, soaked in racist propaganda? Their descendants, you might have seen roaming the Capitol grounds on January 6th, 2021, brandishing Confederate flags.

Cruelty is the point.

In Ohio, a pastor was arrested for opening up his church to the homeless so they wouldn't freeze to death in the bitter cold. Apparently, there is some arcane law that doesn't allow first-floor residency in a commercial zone. And the town, following a complaint from one of its citizens, decided now would be a good time to resurrect this law while the temperature outside was below zero. Their message to the homeless—just fucking die.

Cruelty is the point.

In Texas, with its triple-digit temperatures, Republican Governor Abbott gave final approval to a law that eliminates local rules mandating water breaks for construction workers.

I have no words.

Cruelty is the point.

The Georgia legislature passed a law stating that no one could provide food or water to citizens standing in line to vote, even to an eighty-year-old grandmother, trying to withstand the withering Georgia heat, casting her ballot as guaranteed by law.

Like a cockroach, Jim Crow refuses to die, constantly changing its colors and its machinations of cruelty.

Cruelty is the point.

Republicans in power attempt to stay in power by fostering conflict between races, offering up scapegoats, pitting rich against poor, Black against white. Cruelty is a byproduct. The result of disinformation causes both sides to retreat to their bunkers, sabotaging attempts for common ground, and failing to recognize their common humanity. Republican lawmakers offer rationalizations for why their constituents' lives are miserable—not insight, but cookie-cutter excuses as to why they aren't responsible for their poverty. Trump, the poster child for, "I did nothing wrong" indicted on 91 counts, broadcasts that he is innocent of all charges—every freakin' one. My, my, my, doesn't this guy have the worst luck? Falsely accused 91 times—gotta be a record for bad luck.

The theme here is the unwillingness to take responsibility.

Poor white people blame poor Black people for their condition. Whites look down, searching for scapegoats: Hispanics, immigrants, Jews, Blacks, scapegoats all manufactured by Republicans. Instead of looking up, which is where they would find the invisible forces pulling the strings that sentence them to generational poverty, pollution clusters, denial of a woman's right to choose, lack of medical insurance, their community saturated with guns.

Following their deity, MAGA supporters take responsibility for nothing, clinging to their scapegoats, served up by their false prophet. Irresponsibility breeds cruelty. Adopting scapegoats breeds cruelty because it labels humans 'others,' not human, enabling, and justifying acts of cruelty.

Cruelty is the point.

For admission into this exclusive club of cruelty, Republicans demand loyalty, blind faith, and a willingness to join a mob fueled by disinformation. What's the difference between the January 6th mob with its noose meant for Vice President Pence, and other perceived disloyalists, and the southern mobs who took it upon themselves to hang African Americans for Friday night entertainment?

Cruelty is the point.

Mass shootings continue to spike, despite the fact there are solutions—simple solutions—that would save hundreds of children's lives. But Republican Congressmen subvert each bill that would offer solutions to the holocaust.

> "After Bill Clinton banned assault weapons in 1994, mass shooting dropped by 43%. After the Republican Congress let the ban expire in 2004, they shot up by 239%. We don't need to arm teachers; we need to BAN assault weapons again!"
>
> ~ Lee Turner, Democratic Congressional candidate
> for South Carolina District 04

After each massacre, Republican lawmakers offer their thoughts and prayers, willing to sacrifice children in exchange for campaign contributions from the NRA. Republican lawmakers have blood on their souls, knowingly condoning the execution of our children.

I have no words for this sacrificial cowardice.

Cruelty is the stock and trade of Republicans. They have no vision, no policy, no plan to alleviate the suffering of our citizens. Their cowardice and insecurity breed violence and cruelty: witness the proliferation of armed far-right groups like the Proud Boys, each cell armed to the gills.

Cruelty is the point.

Back in 2017, the Trump administration was confronted with the border crisis. Their solution was to separate children from their parents and lock the kids in cages. If that wasn't cruel enough, the Trump administration went to court to ensure the kids got no soap or toothpaste.

They went to court to argue why kids shouldn't have soap and toothpaste.

I have no words.

Cruelty is the point.

This essay is all about the perpetuators of violence, but we often ignore the damage done to their souls, and how that makes them less human, less kind, more susceptible to disinformation, and primed for the next act of violence. It's a gradient process, the hardening of one's heart, dictating future behavior, each act of violence setting the table for the next brutality.

Cruelty comes from insecurity, a hidden fear of others. When you are terrified, insecure, you latch onto anything that lessens your fear, usually a demagogue who offers up scapegoats to explain how you are not responsible, that 'others' are the source of your discontent.

Each act of violence chisels away their integrity, their goodness, and their empathy, making it easier to embrace disinformation, violence, and scapegoating. There are two victims here: the victims of violence, and the perpetuators of cruelty whose souls are forever blackened by each transgression against humanity. As citizens of the world, we have a responsibility to cleanse, and to repair our brother's soul of this trauma of generational violence.

In South Africa, they had Truth and Reconciliation hearings designed to restore one's humanity. It was a nationwide confessional box that presented South Africans with a path to unburden their sins committed during Apartheid. It prevented the souls of South Africans from falling into the vortex of scapegoats, racism, and disinformation, with truth being the cleansing agent.

America is still under the shackles of racism, fueled and fostered by disinformation. Recently, presidential candidate Nicki Haley, stated that the Civil War was about State's Rights—no mention of slavery. If a presidential candidate is promoting blatant falsehoods that the Civil War wasn't about slavery, then America has a hard row to hoe. These lies about history, race, and culture are passed on from generation to generation, propaganda that serves as a powder keg for violence. We saw a triggered mob in living color on January 6th.

Man is basically good, and each transgression, each act of violence and malice, tarnishes his soul, tainting his native state of goodness. This in turn makes him less human, less kind.

America can cleanse itself of the wildfire of lies, the infestation of disinformation and racism by shedding light on transgressions committed by the perpetuators of violence, which, in turn, will help diffuse and disable the triggers and mechanism of violence. Truth and reconciliation will make America great, not again, but to a new level that honors the ideals our country was founded on.

If cruelty is the point, we can stop it with two words:

Be kind.

All You Need to Know

May 12, 2024

This is all you need to know. They were, and are, doing it now, in plain sight, with unrelenting saturation. But we refuse to look, distracted by their calculated red herrings.

> "In the 60s, the KGB did some fascinating psychological experiments. They learned that if you bombard human subjects with fear messages nonstop, in two months or less, most of the subjects are completely brainwashed to believe the false message. To the point that no amount of clear information they are shown, to the contrary, can change their mind."
>
> ~ Quote by George#VotesBlueAlways

The above two paragraphs explain the phenomenon of Trump, MAGA, and the idea behind big lies.

Remember Hitler's big lie:

> "The big lie is the name of a propaganda technique, originally coined by Adolf Hitler in *Mein Kampf,* who says, '*The great masses of the people … will more easily fall victim to a big lie than to a small one,*' and denotes where a known falsehood is stated and repeated and treated as if it is self-evidently true, in hopes of swaying the course of an argument in a direction that takes the big lie for granted rather than critically questioning it or ignoring it." (https://rationalwiki.org/wiki/Big_lie)

The American people have been assaulted with a daily bombardment of several big lies. The repetition of these big lies created the MAGA movement—or should I say, the MAGA cult—a fountainhead of conspiracy theories. These conspiracies broadcast the idea that Obama is really running the country, or that the deceased John Kennedy Jr. will be reincarnated to lead us to America's Halcyon days. Through this cult, we learn that Trump has been sent by heaven, anointed by the Big Guy himself. And don't forget about the space lasers—I'm sorry, the Jewish space laser—that get into voting machines and altered votes for Biden. And then there is the idea that the January 6th insurrection was an idyllic day of tourism. OK, there was the hanging gallows, but don't let that diminish that day of peace and love. Oh, and don't pay any attention to the Confederate flags flying in the breeze, not racist at all, just good old boys doing good old boy things. It goes on and on, fueled by the Russian propaganda onslaught, saturating social media with the Big Lie that Trump won the election.

It is shocking to see US congressmen and senators embracing Russia's talking points, but they too have succumbed to the Russian disinformation juggernaut.

> "'I think Russian propaganda has made its way into the United States, unfortunately, and it's infected a good chunk of my party's base,' Representative Michael McCaul, chairman of the House Foreign Affairs Committee, told Puck's (Puck News Service) Julia Joffe last week. Representative Mike Turner, chairman of the House Intelligence Committee, went further, telling CNN's Jake Tapper a few days later, 'We see directly coming from Russia attempts to mask communications that are anti-Ukraine and pro-Russia messages, some of which we even hear being uttered on the House floor.'"
>
> ~ Alex Finley

Everyone talks about how divided our country is. We need to look no further than Putin's tentacles and his disinformation factory, his hateful rhetoric in the form of memes have been injected into our nation's soul, cursing through the airways of social media.

"A chief culprit in Congress is Georgia's Rep. Marjorie Taylor Greene. Among the Russian-originated false narratives she has uplifted is the patently false claim that Ukraine is waging a war against Christianity while Russia is protecting it. On Steve Bannon's War Room podcast, Greene even claimed, without evidence, that Ukraine is 'executing priests.' Where would Greene have gotten this wild, concocted notion? We don't have to look far. Russian talking points have included this gaslighting narrative for some time. The twist, of course, is that, according to the International Religious Freedom or Belief Alliance, it is the *Russian* army that has been torturing and executing priests and other religious figures, including 30 Ukrainian clergy killed and 26 held captive by Russian forces."

~ Jay Kuo, *The Big Picture*, May 7, 2024

So what's going on here? The idea of Ukrainians executing priests doesn't even pass the smell test. Is there another fascist technique seeping into our body politic?

"Accuse the enemy of that which you are guilty of."

~ Joseph Goebbels

We've seen it in operation, red meat for the MAGA cult: Biden has dementia; Biden is a fascist; Biden wants to take your guns away; Biden is a pedophile; Biden wants you to pay more taxes; Biden is the head of a criminal enterprise; Biden made millions while in office; Biden is behind Trump's indictments; Biden is lying, etc.

When Trump says these things, he is simply confessing his sins. The New York Times and the Washington Post both tallied Trump's lies at over thirty thousand while he was in office—over thirty thousand!!!! He lies compulsively, shamelessly. Last week, he claimed that outside the courtroom, waiting for him, was a flood of MAGA supporters.

There was one.

Our democracy is hanging by a thread.

Our only hope is to shed light on the disinformation, but more importantly, shed light on the wizard behind the curtain.

About the Author

Curt Strickland is a Boston playwright currently working on a ten-play saga on America, each set in a different decade. Curt is also a landscape photographer, and a former owner at Great American Art, one of the largest commercial art corporations in the nation. Curt believes that art should serve to heal, inspire, provoke, challenge and to offer hope—but, most of all, to connect and remind us of our common humanity.

Curt recently was awarded the William Faulkner Literary playwriting prize for his full-length play, 1968.

In 2020, Curt received a double lung transplant, an event that had profound effects on both his writing and his life. This experience is the basis of a new play he is developing entitled *Double Lung*.

You can view Curt's plays at the New Play Exchange:

https://newplayexchange.org/users/68843/curt-strickland

You can view his political and cultural essays at:

https://curtsview.com

Made in the USA
Thornton, CO
12/30/24 18:02:01

25914b34-5dcc-49f3-b3eb-971b2a243889R01